KANSAS'S WAR

T0307866

THE CIVIL WAR IN THE GREAT INTERIOR

Series Editors
Martin J. Hershock and Christine Dee

Ohio's War: The Civil War in Documents, edited by Christine Dee
Missouri's War: The Civil War in Documents, edited by Silvana R. Siddali
Indiana's War: The Civil War in Documents, edited by Richard F. Nation
and Stephen E. Towne
Kansas's War: The Civil War in Documents, edited by Pearl T. Ponce

FORTHCOMING:

Michigan's War: The Civil War in Documents, edited by John W. Quist
Wisconsin's War: The Civil War in Documents, edited by Chandra Manning

KANSAS'S WAR

The Civil War in Documents

~

EDITED BY PEARL T. PONCE

Ohio University Press

Athens

Ohio University Press, Athens, Ohio 45701
www.ohioswallow.com
© 2011 by Ohio University Press

To obtain permission to quote, reprint, or otherwise reproduce or distribute
material from Ohio University Press publications, please contact our rights and
permissions department at (740) 593-1154 or (740) 593-4536 (fax).

Printed in the United States of America
Ohio University Press books are printed on acid-free paper ⊗ ™

18 17 16 15 14 13 12 11   5 4 3 2 1

Cover art: "Before Dawn" by Samuel J. Reader, from his *Autobiography*

Library of Congress Cataloging-in-Publication Data

Kansas's war : the Civil War in documents / edited by Pearl T. Ponce.
    p. cm. — (The Civil War in the great interior)
Includes bibliographical references and index.
ISBN 978-0-8214-1936-6 (pb : alk. paper) — ISBN 978-0-8214-4352-1
  1. Kansas—History—Civil War, 1861–1865—Sources. 2. United States—History—Civil
War, 1861–1865—Sources. I. Ponce, Pearl T.
E508.K36 2011
978.1'031—dc22
                                                                        2010049464

Contents

Three

Patronage and Policy 50

Four

Kansas's Men in Blue 72

Five

Warfare along the Kansas-Missouri Border 117

Nine

The Promise of Kansas   212

Illustrations

Series Editors' Preface

The Civil War in the Great Interior series focuses on the Middle West, as the complex region has come to be known, during the most critical era of American history. In his Annual Message to Congress in December of 1862, Abraham Lincoln identified "the great interior region" as the area between the Alleghenies and the Rocky Mountains, south of Canada and north of the "culture of cotton." Lincoln included in this region the states of Ohio, Indiana, Michigan, Wisconsin, Illinois, Missouri, Kansas, Iowa, Minnesota, and Kentucky; the area that would become West Virginia; and parts of Tennessee and the Dakota, Nebraska, and Colorado territories. This area, Lincoln maintained, was critical to the "great body of the republic" not only because it bound together the North, South, and West but also because its people would not assent to the division of the Union.

This series examines what was, to Lincoln and other Americans in the mid-nineteenth century, the most powerful, influential, and critical area of the country. It considers how the people of the Middle West experienced the Civil War and the role they played in preserving and redefining the nation. These collections of historical sources—many of which have never been published—explore significant issues raised by the sectional conflict, the Civil War, and Reconstruction. The series underscores what was unique to particular states and their residents while recognizing the values and experiences that individuals in the Middle West shared with other Northerners and, in some cases, with Southerners.

Within these volumes are the voices of a diverse cross-section of nineteenth-century Americans. These include African Americans, European immigrants, Native Americans, and women. Editors have gathered evidence from farms and factories, rural and urban areas, and communities throughout each state to examine the relationships of individuals, their communities, the political culture, and events on the battlefields. The volumes present readers with layers of evidence that can be combined in a multitude of patterns to yield new conclusions and raise questions about prevailing interpretations of the past.

The editor of each volume provides a narrative framework through brief chapter introductions and background information for each document, as well as a timeline. As these volumes cannot address all aspects of the Civil War experience for each state, they include selected bibliographies to guide readers in further research. Documents were chosen for what they reveal about the past, but each also speaks to the subjective nature of history and the decisions that historians face when weighing the merits and limits of each piece of evidence they uncover. The diverse documents included in these volumes also expose readers to the craft of history and to the variety of source materials historians utilize as they explore the past.

Much of the material in these works will raise questions, spark debates, and generate discussion. Whether read with an eye toward the history of the Union war effort, a particular state or region, or the Civil War's implications for race, class, and gender in America, the volumes in The Civil War in the Great Interior help us consider—and reconsider—the evidence from the past.

Martin J. Hershock
Christine Dee

Preface

At the end of January 1864, M. Marshall Murdock, editor and proprietor of the *Osage Chronicle*, wrote that "Kansas politicians may well be likened to a lot of curs, consisting of mongrel whelps, bench-legged fices, and cunning foxhounds." Unfortunately, he continued, "it is a notorious fact that about every other man in Kansas is a politician."[1] Coming on the third anniversary of Kansas's admission to the Union, Murdock's observation was apt. Indeed, although the state had suffered many shortages since its inception—from rain and money to men and munitions— politicians were plentiful. Moreover, their struggle for influence shaped the new state and its response to the American Civil War. As a seminal event in this country's history, the war itself is of such importance that nearly 150 years after the firing on Fort Sumter, we continue to debate its meaning, origins, and legacy.

Kansas's War is dedicated to understanding how Kansans experienced this fundamentally American war. Wartime Kansas was remarkably political, in large part because of its own origins. The struggle over whether Kansas Territory would become a free or a slave state notoriously transformed it into Bleeding Kansas, and its settlement is one of the defining events of the era known as the Coming of the War. Unlike the other states in this series on the "great interior," which enjoyed longer tenures in the country before the war commenced—Ohio having joined the Union in 1803, Indiana in 1816, Illinois in 1818, Missouri in 1821, Michigan in 1837, and Wisconsin in 1848—Kansas was admitted in the midst of the secession crisis. As such, the state did not have an opportunity to recover from its internal strife before being called to contribute to the preservation of the Union. Indeed, the shift from a time of peace to a time of war was not as stark for Kansans as it was for other Americans.

This confluence informs the documents collected. Readers will note the recurrence of names and themes as Kansas's contested settlement shapes the state's war and postwar experiences. Kansas's very organization has dictated those areas represented by this documents collection. Most of the counties organized during the territorial period were in the eastern half of the territory, the most populous being those adjacent to Missouri. During the first decade of statehood, another eighteen counties were organized, largely surrounding those organized previously, moving south and west.[2] As a result, many of the Kansans whose voices are captured in these documents necessarily lived in the eastern and southeastern portions of the state.

The documents themselves have been allowed to stand as they were written midcentury, with scant editing and the retention of the author's original spelling and punctuation. However, I have made three changes for ease of comprehension.

First, I have silently corrected typesetting errors in publications such as newspapers or circulars. Second, repetitive phrases or words which an author used to help a correspondent follow his or her thought as a page was turned or a new leaf was started have been eliminated. Finally, where an author has used an an extra long space to denote a change in subject, I have opted to begin a new paragraph. In all the documents, ellipses indicate where material has been omitted for length, while headnotes provide a context for readers to better understand each document.

Although a young state when the war began, Kansas has a rich and varied history, and a selected bibliography is included for those desiring a greater immersion than this volume allows.

Acknowledgments

I would like to recognize Gillian Berchowitz for her support of this series, Civil War in the Great Interior, as well as its coeditors, Christine Dee and Martin Hershock. In particular, I would like to thank Christine for inviting me to contribute to this volume on Kansas. I have enjoyed our many conversations and this book is better for her insights. In addition, I appreciate the work of the production team, especially Jean Cunningham, Beth Pratt, and Nancy Basmajian, for their work ushering this volume to press. Finally, I would like to thank the two anonymous readers who read this book in manuscript form. Although I have not taken every suggestion, they did point me in important new directions and their assessment of my work was thoughtful and thorough.

The majority of the documents in this volume were collected at three archives in Kansas, and the staffs of each were extraordinarily helpful. Thanks to Mary Nelson at Special Collections and University Archives at the Wichita State University library and to Karen Cook and Sheryl Williams at the Kansas Collection, Kenneth Spencer Research Library at the University of Kansas, Lawrence, for their help in bringing this project to fruition. At the Kansas State Historical Society, the entire staff in the research division made researching this book a pleasure, and I would particularly like to acknowledge Teresa Coble for her good cheer and helpfulness. For their help with permissions, I would like to thank archivist Bob Knecht and Virgil Dean, editor of *Kansas History: A Journal of the Central Plains*. Moreover, Nancy Sherbert, curator of photographs, helped me quickly identify *Breaking Dawn*, the Samuel J. Reader painting on the cover, and secure permission for its use within a compressed time frame. She also drew my attention to a number of images of notable Kansans, some of which I have included.

The history department at California State University, San Bernardino, provided critical funds to travel to Kansas to collect the majority of these documents at the start of this project. At Ithaca College, travel funds from the School of Humanities and Sciences facilitated a trip to Kansas at the close of the project, and the Center for Faculty Research and Development funded two course releases that allowed me to finish writing, editing, and preparing this volume for publication.

On a personal note, I greatly appreciate how much my friends—particularly Jennifer Ahlskog, Angela Branneman, Brett Flehinger, Jennifer Germann, Kurt Graham, Elisabeth Guzman, Cheryl Jung, and Silvana Siddali—enrich my life. Finally, I especially wish to acknowledge my family—Aurora Ponce, Florence Ponce-Cornejo, Lauren Ponce-Cornejo, and Andres Cornejo—for their love and support. I dedicate this volume to my sister, Florence, aware that this simple acknowledgment could never capture all she has done for me or the place she holds in my heart.

Introduction

IN JANUARY 1861, Kansans were less concerned with the secession crisis than with finally having attained their long cherished goal of statehood. Indeed, while Republican Abraham Lincoln's election to the presidency was "glorious," it was not, the *Leavenworth Conservative* asserted, as "important and decisive" as Kansas's admission. As for the departure of so many states from the Union, it was felt that the thirty-fourth state went far to "fill the gap." These sentiments derived from Kansas's singular experience before the American Civil War, for while many Americans were shocked by the aggressiveness of the so-called Slave Power or Slaveocracy, Kansans were not. They were intimately acquainted with civil strife, both ideological and actual. It was this territorial experience that allowed many Kansans to be sanguine about the possibility of war, for they had already survived once, having "stood the test of desertion, and even oppression" during the territorial period.[1] During this critical winter after the election of 1860, Kansas was truly in its infancy, a state few believed had the wherewithal to survive on its own. In the 1850s, Kansas had distinguished itself as a violent, ideologically divided, drought-stricken, underpopulated, indebted territory. Now, with a civil war at hand, the ability of the state to sustain both itself and the nation was uncertain. Yet with few men, fewer resources, and mere weeks into statehood, Kansas responded ably to the crisis of the Union.

When President Lincoln issued his April 1861 militia call in the aftermath of the Confederacy's attack on federal forces at Fort Sumter in South Carolina, Kansas was not asked to provide volunteers. Nonetheless, 650 men stepped forward. When Kansas was asked for 3,235 men in May and July 1861, the state provided more than twice the number of men requested. This pattern served Kansas well, to the degree that a draft would not be ordered in the state until the last conscription call was issued in December 1864. But Kansas had not been properly credited for its volunteers and so Secretary of War Edwin Stanton rescinded the call three months later. By the end of the conflict, Kansas had exceeded its quota by almost 3,500 men, supplying the Union with 20,097 soldiers. This contribution to the war effort is especially impressive, given that the 1860 census revealed only 58,806 men in the territory. Ultimately, 8,498 of these men died in service to their country, a higher mortality rate than any other state in the Union.[2]

In addition to providing more than twenty thousand soldiers, Kansas provided a diversity of troops to the country. The state raised two regiments of American Indians, bringing together loyal members of the Cherokee, Creek, and Seminole nations as the Indian Home Guard (and organizing a third regiment in Indian

Territory). In addition, the state was at the forefront of enlisting African Americans. Although the Lincoln administration resisted the efforts of the state to enroll African Americans, activists in Kansas were eager to include them in what many in the state saw as a war against slavery. In fact, the First Kansas Colored Infantry became the first African American regiment to engage the enemy at Island Mound, Missouri, in 1862; in doing so, they suffered the first African American combat deaths of the war. Finally, while Union general Benjamin Butler formed three African American regiments in New Orleans in 1862, Kansas was the first state to formally muster black troops into the Union army when the First Kansas Colored Infantry was finally accepted into federal service on January 13, 1863.[3]

Populated by settlers from all over the country (but disproportionately from the Midwest and the border states), Civil War Kansas was a microcosm of the nation, but one that, as this leadership on the recruitment of diverse soldiers reveals, had been radicalized by the struggles of the previous decade. Yet Kansas's history reveals a complex attitude toward race. Whereas many of the state's leading politicians had previously advocated freedom for African Americans, their actions had often fallen short of their rhetoric. In 1855, for instance, a convention of freestate men had voted to exclude African Americans from the future state. Less than a decade later, Kansans would be debating whether the word *white* ought to be stricken from the state constitution. Like other Americans, Kansans were divided by emancipation and the extension of civil rights to African Americans. The *Emporia News* admitted that they "possessed more or less of that prejudice so common against the blacks, and do yet; still, we are in favor of doing everything in our power to elevate them." Doing so, the editors argued, was "freedom" and "if we, as a race, can't swim we deserve to sink."[4] Indeed, although prewar Kansas was closely associated with antislavery activity, ideas often outstripped even their experiences and, during the war, Kansans were faced with people, not abstractions. In 1860 only 816 African Americans lived in the territory; by 1865, thirteen thousand had migrated to the state. And these individuals were merely part of a larger migration as refugees—black, white, and Indian—from Missouri, Arkansas, Louisiana, Texas, and Indian Territory poured into Kansas.

For the state's citizens, the war brought both challenges and opportunities. For the first time, money was plentiful in the state as citizens took advantage of the business of war. Indeed, after a few lean years of drought, some Kansans fared better during wartime than they had in the territorial period. But for some prosperity prompted suspicion and those less able to profit from the war occasionally levied charges that such success stemmed from disloyalty. Similarly, while tensions among partisans of different political persuasions did exist, Kansas itself saw little antiwar, copperhead activity.[5] Yet early in the war, Democrats expressed concerns about the nature and goals of the Republican party. As the *Leavenworth Weekly*

Inquirer noted, "We hear much talk about *a* Government; the nigger-worshippers are very solicitous about *a* Government; . . . Now be it understood that we are not in favor of *a* Government; Russia has *a* Government; Turkey has *a* Government; China has *a* Government; . . . But *we,* and the Democracy of this Nation, want *the* Government. We want *the* Government which our Fathers gave us; *the* Government which Abolitionism and Black Republicanism combined, have well nigh ruined, and which will soon be quite ruined, unless the Democracy rescue it from final overthrow and destruction."[6] Although this 1862 editorial urged action, Democrats had little sway in the state. In fact, only one of Kansas's thirty-five counties went for the Democratic candidate in the 1864 presidential election.

Instead, it was far more common for Kansans to express disappointment with the pace of change under Lincoln's leadership rather than with the ideological orientation of the party in office. In advocating a harder war in 1862, the *Marysville Big Blue Union* expressed relief that "the people and the Government are awakening to the fact that it is folly for them to undertake to treat rebels with bullets and sugar-plums at one and the same time."[7] Another newspaper admitted that they thought Lincoln was "too slow, often."[8] Overall, however, Kansas's support for Lincoln was strong and consistent if occasionally impatient. Indeed, the political struggles within the state took a different form than in other Union states with a stronger opposition. In Kansas, the conflict was not between Democrats and Republicans. Instead, Republicans argued among themselves as they vied for influence within the new state. Of their many intraparty debates, one of the most significant was how to best defend the state once the war began.

Even though Kansas was far from the Virginia front, basic geography meant the security of its borders was critical. Indian Territory was directly to the state's south. While fears of an Indian-Confederate invasion proved unwarranted, Unionist Indians did flee into Kansas in late 1861. The following year, the state's soldiers contributed to pacification of Indian Territory and the repatriation of its residents. To Kansas's east was an uncertain, wavering Missouri. Given that Kansas lacked the manpower and means to defend itself, a Confederate Missouri was a grave threat to the state. Should Missouri secede, Kansas would be isolated from the rest of the Union. But despite the risks involved in antagonizing Missourians, their slaves proved to be a tremendous temptation to men like James H. Lane, James Montgomery, and Charles R. Jennison, who placed their radical agendas ahead of their state's and their country's needs. Such aggressive, antislavery "jayhawking" was so detrimental that while Union and Confederate generals agreed on little else, both sides recognized that Kansans' guerrilla activity might very well push Missouri into the waiting arms of the Confederacy. This tension between the two states was heightened by skirmishes fought along the Kansas-Missouri border throughout the war and worsened by the serious depredations committed by residents of both states.

Even for those fascinated by the American Civil War, interest in Kansas's war experience often ends with how the territory inculcated John Brown, its most infamous export, but Kansas's wartime history transcends the story of one abolitionist. A young state, struggling on the frontier, at the edge of the trans-Mississippi theater of war, this volume of the Civil War in the Great Interior series situates Kansas in this nation's most defining conflict while illuminating the uniqueness of its war experience. *Kansas's War* focuses on the state's struggle to meet internal needs at a time when the federal government required an extraordinary commitment of men and resources to preserve the Union. These documents address the new state's main preoccupations: the internal struggle for control of policy and patronage; border security; and issues of race, especially Kansas's efforts to come to terms with its burgeoning African American population and Indians' claims to nearly one-fifth of the state's land.

The documents included highlight Kansans' understanding of the issues at stake in the Civil War—issues that residents understood through the prism of their territorial struggles—while acknowledging that their state's transition from peace to war was not as abrupt as that of their countrymen. From patronage to the raising of regiments, events in Kansas were colored by political competition that spilled over from its territorial days. Bleeding Kansas had contributed directly to the political realignment of the 1850s and to the rise of the Republican Party. Kansas Territory had wrestled with issues of slavery and liberty, the place of African Americans within civil life, and the responsibilities of federal government. Since 1854, Kansans had directly struggled with questions that the entire nation would be forced to confront once the Cofnfederate States of America was formed and war commenced. Yet, despite having engaged such issues beforehand, the Civil War transformed Kansas. These primary source documents illuminate how contemporary Kansans understood their state's transformation in the fires of war.

ONE

Settlement and Strife

$\mathcal{T}$HE SECTIONAL CONFLICT that flared into war in 1861 shaped Kansas more than any other state in the Union. The last state admitted to the United States before the war, it was the first to experience the sectional conflict as more than a philosophical or constitutional disagreement. It was in Kansas that the country first realized that the political conflict between the sections could have a martial aspect, that it could lead to terror, violence, warfare, and even death. Initially, Kansas was like many other new territories, drawing settlers who sought a material improvement in their lives. But while many territorial residents arrived in Kansas to pursue economic opportunity, it is undeniable that the most prominent Kansans were ideologues. Because of this, the territory became a battlefront where Americans died for their beliefs.

Yet the violence that broke out in the 1850s was an unintended consequence of the territory's organization. Kansas had been carved from that part of the original Louisiana Purchase lands north of latitude 36°30', which marked the southern border of Missouri. By the terms of that state's admission, in 1820, future states located north of this Missouri Compromise line would be free while states to its south would be open to slavery. However, when President Franklin Pierce signed the Kansas-Nebraska Act, in May 1854, Kansas was opened to settlement under the doctrine of popular sovereignty, allowing residents to determine their state institutions (notably slavery) for themselves. Although two previous territories, Utah and New Mexico, had been organized through popular sovereignty in 1850, that decision was an outgrowth of the Mexican-American War and a nod to the antislavery tradition in those lands. Pierce's signature jettisoned a congressional compromise in effect for more than three decades. While its geography should have meant a free Kansas, residents now had the option to implant slavery. Within months of the 1854 Kansas-Nebraska Act, the territory became notorious for partisan strife that ranged from voter intimidation to electoral fraud to outright warfare, all in the effort to determine the future state's eventual relationship to slavery.

Although sectional tensions might have led to territorial conflict anyhow, from the start Kansas's condition rendered it unfit for settlement. The territory had not been surveyed, not one acre of land was legally available for sale, and the

area bordering Missouri, where most settlers would enter, was closed to settlement.[1] When Kansas Territory was organized, in 1854, there were approximately
fourteen hundred Americans living in the area: half were missionaries or trad-
ers while the other half were employed by the federal government, many in a
military capacity. However these numbers do not capture the full reality, for while
there may have been few white settlers in Kansas, thousands of American Indians
lived within its borders. Approximately seventeen thousand Indians made Kansas their home, with the Osages (4,951), Pottawatomies (4,300), and Delawares
(1,132) among the most numerous.[2] The Kaws (also known as the Kansa Indians,
after whom the state takes it name), the Osages, and the Pawnees had settled in
the area by the eighteenth century. Over the next century and a half, many more
tribes had been pushed out of the Old Northwest (what is now Ohio, Indiana,
Illinois, Michigan, Wisconsin, and northeastern Minnesota) and into the region
by an Indian removal as effective in the North as it more famously had been in the
South. By 1850 a number of tribes had exchanged their old lands for new ones in
Kansas.[3] As such, although it was home to few whites, Kansas was not the empty
plain that a faraway Congress perhaps thought it was.

Even before passage of the Kansas-Nebraska Act was assured, and despite numerous outstanding Indian claims, outsiders set events in motion. On the East
Coast, Eli Thayer of the Massachusetts Emigrant Aid Company had begun to
organize emigrants to Kansas, and approximately seven hundred settlers made
the journey in 1854 alone.[4] Closer to Kansas, proslavery Missourians were eager to
stake their claims. With their homes nearby, many preferred to sleep mere miles
away in Missouri while making improvements on their Kansas homesteads during
the day. By choosing comfort and not immediately abandoning their homes across
the border, were these Missourians settlers? Not according to many antislavery advocates who claimed that such men were ineligible to vote. Similarly, Missourians
charged that ideologically driven abolitionists were neither legitimate residents
nor eligible voters.

The first two elections held in Kansas Territory—in November 1854, to select
the territorial delegate to the House of Representatives; and in March 1855, to fill
the territorial legislature—were marked by extensive fraud and voter intimidation. As a result, although censuses showed Missouri settlers to be in the majority,
their methods to ensure their victory tainted the results and rendered the outcome unpalatable to free-state activists, who were further alienated by the new
legislature. These legislators voted to unseat free-state men selected in a special
election ordered by the territorial governor to address voter irregularities. In their
place, the legislature seated those proslavery men elected in the original election.
The territorial legislature next moved the legislative seat from Pawnee to Shawnee
Mission, which, located near the Missouri border, had known slavery from at least

the 1830s.[5] Finally, the territorial legislature passed a law protecting slavery such that anyone not favoring the institution was prevented from serving on a jury for certain cases. In addition, antislavery proponents could not freely speak, write, or publish their views, for doing so would render them guilty of a felony.

As a result, by mid-1855 the free-state movement was organizing in Kansas Territory. By September, this Topeka movement had established plans to draft a state constitution, arguing that their disenfranchisement and persecution was so egregious that admission to the Union as a free state was the only appropriate remedy. By November, the Topeka Constitution had been drafted; by December, free-state voters had approved it; by January, they had elected Charles Robinson as governor and Mark Delahay as representative to Congress. By March 1856, the Topeka government had set itself up as a shadow government to the territorial government it decried as illegitimate. The free-state, extralegal Topeka legislature then met in a ten-day session, selected senators, and sent the Topeka Constitution to Congress with a request for immediate admission.

The rest of 1856 proved to be pivotal for the territory. In May, violence broke out soon after territorial chief justice Samuel Lecompte, presiding over the U.S. District Court in Lecompton, impaneled a grand jury to consider the actions of the Topeka government. On May 10 the grand jury issued treason indictments (for usurpation of office, among other charges) for Charles Robinson, James Lane, Andrew Reeder, George W. Brown, Gaius Jenkins, George W. Deitzler, G. W. Smith, and S. N. Wood. In addition, the grand jury ordered the Free State Hotel in Lawrence as well as the town's two newspapers, the *Herald of Freedom* and the *Kansas Free State*, be "abated as nuisances."[6] A few of those named by the grand jury were arrested without incident, while Charles Robinson escaped into Missouri and would later be extradited back to Kansas. Finally, U.S. Marshal Israel Donelson called together a posse to aid in delivering the remaining warrants in the free-state town of Lawrence, and his call was answered by large numbers of eager, and later inebriated, proslavery Missouri volunteers. On May 21, U.S. Deputy Marshal W. P. Fain entered Lawrence, served the warrants, and withdrew from town, and Donelson disbanded the posse.

However, Douglas Country sheriff Samuel Jones, a proslavery adherent who had been shot in Lawrence the week before, then took charge of the posse and, falsely claiming federal duty, led what had become a mob into town. They smashed the newspaper presses, burned the Free State Hotel and other buildings, and terrified Lawrence residents. Because of confusion as to whether Jones was executing a federal order, these actions seemed to have the patina of federal approval. For antislavery proponents who believed Pierce's Democratic administration favored a slave Kansas, the connection between the federal government and the sack of Lawrence seemed obvious.

Three days after the sack of Lawrence, abolitionist John Brown led a small party to Pottawatomie Creek, forty miles south of Lawrence, and they killed five proslavery settlers in revenge. These settlers had not participated in Lawrence events nor did they own slaves. After these back-to-back events, a cycle of action and retaliation had begun and violence erupted throughout the territory. Numerous skirmishes were fought that summer resulting in approximately thirty-eight "political" deaths and earning the territory its Bleeding Kansas sobriquet.[7]

The presidential campaign of 1856 served as the backdrop for these events. Earlier in the year, Republican Nathaniel Banks (formerly a Know Nothing) was elected Speaker of the House of Representatives. Republicans were thus able to parlay their interest in Kansas into action, the most significant act being the House's decision to send a fact-finding committee to the territory on March 19. The Committee to Investigate the Troubles in Kansas was better known as the Howard Committee, after its chair, and included two Republicans, William A. Howard of Michigan and John Sherman of Ohio, and one Democrat, Mordecai Oliver of Missouri. The committee opened public sessions in Lawrence on April 18 and heard testimony for the next two months. Thus, the committee was in the territory during the sack of Lawrence, the Pottawatomie massacre, and the arrest and imprisonment of the Topeka leadership that summer. Ultimately, the committee traveled to several towns in Kansas as well as to Detroit, New York, and Washington. The depositions they took were dominated by impassioned descriptions of the difficulties free-state residents faced. After four months the committee published a majority report running to 1,206 pages that gave the Republican Party ample evidence of Democratic and proslavery misdeeds, which they used to great effect throughout the presidential contest. The campaign of Republican candidate John C. Frémont centered on the failure of Pierce's Kansas policy. Indeed, his party very nearly rode Bleeding Kansas to victory in the first presidential campaign the Republicans contested.

The presidential campaign of 1856 demonstrated the power of Kansas as a symbol. However, the interpretation of Kansas events varied tremendously, depending on one's ideological perspective. Antislavery advocates believed that the so-called Slaveocracy was so intent on obtaining another slave state that the wishes of Kansas residents would be ignored. For proslavery advocates, the admission of Kansas as a slave state represented the willingness of the North to recognize Southerners' equality in the Union.

PROTECTING SLAVERY IN KANSAS TERRITORY

Passed by the Kansas territorial legislative assembly in 1855, this act was designed to protect slavery. Free-state advocates condemned the assembly as unrepresentative and illegitimate; with the passage of laws such as this one, they questioned whether protections other Americans enjoyed existed in Kansas Territory.

AN ACT TO PUNISH OFFENCES AGAINST SLAVE PROPERTY.

Section 1. *Be it enacted by the Governor and Legislative Assembly of the Territory of Kansas,* That every person, bond or free, who shall be convicted of actually raising a rebellion or insurrection of slaves, free negroes, or mulattoes, in this Territory, shall suffer death.

Sec. 2. Every free person who shall aid or assist in any rebellion or insurrection of slaves, free negroes, or mulattoes, or shall furnish arms, or do any overt act in furtherance of such rebellion or insurrection, shall suffer death.

Sec. 3. If any free person shall, by speaking, writing, or printing, advise, persuade or induce any slaves to rebel, conspire against or murder any citizen of this Territory, or shall bring into, print, write, publish or circulate, or cause to be brought into, printed written, published or circulated, or shall knowingly aid or assist in the bringing into, printing, writing, publishing or circulating, in this Territory, any book, paper, magazine, pamphlet or circular, for the purpose of exciting insurrection, rebellion, revolt or conspiracy on the part of slaves, free negroes or mulattoes, against the citizens of the Territory or any part of them, such person shall be guilty of felony and suffer death.

Sec. 4. If any person shall entice, decoy, or carry away out of this Territory, any slave belonging to another, with intent to deprive the owner thereof of the services of such slave, or with intent to effect or procure the freedom of such slave, he shall be adjudged guilty of Grand Larceny, and, on conviction thereof, shall suffer death, or be imprisoned at hard labor for not less than ten years.

Sec. 5. If any person shall aid or assist in enticing, decoying, or persuading, or carrying away or sending out of this Territory, any slave belonging to another, with intent to procure or effect the freedom of such slave, or with intent to deprive the owner thereof of the services of such slave, he shall be adjudged guilty of Grand Larceny, and on conviction thereof, shall suffer death, or be imprisoned at hard labor for not less than ten years.

Sec. 6. If any person shall entice, decoy, or carry away out of any State or other Territory of the United States, any slave belonging to another, with intent to procure or effect the freedom of such slave, or to deprive the owner thereof of the services of such slave, and shall bring such slave into this Territory, he shall be adjudged guilty of Grand Larceny, in the same manner as if such slave had been enticed, decoyed, or carried away out of this Territory, and in such case the Larceny may be charged to have been committed in any county of this Territory, into or through which such slave shall have been brought by such person, and on conviction thereof, the person offending shall suffer death, or be imprisoned at hard labor for not less than ten years.

Sec. 7. If any person shall entice, persuade or induce any slave to escape from the service of his master or owner, in this Territory, or shall aid or assist any slave in escaping from the service of his master or owner, or shall aid, assist, harbor or conceal any slave who may have escaped from the service of his master or owner, shall be deemed guilty of felony, and punished by imprisonment at hard labor for a term of not less than five years.

SEC. 8. If any person in this Territory, shall aid or assist, harbor or conceal any slave who has escaped from the service of his master or owner, in another State or Territory, such person shall be punished in like manner as if such slave had escaped from the service of his master or owner in this Territory.

SEC. 9. If any person shall resist any officer while attempting to arrest any slave that may have escaped from the service of his master or owner, or shall rescue such slave when in custody of any officer or other person, or shall entice, persuade, aid or assist such slave to escape from the custody of any officer or other person who may have such slave in custody, whether such slave have escaped from the service of his master or owner in this Territory or in any other State or Territory, the person so offending shall be guilty of felony and punished by imprisonment at hard labor for a term of not less than two years.

SEC. 10. If any Marshal, Sheriff or Constable, or the deputy of any such officer, shall, when required by any person, refuse to aid or assist in the arrest and capture of any that may have escaped from the service of his master or owner . . . , such officer shall be fined in a sum of not less than one hundred nor more than five hundred dollars.

SEC. 11. If any person print, write, introduce into, publish or circulate, or cause to be brought into, printed, written, published or circulated, or shall knowingly aid or assist in bringing into, printing, publishing or circulating within this Territory, any book, paper, pamphlet, magazine, handbill or circular, containing any statements, arguments, opinions, sentiment, doctrine, advice or innuendo, calculated to produce a disorderly, dangerous or rebellious disaffection among the slaves in this Territory, or to induce such slaves to escape from the service of their masters, or to resist their authority, he shall be guilty of felony, and be punished by imprisonment at hard labor for a term not less than five years.

SEC. 12. If any free person, by speaking or by writing, assert or maintain that persons have not the right to hold slaves in this Territory, or shall introduce into this Territory, print, publish, write, circulate, or cause to be introduced into this Territory, written, printed, published or circulated in this Territory, any book, paper, magazine, pamphlet or circular, containing any denial of the right of persons to hold slaves in this Territory, such person shall be deemed guilty of felony, and punished by imprisonment at hard labor for a term of not less than two years.

SEC. 13. No person who is conscientiously opposed to holding slaves, or who does not admit the right to hold slaves in this Territory, shall sit as a juror on the trial of any prosecution for any violation of any of the sections of this act.

This act to take effect and be in force from and after the fifteenth day of September, A. D. 1855

                                J. H. STRINGFELLOW, Speaker of the House.

Attest, J. M. LYLE, Clerk.

                            THOMAS JOHNSON, President of the Council.

Attest, J. A. HALDERMAN, Clerk.

Kansas, *An Act to Punish Offences against Slave Property, Passed by the Legislative Assembly of the Territory of Kansas, August 14, 1855* (Shawnee M. L. S.: John T. Brady, Public Printer, 1855).

THOMAS WELLS DESCRIBES KANSAS

Thomas C. Wells left Rhode Island for Kansas Territory when he was twenty-three, and his arrival coincided with the March 1855 territorial elections. In a letter to his mother, Wells described the Missourians he encountered. A year later, after returning from a winter spent in the East, he speculated on the fate of Southerners who had relocated to Kansas.

                                        Topeka K. T. Apr 1, /55.

My Dear Mother,

    Here I am in the far famed Kanzas Territory, we left Kanzas City on Monday last at about noon, and passing through Westport, a large Missourian town, we soon came upon the *Indian reserve* (belonging to the Shawnee's) which extends for thirty miles up the Kanzas or Kaw river. . . . The next morning we started for Lawrence City about thirty miles further up the river. . . . We traveled nearly all day among a large party of *Missourians,* number about 200, who were going to Lawrence to *vote* and a pretty rough looking sett they were, some on horseback, some in covered wagons, and others on foot, all hardy, sunburnt, frontier men, and all well armed with guns, revolvers, and bowie knifes. We were often asked what *county* (in Missouri) we came from, and when they learned that we were from the East we had the *pleasure* of being called *"damned Yankee's"* &c but they did not succeed in frightening us or in driving us back, though they assured us that they could fire some twenty shots each, and that they had a six pounder with them. . . . Yours affectionately in haste

                                                   T. C. Wells

                                                Apr. 3, 1856
                                    Steamer Jas H Lucas
                                      Missouri River,

My dear Mother . . .

    We went on board the Steamer J. H Lucas on Monday Morning and engaged passage for Kansas City. . . .

Quite a number of people are on board from South Carolina and Georgia going to Kansas. What think you of that? I will tell you what I think. Nine tenths of them will return home, or at least leave Kansas, before they have been there three months.

They have left their old homes in beautiful springtime, all nature looking green and luxuriated—their warm and sunny homes in the south, for the windy plains of Kansas, as yet brown with the frosts of winter. They have taken the wrong time to emigrate and the new country will not suit them.

And of those who do remain, nine out of ten will ere long turn free state men. They will find it for their interest to do so, and when their interest decides against slavery they will both see and acknowledge that the whole system is entirely wrong. We anticipate no trouble from them. And indeed we expect that the worst trouble is over and that we shall be left comparatively to ourselves, at least we hope so.

The free state people must eventually conquor—the south cannot compete with the North in sending emigrants, and very few of the small number who came from the south dare to bring slaves with them . . .

Yours affect'ly

Juniata Kansas Terr

Apr 13th. . . . We landed at Leavenworth City, instead of Lexington or Kansas. Leavenworth is 50 miles further up the river than Kansas City, and is 15 or 20 miles nearer the Blue than K. The road is also much better, it being the government road from Fort L. to Fort Reiley. . . .

I have got to go down to L again in a few days and get the rest of our things. There has been more trouble in Kansas this winter than I had supposed; the wrongs of the free state people have not been exagerated in the papers. The Lawrence people especially have suffered immensely. For a long time no one could go to or from Kansas City without having his baggage searched, and even now the Missourians frequently break open heavy trunks or boxes to search for sharps rifles of which they stand in great fear. . . .

When we arrived at Juniata we found the government bridge across the Blue had been carried away by the ice. We have to cross on a ferry boat now which is rather expensive and not very pleasant business. Mr Dyer has turned strong pro slavery and they have got a pro slavery minister there of the Methodist Church South, who says "he would as leave sell a nigger as an ox." They have organized a church under pro slavery influence and intend to do all they can to bring slaves into Kansas and drive out the yankees, "for," they say, "they do not want eastern men to rule the territory."

They may do their best however, and they will not succeed, they have a class of people to deal with that are not frightened at trifles and not withstanding their threats and their struggles Kansas will be a free state and and the territory will be ruled by eastern men. . . .

Yours truly T. C. Wells

Thomas Wells Collection 537, Kansas State Historical Society.

A SOUTH CAROLINIAN ENTERS KANSAS TERRITORY

Born in Darlington, South Carolina, Axalla Hoole was a teacher and a captain in a local militia company. He arrived in Kansas in 1856 and remained for almost two years. After his return in December 1857, Hoole rejoined the Darlington Riflemen, which later was mustered into the Confederacy's service as Company A, Eighth South Carolina Volunteers. In 1862 the regiment was reorganized and joined General Braxton Bragg's forces in 1863. Hoole was killed in the battle of Chickamauga on September 20, 1863.

Kansas City, Missouri, Apl. 3d., 1856

My Dear Brother

HERE I am after two weeks travelling, and not in Kansas Territory yet, but it is only 1 1/2 miles off, and I can see into it. . . .

The Missourians (all of whom I have conversed with, with the exception of one who, by the way, I found out to be an Abolitionist) are very sanguine about Kansas being a slave state & I have heard some of them say it *shall* be. I have met with warm reception from two or three, but generally speaking, I have not met with the reception which I expected. Everyone seems bent on the Almighty Dollar, and as a general thing that seems to be their only thought—There was a large box on one of the boats about a week ago coming up the river, which some of the Missourians thought contained Sharp's Rifles, so they sent a deputation to its destination, which was at this place, to have it opened. When they arrived here the person to whom it was consigned refused to let them open it, whereupon they opened it by force—when lo! it contained nothing but a piano. There was a box containing a cannon which a confounded Yankee opened, but closed it up again before any of them could examine it, saying that it was nothing but some cartwheels. His daughter-in-law told me this this morning, hesitatingly, as if her father-in-law had done a smart trick. If she had been a man, I don't know what I should have said, but she was a pretty young woman.

Well, dear brother, the supper bell has rung, so I must close. Give my love to [the immediate family] and all the Negroes. . . . Excuse bad writing for I am very nervous. I am anxious to hear from home. . . Your ever affectionate brother, Axalla.

~

Douglas City, K. T., Apl. 14th., 1856

My Dear Mother

. . . I came to this place last Saturday, after staying at that nasty Abolition town of Lawrence for a week. This is called a City, but there are only four little log houses in it, but it is laid out into lots for a town, and I expect one day it will be. The capital, Lecompton, is two miles from here, but they are going to build the state university at this place. It is situated close on the Kansas river, and I consider it the prettiest site for a town in the Territory.

. . . We are boarding with a very excellent family named Ellison. The old gentleman is the most enthusiastic Proslavery man I have met with.

. . . They are wanting a school in Lecompton but I have not been able to make it up. The fact is, the people here seem to be so taken up with politics, that they can't take time to think of hardly anything else. . . . I don't think I will ever like this country. The timber is too scarce, but the land is very rich—any of it will make from fifty to a hundred bushels of corn to the acre; but then the wind is always blowing, sometimes so hard that a man can hardly keep his hat on his head. . . . But I don't think I will ever like this country well enough to settle here, and I don't think, or at least I am afraid, it will be never be made a slave state, and if it is not, I will not live here on any conditions. . . .

The people in this Territory have very poor houses, generally built of logs with rock chimneys. The one we are boarding in is three log houses built in a row—the middle one of which is the kitchen where the Negroes stay. They have four or five Negroes. . . .

The people here are just fixing to plant their crops. Trees are put out about like they were when we left Darlington. The nights here are still quite cool, but I have not seen frost for some time.

. . . Your ever affectionate son, Axalla.

A. J. Hoole, "A Southerner's Viewpoint of the Kansas Situation, 1856–1857: The Letters of Lieut. Col. A. J. Hoole, C.S.A.," ed. William Stanley Hoole, *Kansas Historical Quarterly* 3, no. 1 (February 1934): 43–46.

IMPRISONED ON CHARGES OF TREASON

On May 21, 1856, a mob sacked the free-state town of Lawrence. George W. Brown, the editor of the Herald of Freedom, *was not in town that day, having been arrested on May 14 on charges of treason. Imprisoned by federal troops near Lecompton, Brown wrote Eli Thayer, the organizer of the New England Emigrant Aid Company (who was elected to Congress later that year), for help. After four months, his case was dismissed without trial.*

Under Guard, Near Lecompton, K. T.,
June 4th, 1856.

Eli Thayer, Esq.,

My Dear Friend:—You have learned ere this of my arrest at Kansas City, while
on the way to the Territory, by an armed mob, and of my confinement here
under guard of United States troops, with all communication cut off with the
business world. You will also have learned of the destruction of the Emigrant
Aid Co's Hotel at Lawrence, of the buring of Doct. Robinson's dwelling; the
stealing of his papers, books and soforth; of his own imprisonment; and of the
destruction of my two hand presses, the power press, all my type and fixtures for
my extensive news and jobbing office; also my private papers and documents,
and my extensive miscellaneous and law library, embracing over a thousand
volumes of the choicest publicatins of the times.

The Demons of the slave power are rampant to day, and all because they
come in the name of law, clothed with authority of the federal government.

The charge of treason against us is the most ludicrous ever brought against
men. All connected with our arrest know it; and yet we have been denied
bail, and shall be compelled to remain here on the open prairie, under a tent,
exposed to an oppressive summer sun, and guarded by United States troops until
September next, unless our friends in the East can contrive sum plan for our
liberation. To remain as we are is to expose us to disease, if not death, before
we can get a trial. The hell-hounds of the South, under the patronage of officers
clothed with authority by Frank Pierce, have temporary supremicy in Kansas.
We are willing they shall run not for a brief season, as we are confident they will
be ultimately chained; we see, too, the end of slavery rapidly approaching, and
deem their late acts in Kansas the crowning work in their destruction. To you to
whom we are already so deeply indebted for past services in behalf of our cause
we naturally look in the hour of affliction. To you we again appeal for sympathy
and aid, and we feel sure it will be received. Your eloquence is needed to arouse
a nation to action. Your energy is demanded to turn the losses of the people of
Lawrence, and their sufferings to account in behalf of freedom.

I beg of you to withhold no effort in favor of our cause. Our triumph is the
triumph of liberty every where. Our enslavement is the death knell of freedom
in this republic—thoughout the world. . . .

Yours Truly,
G. W. Brown

Eli Thayer Collection 519, Kansas State Historical Society.

THE POTTAWATOMIE MASSACRE

After the sack of Lawrence, John Brown, four of his sons, and two other men, executed five proslavery men at Pottawatomie Creek on May 24, 1856. None of the five—Allen Wilkinson, William Sherman, James Doyle, and his two sons, William and Drury Doyle—had owned slaves or had been involved in the Lawrence events. A resident of Franklin County, where the massacre took place, James Hanway, a friend of Brown's and a member of his eldest son's militia, wrote of the massacre in his journal. At the time, Brown's involvement was not widely known.

Killed on Saturday night May 24, 1856 3 men of the name of Doyal—Wm Sherman & Wilkinson—the latter received 6 wounds each one would have proved fatal old man Doyal was shot through the head & stabed in the heart. & his 2 boys where disherated cut about the hands—the younger boy's hands were mangled as if he had held up his hands to defend himself from the blows of the saber—Shermans head was cut by a saber blow, and other.

five men murdered in one night. enticed from their houses with the promise of being kept from violence, as prisoners of war—lead a few rods from their doors then killed. one was flung in the Creek down the bank. (Wilkinson) he was post master—The murderers inquired for Henry, but he was away from home hunting up his cattle this saved his life—At Sherman they seized 3 other men with him took them all out from the house asked them their names, and as they had no knowledge of them, told them to go back again. The question now is who has performed this frightful tradagy men names are whispered—no positive knowledge—Mrs. Doyal disstribed 2 of the men, which disscription is exactly that of Mr. Wilkinson—a man who lives at Shermans for several years says he did not know any of them altho he has lived here 2 yrs and knows most people on the creek. The settlement is plunged into a perfect commotion. A meeting of the settlers was held on the 26 and they mutaley agreed to protect each other from foreign or internal foes all men of real good sense, condemned this midnight assasinations and also the killing of men who are attending to their concerns—one murder by the opposite side, only makes another on the other—

the supposed caused which made the Doyal family the victims, is that the old man & his 2 sons, caled on a man who kept store near Shermans—and told him to pack up his goods, moved off his claims in 5 days or they would kill him—Morse did not move but is still at home, he was arrested by a body of men & as their was no evidenced against him he is at large. Sherman it is said as repeatidly treatened to shoot & exterminate free state men, and as the news of the fall of Lawrence raised a red flag; which was said he ment to intimate that war was commenced & he was in for it—Wilkinson appears to have been a very violent & imprudent man making threat of killing & burning & his wife is a fine woman, sick at the time of the murder and told the Dr. that she has frequently urged him to be more quiet—but could not do it—it appears from general opinion that they were extreme men, and very obnoxious to the free state men—thus violence breeds violence. Again: No sooner the news of the destruction of the Hotel at Lawrence and the two printing presses, than the Border Times a violent paper published at Westport after given a short statement of the pilliage & destruction of Lawrence, comments thus—it says—"This is right, nuisances should be suppressed" and then recommends the pro-slavery party of the Ty to drive and exterminate every "black hearted abolitionist & drive them from out of the Ty."

they advocate assasination—and now that 5 persons have been murdered on their side perhaps they will learn that such hellish sentiments when carried into effect, will work equally to the destruction of the pro slavery men of the territory. Such men are the immediate instigators of all such bloody tragadies as we have witnessed—they should be held responsible at the bar of public opinion

James Hanway Collection 372, Kansas State Historical Society.

KANSAS AS AN OUTPOST IN A LARGER WAR

David Rice Atchison represented Missouri in the Senate from 1843 to 1855, after which he dedicated himself to ensuring that Kansas join the United States as a slave state. He encouraged the enthusiastic participation of Missourians in the first Kansas elections and became active in the Law and Order Party, formed to further this goal. Issued less than two months after the arrival of the Buford expedition (which had brought Southerners to the territory with promises of free transportation, a year's support, and forty acres of land), this 1856 appeal tried to draw more settlers to the territory, recognizing that the four hundred settlers who had accompanied Jefferson Buford would be insufficient.

THE VOICE OF KANSAS—LET THE SOUTH RESPOND.

APPEAL BY THE LAW AND ORDER PARTY OF KANSAS TERRITORY TO THEIR FRIENDS IN THE SOUTH, AND TO THE LAW-ABIDING PEOPLE OF THE UNION.

One of the Committee (Col. Buford) places the manuscript in our hands, and we commend it to the serious attention of the readers of the Review. The cause is one to which, without loss of a single day, every Southern man should contribute. Alabama, South Carolina, and Georgia, have been lavish in their aid. The loss of Kansas will give to the enemies of Southern institutions a victory more signal and more important than has yet been won over us. To avert the mischief, prompt and concerted action at the South is only needed. Those familiar with the state of affairs in Kansas *know* that it can only be abolitionized by the supineness of the people of this section, whose all is at stake in these contests.

The undersigned, at a recent meeting of the party, were constituted a committee, charged, among other things, with the publication of this address.

That a state of insurrection and civil war exists among us is abundantly evident: the "law and order party" on the one side, opposed on the other by the abolitionists, sent out and sustained by the Emigrant Aid Societies of the North. . . .

In territorial politics, the question of free or slave State has swallowed up every other. The abolitionists on the one hand, in accordance with their early teaching, regard slavery as the greatest possible evil; they deem it a monstrous national crime, which their false theories of government impute equally to every portion of the confederacy, and thus believing themselves individually responsible for its existence, they feel bound each to struggle for its overthrow; to such extremes have wicked demagogues stimulated their fanaticism, that their perverted consciences justify any mode of warfare against slaveholders, however much in violation of law, however destructive of property or human life, and however atrociously wicked it may seem to others. . . . And with them it is no mere local question of whether slavery shall exist in Kansas or not, but one of far wider significance, a question of whether it shall exist any where in the Union. Kansas they justly regard as the mere outpost in the war now being waged between the antagonistic civilizations of the North and the South; and winning this great outpost and stand-point, they rightly think their march will be open to an easy conquest of the whole field. Hence the extraordinary means the abolition party has adopted to flood Kansas with the most fanatical and lawless portion of northern society; and hence the large sums of money they have expended to surround their brother Missourians with obnoxious and dangerous neighbors.

On the other hand, the pro-slavery element of the "law and order party" in Kansas, looking to the Bible, find slavery ordained of God; they find there, as by our law, slavery made "an inheritence to them and their children forever." Looking to our national census, and to all statistics connected with the African race, and considering, too, their physical, intellectual, and moral natures, we see that slavery is the African's normal and proper state; since, in that state, that race multiplies faster, has more physical comfort, less vice, and more moral and intellectual progress than in any other.

We believe slavery the only school in which the debased son of Ham, by attrition with a higher race, can be refined and elevated; we believe it a trust and guardianship given us of God for the good of both races. Without sugar, cotton, and cheap clothing, can civilization maintain its progress? Can these be supplied without slavery? Nay, in the absence of slave institutions, must not social distinctions supervene among the free to the detriment of republican equality? This is no mere property question, but a great social and political question of races; it is not a question of whether A. or B. shall be owner, but of whether the slave, still having a master, shall still be a working bee, and not an idle drone in the hive; a question of whether the South shall still be a land flowing with milk and honey, or a land of mendicants and vagabonds; a great question of races; a question of whether we shall sink to the level of the freed African, and take him to the embrace of social and political equality, and fraternity; for such is the natural end of abolition progress. Fanaticism must defend its beneficiaries—first, by sending the federal army to protect them, and ultimately by giving them the right to bear arms, vote, testify, make and administer laws—in short, the right to eat out our substance, to pull us down to their level, to taint our blood, and bring us to a degradation from which no time can redeem us. Thus radical and marked the difference in theory between the two parties, and not less so their difference in practice; while we, in good faith, sustain and uphold the laws, the abolitionists on the other hand, in effect, repudiate and set them at defiance; with open disloyalty they assert the invalidity of the territorial laws . . . ; indeed, more than once, they have openly resisted the marshal in the service of process . . . ; they have repudiated payment of taxes, and have held and published the proceedings of large public meetings in which they resolved to resist, even to blood, the territorial laws, and especially the laws for the collection of the public revenue.

According to testimony under oath lately given before the Congressional Committee, they have secret military organizations for resisting the laws and for carrying out their abolition designs upon Kansas—organizations in which the members are bound by the most solemn oaths to obey their leaders, in all cases, not excepting even murder and treason. . . . By such banditti the murders near Ossawattamie, on Pottawattamie creek, were committed; declarations by the perpetrators cotemporaneous with their foul deeds indubitably show the parentage of these crimes; six victims, whose bodies have been found, fell in that massacre, beside four others missing from the neighborhood, and not yet heard from. Of the six, one was Allen Wilkinson, Esq., a member of the territorial Legislature and postmaster at Shermanville; sick with the measles, for no other offence save that of being a law and order man, he was dragged at midnight from his bed, and from the side of a sick and imploring wife, by a band of abolition assassins, acting as they said in the name of the great northern army; within hearing of the terror stricken wife, with fiendish barbarity, he was flayed alive, his nose and ears were cut off, his scalp torn from his head, and then he was stabbed through the heart. Such is the sworn evidence of his widow lately tendered in Westport before the Congressional Investigating Committee. . . . Besides Wilkinson, Wm. Sherman and brother, and Mr. Doyle and two sons, were proved to have been murdered at their respective homes on the same night and by the same band; one of the Doyles' also had his fingers and arms cut off before he was finally dispatched. Incredible as these things may seem, they unquestionably happened in Kansas

Territory in the latter part of last month; yet what is more incredible, but not less true, is the undeniable fact that these outrages are not, as some pretend, the mere extravagances of a few irresponsible individuals, but on the contrary are justly chargeable to the abolition party, as the legitimate fruit of their party measures and party discipline, and as naturally resulting from the public teachings, advice, and counsel of their chief men and most distinguished leaders. . . .

. . . we firmly believe that our party has a well established, decided, and increasing majority of actual settlers in the territory. This majority, however, we do not believe can be maintained unless something be done to give confidence to our friends, where they are few and weak in number. This can only be done by colonizing large settlements together, under one common head with absolute control; let, say from one to three hundred agriculturalists, mechanics, and laborers so settle together in some suitable point. . . . These measures of mutual defence and future progress, however, require means, and demand aid from our friends abroad. The colonists should be subsisted a reasonable time, and each individual furnished with adequate agricultural or mechanical outfit, so there can be no want of settlers coming and remaining at the points where they are most needed. Funds are required, and for these we call upon our Southern friends—upon all having a common interest—nay, we call on all loving justice and wishing equal rights to each State and section of the Union—we call on the honest free State man, who, sick of the agitation and strife brewed by the abolitionists, desires the restoration of peace and quiet to the country. These can be restored only by restoring to the weaker and attacked section the means of future defence, in restoring the sectional equilibrium disturbed by the measures of 1850. Fanatical aggression cannot be quieted by *giving,* but it may be by *taking away* the power to effect its ends. All fair minds who have looked this question full in the face, know and admit that it is not merely a question of whether Kansas shall be a slave State or not, but a question of whether the entire South shall not become the victim of misguided philanthropy. That man or State is deceived that fondly trusts these fanatics may stop at Kansas. To use that territory as the mere "key to the future"—the mere means of ulterior operations against the whole South—is unquestionably the settled policy of the ultra abolitionists, the head and soul of the aggression, and *whose opinions in the end must leaven and control the whole body*—the whole mass that acts with them. . . .

How can there be other than the most exasperated state of feeling between the two sections? How can civil war be avoided, when honorable committee men countenance such reckless mischief? Look the future in the face like men: if standing up to our rights, to our responsibilities, and to our trust, brings peace and security, so much the better; no other course can effect it. Send us men and means. We must have your help. . . . Friends of the cause must contribute according to their several gifts—we must not meanly abandon our birthright, and, without a

struggle, yield to grasping monopoly this fairest Eden of our common domain—
this land of flowing brook and fertile plain. Kansas is indeed the garden spot of
America, and in every way adapted to Southern institutions; in no other part of the
Union is slave labor more productive; and, in the present imperilled state of our
civilization, if we do not maintain this outpost, we cannot long defend the citadel.
Then rally to the rescue. . . .

DAVID R. ATCHISON [et al.]
June 21st, 1856.

David R. Atchison et al., "The Voice of Kansas—Let the South Respond; . . . ," *De Bow's Review and Industrial
Resources, Statistics, etc.* 21, 3rd ser., vol. 1 (Washington City and New Orleans, 1856), 187–94.

EPHRAIM NUTE ON THE DOY INCIDENT

*On January 25, 1859, John Doy and his son Charles left Lawrence, Kansas Territory,
with thirteen slaves, intending to take them to Nebraska. However, the party was
captured and jailed in Missouri for abducting slaves. After a trial in St. Joseph,
Charles Doy was released, but John Doy was convicted in a second trial. Sentenced
to five years in jail, he was freed by ten friends from Kansas on September 23, 1859.
In these letters, Ephraim Nute, a Unitarian minister in Lawrence who would serve
as chaplain for the First Regiment of Kansas Volunteers during the war, explains
these events.*

Lawrence K.T. Feb 14, 59

My dear friend, . . .

Before this can reach you you will have learned something of the disaster that
befel the last expedition from this place with fugitives, But you are not likely to
get the facts just as they were & I will give you those of most importance. The
party consisted of 13 col.[d] people (11 fugitives & 2 free by birth) with 3 of our
citizens, with two teams (horses & wagons) The col[d] people were put across
the river some 4 miles above this place about 2 o clock in the morning, the
teams crossed the ferry about 2 hours later & took the river road, after taking
in the passengers they took the road toward Oscaloosa & about an hour after
on entering a sort of defile between the bluffs & "the timber" found themselves
surrounded by a party of armed & mounted men. They surrendered without a
blow & were taken over into Missouri, the col[d] people, both free & slaves, have
been shipped for the New Orleans market. One of the white men was released
& returned to Lawrence the others, Dr John Doy & son, are now in close
confinement in Platte city Jail awaiting their trial in charge of stealing a slave
from Weston, (one of the 13). . . .

The whole affair was managed perhaps as well as it could be with the obstacles in the way. The great trouble was the want of funds. This hindered us from sending them forward as fast as they arrived, as before has been done, & so permitted such a large number to accumulate here. . .

Great rewards were offered, spies sent out & men hired in this place to watch & aid in recovering the run away property. We find that every movement was known to the enemy who were gathered at Lecompton the evening before the starting of the train. . . .

~

Lawrence K.T. Feb 24 '59

Dear Friend

Last night one of the captured fugitives of whom I wrote you in my last arrived at this place. As no one appeared to claim him he was lodged for safe keeping in the Jail at Platte city with some ten or twelve other slaves, most of whom had been recently bought up to be taken South. He broke jail by burning out the bars from the window; he walked 10 miles to the Missouri river & crossed on the floating cakes of ice; got 1st on to an island or sand-bar in the middle of the river where he spent two days & nights hid in the young cottonwoods; thence again over the running ice to the Kansas side & walked the 35 or 40 miles to this place in one night. He is a resolute fellow right in the prime of life (35 years old) has a wife who has lived with him here in Lawrence since last September up to the time of their attempted migration to a freer soil in British dominion & their capture by the human blood hounds but 10 miles from this place {He thinks she is now in Lexington Mo, where she is owned,} We have him now hid & are to day making arrangements to have him set forward tomorrow 30 miles to another depot. I think they (there are 2 others to go) will not be taken again without bloodshed. . . .

. . . Dr Doy & son are yet in jail at Platte city, locked up in an iron cell 8 feet square without fire, light or pure air. We are now making every effort in our power for their defence. The x which you sent me has gone for that cause being spent to get Mrs Doy & daughter & other witnesses from this place to Platte city.

You need not be surprised if you hear of an invasion into Missouri & a forcible delivery of our kidnapped citizens out of that vile iron box about the time that this reaches you. . . .

The end is not yet. Yours for the Right

E.N.

John Brown Collection 299, Kansas State Historical Society.

TWO

Joining the Union

$\mathcal{T}$HE SIX YEARS Kansas spent as a territory were marked by a sense of urgency. Aside from the violence, there is perhaps no better evidence of this than the constitutions Kansas residents wrote: the territory prepared one for nearly every eighteen months it spent as a territory. For both sides in the Kansas struggle, admission to the Union offered the answer to their prayers and problems. The ambiguities of popular sovereignty—a policy that seemed more democratic precisely because it placed the determination of a state's institutions directly in the hands of those most affected by the question—had only served to inflame sectional tensions and transform settlement into a race to secure the nascent state for the forces of freedom or slavery. Merely two years after Kansas Territory's organization, an extralegal entity with no official standing sent a constitution to Washington. By virtue of an effective Republican propaganda machine, this Topeka Constitution garnered considerable support during the presidential campaign of 1856.

The Topeka Constitution was an outgrowth of the flawed territorial elections of late 1854 and early 1855. Although proslavery residents were in the majority and thus would have won these two elections, their use of fraud and intimidation to ensure the outcome alienated many free-state residents. Convinced that the territorial legislature had violated their rights and, moreover, that the federal government was complicit in these actions, the free-state movement began a process that culminated in the submission of the Topeka Constitution to Congress in 1856. The constitution itself was typical for the era but included a bill of rights that outlawed slavery in Kansas except as a legal sentence for a crime. Moreover, in direct response to the actions of the territorial legislature, the Topeka Constitution explicitly ensured freedom of speech and the ability to write and publish on all topics. Suffrage was restricted to whites and "civilized" Indians over the age of twenty-one years who had spent six months in the territory. Despite the Topeka movement's reputation as antislavery, the Topeka Constitution excluded free blacks from Kansas.[1] On July 3, 1856, the Republican-controlled House of Representatives voted to accept the Topeka Constitution and admit Kansas to the Union. The Senate, however, rejected Kansas's admission because the constitution was written by a minority of residents acting without proper authority.

The Lecompton Constitution was the second constitution submitted to Congress but the first to have legal standing. It was written by delegates chosen by Kansas residents in the spring of 1857. From the start, free-state residents assaulted the Lecompton process, claiming that the census had been improperly taken and that the delegates therefore did not represent the territory. But the new territorial governor, Robert Walker, supported the process and convinced free-state residents to participate in the process by stressing that the move toward statehood would continue even without their consent or participation.

Written by a largely proslavery delegation, the Lecompton convention proposed a referendum in which residents could not reject the Lecompton Constitution itself. Instead, they could vote only on its form: would the constitution include Article VII, which allowed slavery? If voters agreed, Kansas would be a slave state; if they refused, Article VII would be stricken from the document and Kansas would be a free state. Notably, nothing was said about the emancipation of those 450 slaves already in the territory.[2] On December 21, 1857, 6,226 Kansas voters accepted the constitution with Article VII, while another 569 rejected it. However, free-state voters boycotted the election in favor of one of their own. On January 4, 1858, in a separate election, 10,226 free-state residents voted against the Lecompton Constitution, 138 voted for it without slavery, and another 23 voted for it with slavery.

Democratic president James Buchanan made Kansas's admission under the Lecompton Constitution a party measure. Yet Congress would not accept the controversial constitution outright. Instead a conference committee agreed on a bill that added a major qualification: Kansas voters—all of them this time—would have to reratify the Lecompton Constitution. If they accepted it, they would join the Union with a generous land grant; if not, Kansas would remain a territory until the population standard for a congressional representative (93,420 residents in 1858) was met. Furthermore, there was no mention of a future land grant.[3] Under these conditions, Kansas residents emphatically rejected what they called the Lecompton Swindle on August 2, 1858, by a vote of 11,300 to 1,788.

While Congress was considering the Lecompton Constitution, the Free-State Party, buoyed by winning the legislature in the October 1857 elections, began another constitutional process in 1858. However, this free-state Leavenworth Constitution was ignored by Congress. Undaunted by Congress's repudiation and against the wishes of territorial governor James Denver, Kansans met in the summer of 1859, this time at Wyandotte, to draft yet another constitution, which was accepted by voters on October 4. Moreover, as the 1858 vote on the Lecompton Constitution had heralded, Republicans had gained the upper hand in Kansas Territory and the slate of officers elected under the Wyandotte Constitution in December was dominated by their party. A Republican governor, Charles Robinson, was elected and the state house was composed of sixty-four Republicans and eleven Democrats, while the senate had twenty-two Republicans to only three Democrats. This senate selected Samuel C. Pomeroy and James H. Lane to represent Kansas in the national legislature once Kansas was admitted.[4]

In February 1860 a bill to admit Kansas was introduced in Congress and, on April 11, the House of Representatives accepted it. The Senate, however, waited until after the election of 1860 to take action. Finally, on January 21, 1861, when the Union had already begun to fragment, outgoing president James Buchanan signed the bill of admission and Kansas joined the Union under the Wyandotte Constitution as the thirty-fourth state.

Although Kansas was admitted under its fourth constitution in 1861, the turning point for the territory was the 1858 defeat of the Lecompton Constitution. That lopsided vote revealed the failure of the Democratic Party in Kansas. The actions of two successive Democratic presidents, Franklin Pierce and James Buchanan, had ensured that Kansans would reject both slavery and the party itself. These presidents had secured neither the preferred Democratic, proslavery state nor the fallback position: a free-state, Democratic Kansas. Instead, Kansas was adamantly antislavery with an entrenched Republican Party. In fact, during Kansas's first century of statehood, Republicans served as governor for eighty-two years and the Populists for another four. While the territory had had six Democrats appointed as territorial governor, when allowed to choose for themselves, Kansans allowed Democrats to serve in the state's highest office for only fourteen of the first hundred years.

"WHAT IS KANSAS, WITH OR WITHOUT SLAVERY, IF SHE SHOULD DESTROY THE RIGHTS AND UNION OF THE STATES?"

The choice of Robert Walker—born in Pennsylvania, but having represented Mississippi in the Senate—for territorial governor seemed sure to please Northerners and Southerners alike. But in his 1857 inaugural address, Walker offered opinions sure to displease both sides in the struggle for Kansas.

Lecompton, Kansas Territory, May 27, 1857

Fellow Citizens of Kansas:
. . . The President . . . expressed to me the conviction that the condition of Kansas was fraught with imminent peril to the union, and asked me to undertake the settlement of that momentous question which has introduced discord and civil war throughout your borders, and threatens to involve you and our country in the same common ruin. . . .

The people of Kansas, then, are invited by the highest authority known to the constitution to participate freely and fairly in the election of delegates to frame a constitution and state government. The law has performed its entire appropriate function when it extends to the people the right of suffrage, but it cannot compel the performance of that duty. Throughout our whole union, however, and wherever free government prevails, those who abstain from the exercise of the right of suffrage authorize those who do vote to act for them in that contingency, and the absentees are as much bound under the law and constitution, where there is no fraud or violence, by the act of the majority of those who do vote, as if all had participated in the election. Otherwise, as voting must be voluntary, self-government would be impracticable, and monarchy or despotism would remain as the only alternative. . . .

I cannot too earnestly impress upon you the necessity of removing the slavery agitation from the halls of Congress and presidential conflicts. It is conceded that Congress has no power to interfere with slavery in the states where it exists; and if it can now be established, as is clearly the doctrine of the constitution, that Congress has no authority to interfere with the people of a territory on this subject in forming a state constitution, the question must be removed from congressional and presidential elections.

. . . If this principle can be carried into successful operation in Kansas—that her people shall determine what shall be her social institutions—the slavery question must be withdrawn from the halls of Congress and from our presidential conflicts, and the safety of the union be placed beyond all peril; whereas, if the principle should be defeated here, the slavery agitation must be renewed in all elections throughout the country with increasing bitterness, until it shall eventually overthrow the government. . . .

And let me ask you, what possible good has been accomplished by agitating in Congress and in presidential conflicts the slavery question? Has it emancipated a single slave, or improved their condition? Has it made a single state free, where slavery otherwise would have existed? Has it accelerated the disappearance of slavery from the more northern of the slave-holding states, or accomplished any practical good whatever? No, my fellow citizens, nothing but unmitigated evil has already ensued, with disasters still more fearful impending for the future, as a consequence of this agitation.

There is a law more powerful than the legislation of man, more potent than passion or prejudice, that must ultimately determine the location of slavery in this country; it is the isothermal line, it is the law of the thermometer, of latitude or altitude, regulating climate, labor, and productions, and, as a consequence, profit and loss. Thus, even upon the mountain heights of the tropics slavery can no more exist than in northern latitudes, because it is unprofitable, being unsuited to the constitution of that sable race transplanted here from the equatorial heats of Africa. Why is it that in the union slavery recedes from the north and progresses south? It is this same great climatic law now operating for or against slavery in Kansas. If, on the elevated plains of Kansas . . . should render slavery unprofitable here, because unsuited to the tropical constitution of the negro race, the law above referred to must ultimately determine that question here, and can no more be controlled by the legislation of man than any other moral or physical law of the Almighty. . . .

If, from the operation of these causes, slavery should not exist here, I trust it by no means follows that Kansas should become a state controlled by the treason and fanaticism of abolition. She has, in any event, certain constitutional duties to perform to her sister states, and especially to her immediate neighbor, the slaveholding state of Missouri. Through that great state, by rivers and railroads, must now, to a great extent, our trade and intercourse, our imports and exports. Our entire eastern front is upon her border; from Missouri come a great number of her citizens; even the farms of the two states are cut by the line of state boundary—part in Kansas, part in Missouri; her citizens meet us in daily intercourse; and that Kansas should become hostile to Missouri, an asylum for her fugitive slaves, or a propagandist of abolition treason, would be alike inexpedient and unjust, and fatal to the continuance of the American union. . . .

Our country and the world are regarding with profound interest the struggle now impending in Kansas. Whether we are competent to self-government; whether we can decide this controversy peacefully for ourselves by our own votes, without fraud or violence; whether the great principles of self-government and state sovereignty can be carried here into successful operation, are the questions now to be determined; and upon the plains of Kansas may now be fought the last great and decisive battle, involving the fate of the union, of state sovereignty, of self-government, and the liberties of the world. If, my fellow citizens, you could, even for a brief period, soften or extinguish sectional passions or prejudice, and lift yourselves to the full realization of the momentous issues intrusted to your decision, you would feel that no greater responsibility was ever devolved on any people. It is not merely shall slavery exist in or disappear from Kansas, but shall the great principles of self-government and state sovereignty be maintained or subverted. . . . Do you love slavery so much, or hate it so intensely, that you would endeavor to establish or exclude it by fraud or violence, against the will of the majority of the people? What is Kansas, with or without slavery, if she should destroy the rights and union of the states? . . . Who can decide this question for Kansas, if not the people themselves? and if they cannot, nothing but the sword can become the arbiter. . . .

. . . if you cannot thus peacefully decide this question, fraud, violence and injustice will reign supreme throughout our borders, and we will have achieved the undying infamy of having destroyed the liberty of our country and of the world. We will become a by-word of reproach and obloquy, and all history will record the fact that Kansas was the grave of the American union. Never was so momentous a question submitted to the decision of any people, and we cannot avoid the alternatives now placed before us of glory or of shame. . . .

Is it not infinitely better that slavery should be abolished or established in Kansas, rather than that we should become slaves and not permitted to govern ourselves? Is the absence or existence of slavery in Kansas paramount to the great questions of state sovereignty, of self-government, and of the union? Is the sable African alone entitled to your sympathy and consideration, even if he were happier as a freeman than as a slave, either here, or in St. Domingo, or the British West Indies, or Spanish America, where the emancipated slave has receded to barbarism, and approaches the lowest point in the descending scale of moral, physical and intellectual degradation? Have our white brethren of the great American and European race no claims upon our attention? Have they no rights or interests entitled to regard and protection? Shall the destiny of the African in Kansas exclude all considerations connected with our own happiness and prosperity? And is it for the handful of that race now in Kansas, or that may be hereafter introduced, that we should subvert the union and the great principles of self-government and state sovereignty, and imbrue our hands in the blood of our countrymen? Important as this African question may be in Kansas, and which it is your solemn right to determine, it sinks into insignificance compared with the perpetuity of the union and the final successful establishment of the principles of state sovereignty and free government. . . . The minority, in resisting the will of the majority, may involve Kansas again in civil war; they may bring upon her reproach and obloquy, and destroy her progress and prosperity; they may keep her for years out of the union, and, in the whirlwind of agitation, sweep away the government itself. . . . Is Kansas willing to destroy her own hopes of prosperity merely that she may afford political capital to any party, and perpetuate the agitation of slavery throughout the union? Is she to become a mere theme for agitators in other states, the theater on which they shall perform the bloody drama of treason and disunion? Does she want to see . . . revolution and civil war inaugurated throughout her limits? Does she want to be "bleeding Kansas" for the benefit of political agitators within or out of her limits, or does she prefer the peaceful and quiet arbitrament of this question for herself? . . .

Those who oppose slavery in Kansas do not base their opposition upon any philanthropic principles or any sympathy for the African race. For in their so-called constitution, framed at Topeka, they deem that entire race so inferior and degraded as to exclude them all forever from Kansas, whether they be bond or free, thus depriving them of all rights here, and denying even that they can be citizens of the United States; for, if they are citizens, they could not constitutionally be exiled or excluded from Kansas. . . .

I have endeavored heretofore faintly to foreshadow the wonderful prosperity which would follow at once in Kansas the peaceful and final settlement of this question. But if it should be in the power of agitators to prevent such a result, nothing but ruin will pervade our territory. . . .

Nor will the mischief be arrested here. It will extend into every other state. Despots will exult over the failure here of the great principles of self-government and the approaching downfall of our confederacy. The pillars of the union will rock upon their base, and we may close the next presidential conflict amid the scattered fragments of the constitution of our once happy and united people. The banner of the stars and stripes, the emblem of our country's glory, will be rent by contending factions. We shall no longer have a country. The friends of human liberty in other realms will shrink despairingly from the conflict. Despotic power will resume its sway throughout the world, and man will have tried in vain the last experiment of self-government. The architects of our country's ruin, the assassins of her peace and prosperity, will share the same common ruin of all our race. They will meet, whilst living, the bitter curses of a ruined people, whilst history will record as their only epitaph: These were the destroyers of the American union, of the liberties of their country and of the world.

But I do not despair of the republic. My hope is in the patriotism and intelligence of the people; in their love of country, of liberty, and of the union. . . . For, recollect, my fellow citizens, that it is the constitution that makes the union; and unless that immortal instrument, bearing the name of the father of his country, shall be maintained entire in all its wise provisions and sacred guaranties, our free institutions must perish. . . .

Robert J. Walker, "Governor Walker's Inaugural Address," May 27, 1857, in *Transactions of the Kansas State Historical Society, 1889–'96*; . . . (Topeka: Press of the Kansas State Printing Company, 1896), 5:328–41.

PURSUING WOMEN'S RIGHTS IN TERRITORIAL KANSAS

The Moneka Woman's Rights Association was formed in 1858, and its secretary's book reveals their belief that women's rights were tied to the territory's fate. This association worked to influence territorial politics and supported efforts to shape the Wyandotte Constitution. While women were denied the vote, the final version advanced the cause of women's rights, for Article XV, Section 6, recognized the rights of women to their own property and to their children.

EXCERPTS FROM "SECRETARY'S BOOK OF THE MONEKA WOMANS RIGHTS ASSOCIATION"

Moneka Feb 13th. . .

Preamble and Constitution of the Moneka Women's Rights Association.

Because, Woman is constitud of body and mind and has all the common wants of the one and the natural powers of the other

Because she is a social being and has all the relations of life to sustain which belong to an Associated condition of existance—and

Because she is a progressive being ever out-growing the past and demanding a higher and greater Future—or in other words,

Because she is a Human Being and as such is endowed by her Creator with the full measure of human rights whether educational, social or political; and

Because by the present arrangement of the world she is shut out of Colleges and the higher order of educational institutions, thereby deprived of great opportunities for intellectual improvement—shut out from most of the lucrative professions and the mechanic arts, thereby deprived of the facilities for the accumulation of wealth and enjoyment of social life,—made subject to laws which she has no voice in making and which deprive her of the ownership of property & of herself, and give even her *daily earnings* to the control of others; dragged before courts to answer for crimes, against laws to which she has never given her assent, to be tried as a criminal in Halls where she can neither sit as judge or juror, or officiate as counsel; and

Because, from the Pulpit and the Rostrum woman is called upon to give character to the rising generation and charged with the responsibility of shaping the destiny of the race,

Because she is demanded to make statesmen to wield the fate of Nations, and divines to wake the wor[l]d to glory,

We therefore form ourselves into an Association to be governed by the following Constitution

Article First

This association shall be called The Moneka Women's Rights Society

Article Second

It shall be the object of the Society to secure to woman her natural rights and to advance her educational interests. In furtherance of these objects the Soc. shall consider what womans natural rights are, and the means best calculated to secure them. It shall also encourage lectures on this subject in the Society and else where; and give its support to some paper devoted to the elevation of Woman . . .

The following resolutions were then offered and adopted.

1st Resolved That we will exert whatever influence we can over the public sentiment of this Territory that the Constitution about to be formed may prohibit the distillation of all alcoholic liquors within its boundaries

2nd Res. That we will invite to our Territory such women lecturers as are accustomed to public speaking to labor with us in procuring this desirable end and we will sustain them when they come.

3rd Resolved That Kansas cannot be truly free while the words "white" or "male" are found within the limits of her constitution.

4th Res. That the Secretary be instructed to correspond with the Editor of the Lilly and ascertain what tracts are on hand, if any, that treat of Women's Rights &c and ascertain on what terms they can be obtained. . . .

Moneka Feb 27th 1858 . . .

The following forms of petition were then presented.

To the Constitutional Convention

We the undersigned citizens of Kansas respectfully petition the Convention now assembled to frame the organic law of the State of Kansas for the *citizens* without any invidious distinctions

To the Legislature of Kansas,

We the undersigned citizens of Kansas respectfully petition your honorable body to enact such laws

1st As will secure to woman the property which she possesses before marriage

2nd Also a just proportion of the joint property of the husband & wife acquired during marriage

3rd Also at the death of the husband or wife that the same laws shall govern the widow or widower in the possession and disposal of the estate and children belonging to them jointly.

4th That no bond or security given for another shall be valid without the signature of the wife. . . .

Moneka May 13th 1859
Society Met & organized. . . .
    The Sec then read the following form of petition prepared by Mrs. Nichols of
Qunindaro

Petition

To the Constitutional Convention of Kansas

Greeting
    We the undersigned citizens of Kansas Territory do respectfully represent to
your Honorable Body that, whereas—the *women* of the state have individually an
evident common interest with its *men* in the protection of *life, liberty, property* and
intelligent culture; and whereas by inherent laws and the "universal concent of mankind" their inalienable relations to humanity do involve them in greater and more
complicated responsibilities; and whereas, in virtue of these common interests
and responsibilities, they have pressing need of all the Legal and Constitutional
guarantees enjoyed by any class of citizens—and whereas the enjoyment of these
guarantees involves the possession of *equal political rights—*
    Therefore we the undersigned being of full age, do respectfully petition and
protest against any constitutional distinctions based on differense of sex. To this
end your petitioners will ever pray
Res That we will circulate this petition and request Mrs. Nichols to present the
same to the Constitutional Convention. . . .

Moneka Dec 19th 1859 . . .
The following forms of petition were then presented
    To the Honorable Senate and House of Representatives of the State of Kansas
We the undersigned, Petitioners, inhabitants of Kansas male and female having
attained the age of legal majority believing that Woman both married and single
should enjoy the same rights as men, in regard to the holding, conveying, and
devising of real and personal property, and the guardian-ship of children, do earnestly request your Honorable Boddies to frame the Laws of the State of Kansas
in these particulars so as to fully establish the legal equality of Women with men—
    To the Honorable Senate and House of Representatives of the State of Kansas
Whereas Governments derive their just power from the consent of the Governed,
we your Petitioners male and female inhabitants of Kansas do earnestly request of
your Honorable Boddies to propose to the people of the State such amendments
of the Constitution of the State as will secure to Females an equal right to the
Elective Franchise with males

After some discussion it was

Res That we accept and adopt these forms of petition for circulation The Society then adjourned to meet at the Accademy in Moneka on Saturday the 7th day of Jan. 1860 . . .

Moneka Jan 7th 1860 . . .

A Resolution was offered and accepted that Mrs. C. I. H. Nichols be requested to attend the Ter Leg for the purpose of advancing our cause as far as practicable. . . .

History, Linn County, Kansas State Historical Society.

THE *FORT SCOTT DEMOCRAT* ON HARPERS FERRY

John Brown's attack on Harpers Ferry galvanized the nation, but Kansans paid particular attention because he began his abolitionist career in the territory. The Marais des Cygnes massacre occurred when proslavery Charles Hamilton and his men lined up and shot eleven men, killing five, on May 19, 1858. It garnered national attention and led John Greenleaf Whittier to write "Le Marais du Cygne," a poem published by the Atlantic Monthly *that September.*

DEVELOPMENTS.

The Harper's Ferry affair has served fully to develop the motives of those who were mainly instrumental in keeping up disturbances in Southern Kansas, during the past two years. It has long been evident that there was some object behind the declared one of driving out the Pro-slavery men. It is true that the desire for plunder was a leading cause. They relied on the excited state of the public mind for protection from punishment for their crimes. But the leading object was war— civil war, the most dreadful and bloody that ever was waged. A systematic plundering of emigrants from Missouri and other southern states, would be the most likely means of effecting this end. They hoped to incite another Missouri invasion, and the ball would be set in motion. The fire thus kindled would have swept far and wide until the whole Union would have been in a blaze.

The end was a diabolical one—the instruments fit. Happily, however, with the exception of the terrible tragedy of the Marais des Cygnes, Missouri maintained the integrity of her Border, and after the raid in which Cruze was killed and his negroes carried off, the war was transferred to another field, with what success the public are aware.

Fort Scott Democrat, November 10, 1859.

DROUGHT IN KANSAS TERRITORY

These documents present a picture of Kansas shortly before statehood. Afflicted by drought, grasshoppers, sickness, and shortages, Kansans needed relief. Money was a serious issue as Kansas became a state, with $100,000 of debt from its short territorial period.

MISCELLANEOUS ACCOUNTS OF CONDITIONS RESULTING FROM DROUGHT

It is unclear who conducted these interviews or made the annotations, but William F. N. Arny likely solicited this report. Born in the District of Columbia, Arny moved in 1850 to Illinois, where he became a leader in the Republican Party before emigrating to Kansas in 1857 and becoming involved in relief efforts. In 1861, Arny became territorial secretary of New Mexico.

MISCELLANEOUS.

Moseley of Greenwood County, a celebrated buffalo hunter said he had just bought a claim for $200 that 6 months ago the man would not have taken $1000. he gave only 25$ in money the balance in trade. There is not a bushel of old corn in the County.

I lived on the Little Arkansas there was a number of families there but now for the extent of 15 miles square not a white–settler remains I do not believe there are three families that have any corn in Greenwod County. Where I am now staying they have no groceries and no money—the people are depending on Buffalo for meat and for bread they have to buy it with wolf skins The wolf skins are a legal tender but you have to catch them first. The people have lost the seed that they planted

A colored man is living in Otoe County by the name of Buckner—Judge Buckner moved from Kentucky to Missouri and at his death he willed to Buckner "The negro" his freedom—he then went to Iowa prejudice drove him to north Kansas and from there he moved to Whitewater on the Osage Lands, west of Butler County in Otoe County He has about 50 head of cattle. some horses. and has 20 acres under cultivation and was doing well till the drougth came on—has now hardly any thing so far as crops are concerned. he is the only person who has not deserted that neighborhood.

Thomas A Hill Greenwood County says the whole county will not produce a bushel of corn to the acre, 80 or 90 families have left, and others want to go but are not able.

Revd. Henry Moys Methodist, Elmendaro says Madison County—will probably raise a half a crop on the Verdigris the people will not have half enough to do. he found a family whose crop had failed and who has not the means to get away.—The settlers are losing their cattle by Texas Fever. some have lost all the cattle they have. Knows of but one or two persons who have corn in the bounds of his circuit.

John L Pratt of Chelsea Butler County. no crops in his County not a cucumber even no old corn in the county—not much money and what could be raised has been used for preemption of land many persons were compelled to mortgage their claims and others gave up entirely and left the country 640 persons in the County and there is not a dollar in money to the man 15 Townships of Land were offered for sale at Fort Scott on the 13th of August and the people were compelled to go about 150 miles to Fort Scott to pre=empt their land.

Buffalo meat is a legal tender There is not a grain of old corn on hand on Walnut Creek an extent of 65 miles. except what has been hauled from Cottonwood a distance of 50 miles. The Grasshoppers came to that Country in a cloud about 2 weeks ago and after destroying the Corn and Buckwheat are now eating the leaves of the trees he saw clouds of them in the sky on the day they came as high up as he could see—the wind blew from the Northwest at the time.

H I Hunter of Madison County. has 8 acres of corn which he thinks will average 15 bush of corn to the acre very wormy on the same ground he raised last year 20 Bushels to the acre wheat

through this section is an entire failure—in his township there is some old corn—on the Verdigris the crops are an almost entire failure one man B. F Vanhorn has a large field of Corn which he has offered to sell for 25 cents an acre. On the upper part of the Verdigris some weeks ago after a rain came there was some hopes of a crop but since the continuance of the dry weather the crops will be an entire failure—Thinks there is not corn enough in the country to do the people. said Mr. Huntly has 500 bushels old corn which he intends to keep for his own use will not sell any the population on these creeks is about 500 persons. One shower only fell in 9 months money is scarce and people cannot sell cattle or Hogs for even less than half what they could be sold for some time ago. many borrowed money to pre-empt and have mortgaged their claims—

Myrock Huntley (*speaks for himself!!*—Last year he had 30 acres which averaged 75 bushels to the acre this year he has 40 acres no corn nothing but fodder has about 400 acres with his two sons and himself which will produce nothing but fodder. 5 acres of Fall wheat 12 acres of spring wheat which was not harvested. There is not enough old corn to bread the people no money and corn is legal tender part are going away others will stay a few will have bread and water. The settlers entered land on shares and are free from debt. He is selling corn at 50 cents and will continue as long as he has any to spare will sell only in small quantities for breads—Bread stuff and groceries will be needed

Judge Graham Madison County.—Fall and spring wheat sown none harvested. Corn crop in his neighborhood will average ten bushels to the acre. is much injured by the worm. very little old corn in the country only ten bushels in the Mill. if it does not rain in a week there will be no potatoes—The population of the County cannot be sustained by the present crop. Cattle disease very severe about 53 head of the best cattle died in one week.

met *Peter Welsh* on the Road for provisions lives in the Osage Country—has lived 30 years in this Country and never saw any thing like this. has now to haul provisions for his family 150 miles. The Osage Indians have gone to the Buffalo Country to keep from starving—*Chetopa* the Chief 93 years old never knew till this year a want of grass for the ponies to live on and corn has always been raised till this year. unless there is some help for southern and western Kansas it will be depopulated, houses are vacated people moving out women have been compelled to cut squashes with blooms on to cook for their children—

met 5 wagons and 24 persons from Walnut Creek—Wm Thurman said he had a good place and was well fixed but the troubles now are worse than in 56. he could not stay and starve. The people are now living on Corn Breads and corn coffey last spring he was offered 700$ for his improvements he now sold them to leave for 1 yoke of Cattle—and a wagon not in all worth more than $100. tho teams have driven for a week and have not been able to get feed "Folks have staid till they have worn out their clothes and have nothing to eat and are compelled to leave or starve"—and they find men who will give nothing and report false so as to speculate on the necessities of the people

John T Jones Ottawa Creek has lived in Kansas 24 years. has never seen any thing like the present condition of Crops. last year raised 50 acres of corn which averaged 60 Bushels to the acre this year he will not have an average of 5 bushels to the acre since he has been here till this year the seasons have been as good as in any of the western

Copy.

"Owl Creek Woodson Co Kansas
September 14th 1860

To Thaddeus Hyatt.
Dear Sir.—Men under some circumstances become desperate and men of any honor, men of sensitive feelings would scarcely appeal to strangers until the last resort had failed until hope had well nigh fled—Sir we are bold but it is a boldness that desperation gives, we ask of you aid, we ask of you a little money *to buy bread;* You have seen our faces, you saw us at Leroy we come to you with no lie—there is no collusion there is no illusion nor delusion about it we must have aid from some source—We raised no crops neither of us have a team, not a dollar in money. how can we get away?—no employment it is not a tale of false

woes, our oaths will verify it dozens of our neighborhoods testify to it—S N Howe lost well nigh all he had by fire—I have lost *more* than all. I came here full of hope full of determination to have, to adorn and beautify a home—but *she* who was the life the light the joy the pride of my *home* and heart—the mother of my children now sleeps beneath the clay—she who has lain upon my arm who has welcomed me home a thousand times who never murmered now lies beneath the soil of Kansas and sleeps the sleep of death.

do not cast this to one side and say "what stuff to a stranger"—I know something of your history you are not to me altogether a stranger—nor to humanity—We ask it not for ourselves but for our hungry ragged destitute motherless children and although it may create a smile we say we do not wish to *beg* we do not ask it as a pure gift—We are willing to work we are willing to give bond with as good security as the County affords Can you will you."

Leroy Coffey Co KS"　　　　Sam S Howe
"E Condit"

"PS. No rain yet—indeed rain would do but little good vegetation is dead. A general exodus seems about to take place without my exaggeration. Whatever whole neighborhoods are being deserted". "EQC"
"The utterly helpless and the utterly hoggish still remain."—

Copy.

"Chelsea K T. Sept 20th 1860

Mr W.F M Arny–Dear Sir
　　Your letter of the 7th was duly received and in order that I might make correct statement in regard to the true condition of our country, I have visited many families and had others to do the same within the Counties of *Butler Hunter and Otoe* and am truly sorry to report the destitute condition of our country I was satisfied it was bad enough, in fact it is truly alarming as to crops. there are none—it is a complete failure there will not be twenty bushels of Corn raised in the three counties named, and not to exceed that amount of wheat, no potatoes the Buckwheat crop is entirely destroyed by grasshoppers, in *Butler County* there is about six hundred inhabitants in *Hunter* one hundred in in Otoe one hundred and fifty and at least three fourths of that number are almost destitute of money clothing and provisions.—very few have more stock than can supply their immediate wants. some indeed have been deprived of their last cow, by a disease that has prevailed in this country to some extent called Spanish fever—I find many families that have not more than one bushel of corn meal in the House that with some Buffalo meat and the milk they get composes their daily food—the

facts as they really exist are that the people are in a suffering condition and unless
supplies are furnished from some source much suffering will be the result most
of the settlers have been here over two years. have raised nothing their means are
exhausted they would gladly work—but can get no work to do. that would bring
subsistence, and the land sales being forced upon them had much to do in draining
them of their last dollar. there is no false conception in this matter as my friend of
the "news" has it.—but it is real and this state of things does not only exist in these
counties just named but is general throughout Southern Kansas. that is according
to my observation I have travelled about seven hundred miles since the 1st of July
and with a very few exceptions there is but little difference south of the *Kaw River* I
heartily concur in the statement made by C.H.S. in a letter to the *New York Tribune*,
and am truly glad that you have taken it upon yourself to act in this matter. and
sincerly hope that your efforts may be crowned with success, and that speedy relief
may be had for the sufferers in *Kansas* for which they will ever be grateful.

"Yours truly"

"*J. C Lambdin*"

Judge Lambdin is a senator elect under Wyandott State Constitution.—
There are 6 or 8 families in Otoe County of Colored persons who have been
driven from Arkansas by the Law compelling "Free negroes to leave the state.
these families are represented as industrious but now in want—owing to the
present drougth.—

Thaddeus Hyatt Collection 401, Kansas State Historical Society.

THADDEUS HYATT'S APPEAL FOR KANSAS RELIEF

*The president of the National Kansas Committee, Thaddeus Hyatt, had been involved
with Kansas Territory since its inception. A prosperous New York merchant, Hyatt
vigorously supported the free-state cause, funding settlers and antislavery activity. He
was jailed for refusing to testify before the Senate committee investigating the Secret
Six, who were suspected of funding John Brown's attack on Harpers Ferry, in October
1859. In 1860 Hyatt focused national attention on the suffering in Kansas by writing
President James Buchanan for aid.*

Washington D.C.

Octr. 16, 1860

To James Buchanan
President of the U.S.A. Sir:

Having just returned from the Territory of Kansas, where I have been an
eyewitness to the deplorable and starving condition of that scorched and famine

stricken land, I come to implore of the Executive as an act of clemency in behalf of its suffering inhabitants, that all Government lands now offered for sale in that Territory may be witheld from market, and more especially those lands embraced in (proclamation No 669) what is known as the New York Indian Reserve.

You need be informed Sir, of but half the desolations and heart rending scenes I have witnessed among that heroic & industrious but unfortunate people to arouse your utmost sympathies.

Thousands of once thrifty and prosperous American Citizens are now perishing of want; winter is upon them; of clothing they are nearly bereft; food they have not to last them through the cold season that is approaching; of over a hundred thousand people upon Kansas soil six months ago, at last one quarter or a third have left; of the remainder it is safe to say that 40,000 at this moment see nothing but exodus or starvation at the end of the sixty days now just before them; from 10 to 20 thousand look with only despairing eyes upon November; thousands cannot subsist a month longer unaided; other thousands are living upon the little which their neighbors deprive themselves of to give to them; neighbors equally unfortunate, and with whom the starvation is merely a question of but a few days longer; while still other thousands if not at once relieved must perish from hunger or the diseases that follow in its train. Some have already died; others are daily dying; . . .

Had the blood of this poor people in 1860 been as valuable for coinage into votes as it was in 1856 your Department would have long since been made aware of their miseries, and it would not have remained for the discharge of a mere mechanical duty to have brought to your notice the sickening fact that the mere discharge of the duty was in its terrible workings a practical cruelty such as no Despotism on Earth would intentionally be guilty of, and such as being once brought to the notice of your Department it cannot but rejoice to have escaped committing.

Commending these facts to your careful consideration, I have the honor Sir, to subscribe myself

Very Respectfully Yours
—Thaddeus Hyatt—

Thaddeus Hyatt Collection 401, Kansas State Historical Society.

"THE IRREPRESSIBLE CONFLICT GROWS WARM"

Edited by Chares F. De Vivaldi, the Western Kansas Express was located in Manhattan, in the central part of the state, and published its first issue in 1859. A member of the Frontier Guard, which protected the White House in April 1861, De Vivaldi was appointed consul to Santos, Brazil, by President Lincoln later that year.

THE IRREPRESSIBLE CONFLICT GROWS WARM;

The Southern press comes, this week, flaming with sentiments of treason, rebellion and secession. Speeches glowing with local patriotism, egotistical arrogance, and based on inverted political principles, from which are evolved reasonings and conclusions which are exciting the derisive laughter of the civilized world, are flowing glibly from a thousand Southern tongues.

In adopting and maintaining the slave system, the Southern States have espoused a philosophy, which stands arrayed against the eternal laws of equity, the instincts of humanity, and the mandates of the Supreme Ruler. They feel that the issue is upon them,—that the conflict is *indeed* irrepressible, and they struggle like desperadoes in a bad cause. The tide of popular sentiment has turned upon this vast system of fraud and oppression, under which growning millions are crushed to hopeless bondage, and drawing around its boundaries and limits, has frowned upon it, its withering rebuke.

The advocates of Slavery have adopted a variety of novel and interesting ways, of testifying their devotion to its interests. The man who can talk treason the loudest, and raise the biggest fume, fuss and furor, is placed in the front rank of its distracted hosts, while the State which will hurry along the dark path of nullification, and precipitate herself into the gulph of rebellion, and involve (so far as she is concerned,) a constitutional government, reared by the unrivalled wisdom, and patriotism of the Fathers, on the immutable principles of equity, in a defeat and ruin, is applauded as the champion of the rights of the South. The execution of lynch law, mob law, and an utter disregard of all law, founded on right, is a sufficient attestation of loyalty and devotion to her dark behests. And the destruction of a healthful literature, and scruntinizing censorship are acceptable offerings to this rapacious molock.

To perpetuate its tyranical rule, slavery adopts the means of despotism, and interdicts the liberty of speech, publication and action. Superstition and despotism are ever associated. An *unenquiring credence,* which is the essence of superstition, enfetters mind and renders the rule of tyranny safe and lasting. . . .

The Slave States to consolidate, and perpetuate their peculiar institutions, will, in addition to seceding from the Union, be under the necessity of raising along the whole of their frontier an impassable barrier, entirely prohibit all civil and commercial intercourse with neighboring nations, extirpate from the human bosom every instinct of humanity, and reverse the eternal laws of the Universe.

The great agitation, which, growing out of the system of Slavery, is convulsing the country, and threatening the stability of our Republican Institutions, and the subversion of the constitution, is not a war of sections merely, not a contest between northern abolitionists and southern slavery propagandists, but a conflict of truth with error, an antagonism of injustice with the fundamental principles of right, the settled convictions of mankind, and the jurisprudence of the civilized world.

Western Kansas Express, December 1, 1860.

"FREEDOM & OPPRESSION GRAPPLED HAND TO HAND"

Motivated by antislavery convictions, Reverend Peter McVicar, a Canadian who had moved to Wisconsin as a young man, came to Kansas in the territorial period and became pastor of the Congregational Church and Society of Topeka. Delivered five months apart, these sermons connect the crisis of the Union with Kansas's struggle against slavery. The blow on one of "New England's noblest sons" occurred when Congressman Preston Brooks felled Senator Charles Sumner in retaliation for the latter's 1856 speech on Kansas.

FIRST THANKSGIVING SERMON, . . . , NOV. 29, 1860 . . .

This day, however, calls us together not only as individuals & families—but also as citizens of Kansas, as members of our *adopted* territory. Many of you come here in troublous times—Many came from the peace & quietness of Eastern New England homes, to establish here those principles of freedom & religious liberty which have been & are to-day the glory our land.

Dark & threatening were the clouds that hung over the early settlers of this Territory. The question was *not* one of individual or personal interest. It was a question between liberty & slavery—Here Freedom & Oppression grappled hand to hand—The struggle was severe—The bones of our brethren that to-day be buried in our soil, will testify that it was not a *bloodless* struggle—We at the East also felt the blow, as in our national Hall it fell heavily on one of New Englands noblest sons—But let the past bury the past.

We come not to-day to recall animosities. We come rather to forgive the past, & look out upon the prospect of the present & the future—Sufficient forces that Freedom has gained the day. That free labor has been established on our soil—The night is spent, the clouds are broken & passing away—the dawn has come—& Kansas the child of political sufferings, will soon we trust be admitted into the family of states—herself also a *free* state— . . .

Sermon, Topeka, April 28–1861– . . .

The discord of to-day then is the ripening fruit of slavery, is the legitimate tendency of things since the introduction of the system of oppression unto our Continent. The disension of the present is nothing more & nothing less than the dominant & reckless spirit of slavery manifesting itself on a *large* scale. As long as the South could have her own way of concessions & repeals & compro[mi]ses from the North, so long the friends of slavery were comparatively quiet. The South like a spoiled child was willing to remain in the family so long & only so long as the general welfare of the household was subservient to its whims & caprices.

This contest is not a contest between the North & the South as sections, but between freedom & slavery, as principles. The increase of slave sentiments at the South, refusing to be governed by the enlightened decision of the nation & restless under the check of a corresponding increase of free sentiment at the North, has resulted in the Secession of 1861. . . .

The attitude of the seceding states & all who sympathize with them is nothing less than *rebellion*. It is not an opposition to a particular act or law. It is not a refusal to obey in this or that thing, for then it would only be an insurrection. But this secession is rebellion in its boldest form. It is an open & avowed renunciation of all national authority, a determined seizure of arms to traitorously resist established government. Nor is this all.

The secession is rebellion on the part of a *minority*—& that too under a *republican* form of Government. There is no doubt that there may come times when even a minority shall have the right to rebel & resist established Government. The wrongs may be so intolerable as to justify such a course. . . .

The attitude of the seceding states is rebellion without any *sufficient* reason. All their greivances may be summed up in the fact that one of the best statesmen of the Nation has under a Republican form of government, been constitutionally elected by a majority of the people to the Presidency of the United States. This is the burden of complaint as alleged by themselves. They are then in the strange & execrable position of revolusionists without any cause for revolution. But their attitude is still worse then this. For it is rebellion not merely without any just cause for it. . . . *It is rebellion in behalf of slavery.* . . .

. . . *What is our duty in the present emergency?*

To this question there can be but one answer & that is *To Maintain the Government.* For eighty-five years it has had an existence. It has come down to us baptized with patriotic & ancestral blood. It is the embodiment of principles of civil & religious liberty for which the nations of the earth are struggling. Our nation is one family. . . .

We have also this additional encouragement from the fact that God has apparently raised up the fit man for the emergency & has placed him at the head of the nation. Never perhaps, has an Executive engaged the implicit confidence of the Free States & even the respect of the South more than Abraham Lincoln does today. A man of calm judgment, of decisive purpose, surrounded by the Military & Legislative wisdom & experience of the nation. A man also who humbly relies on the strength of God for success & whose administration may be said to have been inaugurated by prayer.

. . . Let the Government so long as it unflinchingly prosecutes the right, have the warmest sympathy of the citizen, the sincerest prayer of the Christian, &, if it must needs be, the *best blood in the nation.*

We are, however, to avoid any undue excitement. This is not a time which calls for a war spirit, but for decided purpose & calm action. Our side of the struggle is to restore peace & preserve harmony, by putting down the spirit of rebellion.

We are to prepare & hold ourselves in readiness for the call of our country. . . .

Peter McVicar Collection 429, Kansas State Historical Society.

THE THIRTY-FOURTH STATE JOINS THE UNION

Local newspapers welcomed the news that Kansas joined the Union on January 29, 1861, but placed the Union's precarious situation in the context of the territorial struggle of the 1850s. The first editorial is from the Lawrence Republican *and the second is from the* Leavenworth Conservative.

KANSAS A STATE.

Two days ago Lawrence was electrified by the announcement of the admission of Kansas to the Union. She had been a virgin Territory so long, we feared the fate of all over-ripe maidens; but as some women, like fruit, are sweetest just before they begin to decay, Kansas, in her maturity, was more attractive than in her youth. After a long candidacy, she has formed a union—a union, too, for weal or woe with discordant and belligerent States. She will take her stand by the side of those sisters who are loyal to the Constitution, and join in their appeal to those who are disaffected, first in the gentle tones of love, and then, if need be, in the stern voice of war.

But it is not meet for us to conjure visions of terror to the bridal feast—to mingle strains of sorrow with your joyous epithalamium. Let men shout till the welkin rings; let women smile till the prairies blossom and the birds sing as though it were not winter.

A little while, and Charles Robinson assumes his official robes, with more prestige than Governor ever had since the days when Isaiah sang his paean over young Hezekiah's accession. He goes into office elevated by the suffrages of "the wisest and the bravest and the purest people under the sun." He stands at the head of, we trust, the never ending column of Kansas Governors. After long years of suffering, under the despotism of a Democratic administration; after a long series of insults and abuses from delegated Governors, Kansas is free, and has a Chief Magistrate of her own choosing. May he be unto us all as a pillar of fire by night, and as a pillar of cloud by day.

Although Kansas is the youngest, she is by no means the weakest of the States. She has grown strong from defending herself, and from long wrestling with the Lord in prayer. She has taught Slavery to more dread her hug than the Spanish Protestant did the Maid's of the Inquisition; and when she speaks her sovereign voice, at home and in the National Senate, treason will be sicklied o'er with the pale cast of fear.

The men of Kansas are conservative, but if any people under our broad aegis have cause of irritation, they are the members of the new State. They are those whose rights have been violated, whose interests neglected, whose humanity outraged, yet they are those who most love the Union and the Constitution. If, then, we are devoted to the federal government—if, after all our abuses, we love it still, can we submit to its overthrow by men who have never felt a wrong or knew an injury? No! a hundred thousand times, no! for such is the answer of every human being in Kansas. . . .

LET US ALL REJOICE!

In the troubles of Kansas was created that great party which, at the last national election, gave to the nation a President. Our position, as the battle ground upon which the new slavery issue was fought, gave us a prominence for which subsequent events developed our fitness. Upon us—a new people—emigrants, and soldiers of fortune all, was precipitated the most momentous question which has ever yet agitated the American people. We met the issue. The history of Kansas, even now, stands prominent in the annals of the nation. To rehearse the story of the struggle between slavery and freedom in this Territory, would be but to recount a story familiar to the whole civilized world. Now is not the time or place for such a history.

The election of Lincoln, glorious as was the triumph, was, in our estimation, far less important and decisive than the admission of Kansas. Against our devoted people have been arrayed the whole force of the slavery power. The ingenuity of the pro slavery partisans has been exerted to its utmost to prevent the recognized expression of the will of the Free State people of Kansas. Every resource having been exhausted, the persistent, manly efforts, and the godlike courage of our people have at last prevailed, and the glorious reward, so gallantly earned, has been doled out to us with an unwilling hand. Yet we accept the boon—accept it gratefully, and hasten to take our place as a free State in the glorious Confederacy. Knowing, as we do, the resources of our State, and the courage and endurance of our people, we feel that this accession will go far to fill the gap made by the seceding States.

Our people have an abiding love for, and a loving faith and confidence in, the Union.—This love and faith has been bred in the bone—it has stood the test of desertion, and even oppression; but is as strong and confident as ever. For them, we send greeting to the sister States, and if ever the time should come when the Union and the Constitution should call for defenders, we pledge the faith and the strong arm of that gallant people, who, for the institutions they loved, have heretofore trod the wine-press of oppression, and come out unscathed in honor from the trial.

Then, to our Republican brethren of Kansas we send one joyous greeting—to Republicans everywhere we extend the same joyous greeting. The grand culminating triumph [of] Republicanism has been achieved. Kansas has been admitted.

"When Kansas Became a State," *Kansas Historical Quarterly* 23, no. 1 (Spring 1961): 8, 4.

A DEMOCRATIC SHEET FINDS A POLITICAL EQUILIBRIUM

For some Democrats in Kansas, the outbreak of war led to difficult decisions, but the editor of the Fort Scott Democrat *stated that despite party affiliations, Union was foremost. Furthermore, relations with Missouri, a mere five miles from Fort Scott, had to be ameliorated.*

March 9, 1861

THE UNION—OUR POSITION

Hitherto our paper has done battle, constantly and actively, for the Democratic party. It has been a loyal soldier, not very brave, perhaps, nor greatly effective; but, at all times, earnest, zealous, devoted. We have stood in the fight unshrinkingly, and gone down only with the flag, when our cohorts were scattered, and the battle irretrievably lost. Party principles and party success have been, to us, the dearest of all things secular in the past.

The principles of our party are as dear to us now as ever. We believe in them as firmly and religiously as before. But another question has arisen, more engrossing and absorbing than all others combined, which overrides party allegiance, and absolves us from fidelity to partizan interests. Before such a question party is powerless and ineffectual. We have but *one duty*—that is, TO OUR COUNTRY. No party dispensation can absolve us from our imperative duty to the Constitution and Union of the States.

We propose, therefore, to lay aside our party harness for the present. We do this, because we believe it to be the first duty of every citizen, in view of the present disintegrated condition of the Union, to ignore all minor considerations, until the Union is restored or reconstructed; or every possible effort made in its behalf. We do not, by any means, give up our principles, for when the proper time arrives, we shall buckle on the harness again, with joy which will only be brighter because of the sorrowful forebodings with which we lay it down.

We are not willing to give up the Union for five hundred parties, even if it were possible for each one to be as good as the old Democratic party. We will, therefore, yield a liberal and cordial support to any party, man, or set of men, whose efforts honestly tend to the preservation of our glorious Union.

And now, as the destinies of our country are committed, under constitutional usage and sanction, to Mr. Lincoln, we stand prepared and pledged hereby, to support with patriotic zeal and earnestness, any and all measures of his Administration, having in view the restoration of peace to the distracted interests of our Country. Our support will not be stinted or grudging, but cordial, spontaneous, and sincere. . . .

We are the youngest of the sisterhood of States—not very blooming, indeed, at present, but rather scarred and weatherbeaten, like the veteran of an hundred battlefields; but for that very reason we have a greater necessity for quiet and repose, to rejuvenate our withered bloom, and recuperate our exhausted energies.

We are prepared, therefore, to go hand in hand with patriots both in and out of the Republican party, so long as wisdom and moderation prevail in their councils, and there remains a reasonable hope of their being able to give peace to our distracted country and half-ruined State. We will fight as hard as any Republican, for any portion of their policy, that will probably lead us nearer the end we have in view. We can freely give up party for the sake of our common country. And we are satisfied that in this we fully and faithfully represent the feeling of the Democracy of Fort Scott and Bourbon county. We have conversed with many, and the universal reply is "we will give up anything for the sake of the Union."

Peace with our neighbors, and quiet within our own borders we *must have;* and the Union restored or reconstructed, if within the limits of human possibility.

Such is our creed, and we are in for any man or party that fights for it.

May 4, 1861

KANSAS AND MISSOURI.

Whatever course the border Slave States may pursue in relation to the secession issue, there never was a time when the mutual interests of Kansas and Missouri demanded the maintenance of a peace policy on this border, more than at the present. The bloody records of the past show, that the people of each State are alike zealous in the guardianship of what they believe to be their just rights, jealous of any foreign interference.

There are many reasons why Kansas should maintain a peace policy, at this time, which are patent to the most casual observer.—For the next five months, at least, we shall be dependent, for our subsistence, on provisions brought in from

Illinois and other Western States. Those provisions can only come through Missouri, and in the event of a war, would be liable to stoppage at any time. Our only direct communication with the East is across Missouri. True, we can get out by way of Nebraska and Iowa; but it embraces a stage transit almost equal to a journey to California.

Kansas is too poor to support a war. With the heavy burden of a State government newly organized and our people still suffering from the terrible drouth scourge of last year, nothing but the most extraordinary circumstances—such as foreign invasion—would justify a heavy additional expense, for military purposes. The organization of the Volunteer Militia, however, and their proper equipment with the arms furnished by the Federal Government to the State, is a movement which can be made with comparatively trifling cost to the State, and without necessarily exciting suspicion abroad.

On the other side, there are many, no less potent reasons, why Missouri should keep the peace.—She has fifteen hundred miles of Free State border, which, the moment she makes a single aggressive step, will be in constant danger of invasion. She has not the men, arms or money to protect it, nor can she obtain them. But what has Missouri to gain by a war on Kansas? Nothing; absolutely nothing. On the contrary, she has everything to lose. There no spoils to tempt cupidity or avarice. She may lay waste our towns and villages, and destroy our growing crops, but she cannot conquer us, and swift and sure vengeance will return upon the heads of the aggressors. She may ruin Kansas, but she will share that ruin with us. . . .

Fort Scott Democrat, March 9 and May 4, 1861.

"I BEGIN TO THINK KANSAS FATED"

As this letter attests, when war arrived, many Kansans were already weary from the territorial period. The Kent family came to Kansas from New Hampshire by way of Illinois. In this letter, Richard Kent, who remained behind in Alton, responds to a letter from his father, Adrial Kent, about the troubles in Kansas. In 1861, the elder Kent was serving as postmaster of Burlington; after his death in October, he was succeeded by another son, Richard's brother, Orson Kent.

Alton September 23d 1861

Dear Father

I received a letter from you a few days since. the first I had heard for some time was glad to hear that you had got so much better. And sorry that the troubles had commenced around you. I was in hopes Kansas would get along without having any fighting on her soil, but it seems to have been otherwise ordered. I begin to think Kansas fated. first war. then famine. then war again for a change. I should really like to know what is to come next.

We received the news this morning that Lexington had been taken by Genls Price and Jackson. Col Mulligan being obliged to surrender. after holding out until there was no hope. And falling short of water. About 5,000 men left St Louis yesterday for the Missouri River somewhere. It seems a pity that Col Mulligan could not have been reinforced, but I suppose there is some good reason for it. I am unwilling to think that Genl Fremont did not do all in his power. Although the curses that He is receiving to day would ruin any man, if there was any virtue at all in them. Some even say that they would like to see Frank Blair take his place. I would rather have Fremonts *right hand* than all of Frank Blair. So long as all was getting along smoothly People could not say enough in His praise, but when there is any reverse, they are equally willing to curse him. . . . .

There is nothing particularly new going on here. Soldiers still continue to pass through here no less than four full Regts passed down last week. aside from a good many Co and squads. I hope our fortunes will turn before long. It is high time they did so.

Please write soon.

In trust from
Your Son
Richard A Kent

Orson Kent Miscellaneous Collection, Kansas State Historical Society.

"NO MAN IN KANSAS DARES RAISE A SECESSION FLAG"

This editorial from the Olathe Mirror *reveals the tension found in border towns. The seat of Johnson County, Olathe was about twenty-five miles southwest of Kansas City, Missouri. As editor John Francis noted, even though Olathe had been founded in 1857 under a charter granted by the "bogus legislature," by 1861 proslavery sentiments were not welcome. Although even then June had only thirty days, this editorial nonetheless appeared in the June 31, 1861, edition.*

June 31, 1861

PERILOUS TIMES.

While Missouri is driving Union men from her midst, destroying or taking possession of their property, Kansas confines herself within the limits of her "treason law," and rests in peace. The fact that no man in Kansas dares raise a secession flag, or wear a cockade showing sympathies with traitors, is significant. That law has accomplished everything desirable in reference to quieting the secessionists of Kansas. If Missouri had desired peace within her borders, why didn't she pass a law against raising the stars and stripes, or the federal flag within her limits, and not persecute men who love the Union and its glorious flag that has gracefully waved over it for nearly a century. There are secessionists in Kansas—but the treason law prevents them from doing any injury, by word or deed. In many parts of Missouri, a man dares not say that he is for the Union, in Kansas, no man dares raise a secession flag, or wear a secession cockade, or express his sympathy for Jeff. Davis and his bogus government. Who will not say these are perilous times?—When we shall have passed through this ordeal, the Union will still exist, be more enduring and better united to show the world, that free institutions are not a mockery.

Olathe Mirror, June 31, 1861.

THREE

Patronage and Policy

*W*HEN KANSAS ENTERED the Union in 1861, it was a small, deeply indebted state with barely one hundred thousand residents. Kansas had acquired
its debts largely because the cost of funding multiple constitutional conventions
and the need to routinely investigate electoral fraud vastly overtaxed its slim
coffers. In addition, Kansas had just suffered through a severe drought and it
was widely expected that the new state would struggle to meet its fiscal responsibilities.[1] Indeed, there is little doubt that Kansas would have struggled to find
its footing in the federal system in the best of circumstances. Kansas did not
have the luxury of time, however, and these challenges would quickly pale in
comparison to those the new state faced when war broke out shortly after its
admission to the Union. As the Civil War raged on, its battles largely fought
outside the state's borders, Kansas experienced a political war of its own within
state lines.

This war was made worse by its territorial history and by an ongoing struggle
for power, place, and prestige within Kansas that continued during the war in a
heightened atmosphere of suddenly and significantly raised stakes. In the four
years of the Civil War, Kansas had three executives: Republicans Charles Robinson, Thomas Carney, and Samuel Crawford. Although the conflicts within the
state were among Republicans, they were hard-fought, intraparty battles for control of federal patronage. In addition, Kansans witnessed an odd and detrimental
tug-of-war between the governors and Senator James H. Lane for control over
how Kansas's regiments were raised, commanded, and dispatched.

Lane's rivalry with Charles Robinson went back to the territorial era, when
they had struggled for control of the Free-State Party. Robinson had come to the
territory as an agent of the New England Emigrant Aid Company and quickly
became a political powerhouse, being elected governor under the Topeka Constitution submitted to Congress in 1856. But Robinson was challenged for leadership
from an unexpected rival. A Democratic congressman from Indiana, Lane had
been a victim of his yes vote for the Kansas-Nebraska Act of 1854 and left Indiana
to resurrect his career in Kansas. Initially, he supported the proslavery territorial
legislature and attempted to organize the Democratic Party in the territory. Meet-

The Honorable James H. Lane, Senator from Kansas.
Courtesy of American Memory, Library of Congress.

ing with little success, Lane soon abandoned the party to become an influential leader in the free-state movement instead.

The contrasts between the two men were as extreme as their politics and methods. Historian Albert Castel perhaps captures the rivalry best when he describes Charles Robinson as "ambitious, hardworking and strong-willed," while saving the colorful language for James Lane, whom he depicts as "vulgar, tempestuous, of fluctuating courage, and utterly unscrupulous," a "cynic who posed as a zealot, a demagogue who claimed to be a statesman."[2] Even when assessed with a more sympathetic eye, there is little doubt that Lane was an opportunist of the first order who managed to leverage himself into a position of tremendous power within Civil War Kansas. Lane's influence was due entirely to his ability to ingratiate himself with the new Republican president, Abraham Lincoln. A friendship with Mark Delahay, a close friend and cousin to Lincoln, provided Lane's initial access to the president. And at a time when many of the territory's political leaders preferred the Republican Party's better-known men for the presidency, Lane had campaigned for Lincoln.

Although Lincoln refused Lane's offer of a bodyguard escort after his victory, Lane soon made himself indispensable. In Washington with a large contingent of Kansans seeking appointments, Lane organized the Frontier Guard to help protect the capital in the aftermath of the firing on Fort Sumter. After two weeks, the Frontier Guard was mustered out, but his service won Lane unprecedented access to the new president. By the end of April 1861, Lane was handling the appointment process for Kansas and the president often endorsed his choices without reading what he was signing.[3] One of the most interesting aspects of this relationship is Lincoln's continued support of Lane even after it became clear that Lane's excessive ambition greatly affected state politics and demanded considerable attention from the president and his secretary of war, Edwin Stanton.

As a result of this relationship with Lincoln, Lane controlled patronage to the detriment of Samuel C. Pomeroy, Kansas's other senator, and Martin Conway, its congressman, as well as Governor Charles Robinson. This stranglehold that

Lane had on the state's patronage was a source of tremendous dismay for Kansas's leading citizens, who wanted to share in the spoils of statehood. But even this power was insufficient to temper Lane's ambition as he tried to control military affairs along with political patronage. Lane managed to wrest control of the commissioning of staff and field officers from the state's governors (who ought to have had this power by right and tradition). In addition, Lane interfered with the naming of the commanders for whichever department Kansas belonged to during the course of the war (it had several homes). For instance, Lane convinced Lincoln that Kansas needed a department of its own and managed to get a friend with scant military experience named as its head in May 1862.[4] More seriously, Lane prevented Governor Thomas Carney from providing Lincoln with two needed regiments and from recruiting a home guard to protect the border because he worried that Carney would control the resultant patronage. This latter decision proved costly to the state for, as the warfare of 1863 and 1864 proved, Kansas's border was inadequately defended and the state desperately needed more men under arms.

The rivalry between Lane and Robinson took a peculiar turn when Lane, not content to be merely a senator, accepted a commission as brigadier general. After declaring Lane's Senate seat vacant, Governor Robinson appointed former territorial secretary Frederick Stanton to replace him. Stanton promptly presented his credentials to the Senate, thereby enraging Lane. Lane retained his Senate seat by denying that he had accepted or intended to accept the military commission. After the Senate refused to seat Stanton, Lane managed to get the governor of Indiana to commission him as a brigadier general and returned to Kansas, filled a brigade, and went to war along the border and against the governor. Lane's efforts to undermine Robinson included a flurry of charges, including treason and willfully depriving him of needed artillery to defeat Confederate general Sterling Price. His campaign against Robinson culminated in impeachment charges against the governor based on the latter's handling of bond sales to finance the militia and state expenses in 1861. Robinson was acquitted of these charges the following year, but his reputation never recovered. As Robinson had noted shortly after the war began, it was "a delicate matter to harmonize all the Union elements in Kansas,"[5] and his inability to do so ended his gubernatorial career.

The second governor of Kansas was merchant Thomas Carney, a little-known latecomer to Kansas who reputedly was the richest man in the state and who, more significantly, had Lane's support. However, once in power, like Robinson before him, the new governor soon came into conflict with Lane over control of Kansas's regiments. Ultimately, Carney's ill-advised play for Lane's Senate seat doomed him to serve a solitary term. Carney was selected for the Senate in the spring of 1864, but Lane successfully argued that the legislature's action a year

in advance of the end of his term was unconstitutional. He forced Carney to re-
nounce his claim to the seat, and the resulting imbroglio resulted in the governor's
loss of influence. In the end, Carney secured neither the desired promotion nor a
second nomination for governor.

Carney was replaced by Samuel Crawford, who was only twenty-nine when
he took office as the state's third governor, in January 1865. His election was an
odd one and perhaps would not have happened without the influence of military
events along the border. Arriving in 1859 from Indiana, Crawford was elected to
the Kansas house of representatives under the Wyandotte Constitution. However,
Crawford served only six weeks before joining the military; he was given command of the Second Kansas Colored Infantry with the rank of colonel.

Nominated in September 1864 on a pro-Lane ticket, Crawford became governor
despite being out of the state for almost four years. He was helped immensely
by his active pursuit of Confederate Sterling Price shortly before election day.
Political tensions in the state were such that when rumors circulated that Price
threatened to invade Kansas, many believed it to be a political trick fomented to
offset Lane's recent dip in popularity.[6] Regardless, Price was chased from Kansas
and Lane rebounded. He was overwhelmingly reelected for a second Senate term
in 1865, garnering eighty-two votes while only sixteen legislators opposed him.[7]
But Lane's resurgence was short-lived.

In Washington, Lane had supported President Andrew Johnson's Reconstruction policies, a decision at odds with many Kansans who supported the more
radical Congressional program. On the journey from the capital to Kansas, Lane
apparently was deeply depressed, confiding that "he had felt compelled, in order
to preserve, if possible, the harmony of the Republican party, to take a course
which had brought down upon him bitter denunciations from former friends, and
that wrong motives had been unjustly imputed to him."[8] On July 1, 1866, after arriving at a farm near Leavenworth, the Senator shot himself in the head and died
ten days later. Although it is impossible to know why Lane killed himself, within
Kansas, the tie between Lane's despondency and his status in Kansas was clear. As
the *Wyandotte Commercial Gazette* noted, "Lane lived upon the smiles of the people
of Kansas and when he came to the conclusion, whether correctly or not, that he
had lost their confidence, his mind gave away, and with his own hand he did what
thousands of border ruffians and rebels would gladly have done if they could slew
Jim Lane."[9] With his suicide, Lane left a political vacuum in Kansas that his fellow
Republicans welcomed and scrambled to fill.

"THOSE HAVING NO GUNS MUST USE BROOMSTICKS"

*For many Kansans, war came as no surprise, as they had long been fighting against
the slave power. This letter from George Collamore expressed Kansans' unique*

understanding of the war while alerting avid abolitionist George Stearns that the state lacked the ability to defend itself. Collamore became mayor of Lawrence in 1863, while Stearns chaired the Massachusetts State Kansas Aid Committee during the territorial period.

Leavenworth, K. May 2, 1861

My Dear Sir,

. . . I think you cannot understand our situation, nor can any other person living out of Kansas—My means of knowledge concerning matters in every part of this state is by no means meagre—. . . . The situation of Kansas is by no means safe. Never has she been so poorly provided for arms and ammunition as now. And should she be attacked by Missouri we could make but a poor defense. Nearly all the sharps rifles have been taken to Pikes Peak.

We have not only the Missourians to fear but the Cherokee & Osage Indians on the south and several Indian Tribes on the west. . . . We cannot spare a man out of Kansas and I truly believe stand in need of more men to defend ourselves in case of troubles and that too if we were properly prepared & armed—There has been much apprehension lest the Missourians should take Fort Leavenworth

At the arsinal of fort S[cott] there is small arms, this includes many revolvers 1100 of which arms are muskets 800 sharps rifles—the balance various kinds and many of them out of order. About 1000 rounds of ammunition and 20 cannon mostly of small size. These arms should be placed at the disposal of the Gov. of this State. . . . It would not be advisable to moun a raid on Missouri or any other plan if we were fully armed—The prospect of an abundant crop is every where seen in this state and more seed has been sown and planted than ever before and the people, for a wonder, *feel times worst* more than ever.

And should the war continue, of which I have no doubt, provisions will advance and they will receive a handsome reward. It is our duty and it is for our interest to remain on friendly terms with Missouri if we can—They talk friendly and at the same time are making great preparations either for defence or for an attack, the latter I think. . . . If they [arms and other articles] are not shipped here soon I fear they will be cut off unless the Goverment take possession of the Saint Joseph & Hannibal R. R. which they should do at once—I ask that they may be sent as a matter of Caution and not for the interest of Kansas alone but for the good of the whole people. . . . I would advise in all our movements secrecy. Mr Wigfall from Fort Scott, Bourbon Co. called on me yesterday at Lawrence, on his way to Topeka to see the Governor relative to arms and ammunition, he fears more from the Indians than from the Missourians—

Nightly drills go on throughout this State those having no guns must use broomsticks or such other articles as come handy—It is not generally known how poor off we are for arms—. . . . There are in town only about two hundred kegs powder.

This is watched by six men every night and should an attack be made at night the powder could be easily seized and carried off—Our situation is such that I am about to purchase 100 kegs of this powder and have it carry so by night to Lawrence and placed in a secure place.

The price asked is ten dollars per keg—And as this is a private affair the question arises where shall I git the money to pay for it? And still I feel it my duty to do so—if *I* dont no one will—What is every bodys business is no ones business—This powder is too near the boarder to be safe—I think I may purchase it. . . .

Let me hear from you without fail at once & oblige.

Yours Truly,
Geo. W. Collamore
To
Geo L. Stearns, Esq.
Boston.

George L. Stearns Collection 507, Kansas State Historical Society.

"AN EFFORT IS BEING MADE TO GET UP A PANIC"

Charles Robinson was the first governor of Kansas, serving from February 9, 1861, to January 12, 1863. In this letter, he asks Major General John C. Frémont to return arms to Leavenworth and reassign Lane's Brigade (composed of the Third, Fourth, and Fifth Kansas Volunteers), which was led by James Lane, his old rival in free-state politics. The brigade was known for its depredations against Missourians, not all of whom were necessarily rebels or Confederate sympathizers.

Topeka, Sept 1ˢᵗ 1861

Maj Gen'l J. C. Fremont—
Dear Sir—

An effort is being made to get up a panic in our state, & I am told messengers have been sent to you representing a fearful state of things on our border—As some parties are interested to have war on our border, & consequently may not be impartial in their reports, I desire to say that we are in no danger of invasion, *provided* the government stores at Fort Scott are sent back to Leavenworth, & the Lane Brigade is removed from the border—It is true small parties of secessionists are to be found in Mo, but we have good reason to know that they do not intend to molest Kansas, in force, until Jackson shall be reinstated as governor

of Mo. Indeed, when a short time since a guerilla party came over & stole
some property from our citizens, the officers in command of the confederates
compelled a return of the property & offered to give up the leader of the gang
to our people for punishment. But what we have to fear, & do fear, is that Lane's
"Brigade" will get up a war by going over the line, committing depredations,
& then returning into our state. This course will force the Secessionists to put
down any force we may have, for their own protection, & in this they will be
joined by nearly all the Union men of Mo—

   If you will remove the supplies at Fort Scott to the interior, & relieve us of the
Lane brigade, I will guarantee Kansas from invasion from Mo. until Jackson shall
drive you out of St. Louis. . . .

Very Respectfully—
Your obt. sevt.
C. Robinson

Charles Robinson Collection, Kansas State Historical Society.

TWO NEWSPAPERS ASSESS LANE'S DEFENSE OF HIS BRIGADE

*In October 1861, James Lane took to the stump to defend himself, while attacking
Charles Robinson as a traitor. Two reports on his speech contrast notably. Given that
the editor of the* Leavenworth Daily Conservative, *D. W. Wilder, was a secretary
of the meeting, the enthusiasm his piece reflects is expected, but it also captures Lane's
oratorical style and self-perception. For the second article, the* Wabaunsee Patriot
sent a correspondent to Leavenworth who produced a more measured report.

"JAYHAWKING FOR THE GOVERNMENT"
GEN. LANE ADDRESSES THE CITIZENS OF KANSAS!
IMMENSE GATHERING IN STOCKTON'S HALL!
THE WANTS OF KANSAS!
TRAITORS EXPOSED!
THE PEOPLE STAND BY OLD JIM!
FULL REPORT OF HIS SPEECH.

   Last evening Stockton's Hall was crowded to its utmost capacity by an audience
anxious to hear the great military chieftain. Every nook and corner was filled long
before the hour for which the meeting was called together. . . .

   Gen. LANE on coming forward was received with rapturous applause. He began
by saying:

I have come here to-night, not to make a speech to you, but to have a plain talk about Kansas matters, and matters relating to the best interests of the country. This is a period in our history, when every man is called upon to act and to act cautiously. It is not expected that every man will join the army, but those who remain at home are not to forget that they may be called upon to act for those in the field. I ask every Kansas man who is here to give his protection to the Kansas soldier. I am uttering no words for myself—it is for the soldier who fights your battles.

Two months ago the Kansas Brigade was organized. I was put at the head of it with the respect, the confidence, aye, the love of every man in that command. Every day since it entered the field it has been actively engaged for the protection of Kansas and the Government. It has not been whipped, it has not surrendered. Why is it that these creatures at the Fort sneer at it? They abuse the Kansas Brigade because it has not surrendered to the enemy. They sneer at the Kansas Brigade because we have never engaged the enemy without whipping them like the devil.

Go to Nevada where 56 of the Kansas Brigade met and defeated 200 rebels; go to Ball's Mill where 130 Kansans whipped 350 traitors; go to Dry Wood where 400 men under Montgomery for two hours fought 7000 of the enemy and drove them back from your soil; go to Morristown, the death-bed of our gallant Johnson, where 400 of the Kansas Brigade drove 600 traitors from their entrenchments; go to Osceola, one of the strongest natural points in Southern Missouri, where, after eighty miles march through the enemy's country, we met a greatly superior force, beat it and took and destroyed more than a million dollars worth of property. Go to these fields and tell me why the Kansas Brigade is sneered at.

Our sin is that we have never been whipped. That Brigade is conspired against. This last Sabbath was desecrated by a conspiracy at the Fort between Robinson and Prince to destroy the Kansas Brigade. Charles Robinson and Capt. Prince conspired to destroy it. They were guilty of treason baser than that of Price. [Great cheering.] I have come here to talk plainly to you. [Cries of "That's right," "Let us have it."] What is the charge they make against the Kansas Brigade? We are jayhawkers!

I stated in Washington that the institution of Slavery could not survive the march of the Federal Army—that there would be an army of one color marching into the Slave States and an army of another color marching out. I said further, that confiscation must follow treason as thunder follows the lightning's flash.

Confiscated property goes to the Government, and this rule has been adopted by my Brigade. If we are jayhawkers, we are jayhawking for the Government.

Now if—oh! the dirty puppy—if that creature Prince, or that still dirtier creature, Robinson, can find an instance of a violation of this rule in my command, the guilty man shall be hung.

But they say we steal slaves—great God Lieut. Col. Blunt, of Montgomery's regiment has just returned from the interior of Missouri and they tell me he comes

back with more slaves than white men. ["Good," "Good," and cheers.] Secessionists get no slaves from the Kansas Brigade. When a Union man comes to my camp
to recover slaves, I tell him to look upon the camp as naked ground. "Resort to the
same measures that you would if I were not here." If he fails to recover his slaves
we give him a certificate—as a voucher to the Government—that such a man lost
such a slave by the march of the Kansas Brigade.

Slavery disappears before my Brigade [Applause.] I guess that's true. [Renewed
Applause.] But it disappears on the principle I have laid down. I venture to say that
if I were to tell Montgomery or Blunt or Stewart or Williams or Bowles, "you
shan't take those slaves," the reply would be "slaves are men, and you shan't make
me nigger catcher for traitors." [Great cheering.]

Is there a man here who would act as slave-catcher for Price? I wonder if that
dirty dog Prince would do it!—This is the sin, this is the charge against us. We
march to crush out treason and let slavery take care of itself. If they don't want
slavery to perish let them lay down their arms—or do the other thing—keep
Lane's Brigade out of Missouri. [Rapturous Applause.] In my opinion this war will
never be successfully carried out so long as an army marches through slave States
as a boat goes through a flock of ducks. They fly up on its approach and nestle
down as soon as it has passed. The boat is safe and so are the ducks. When you
march through a State you must destroy the property of the men in arms against
the Government—destroy, devastate, desolate. This is a war.

Take the Union man by the hand, but lay waste the property of traitors. Why
is so much sympathy shown for traitors and none for Union men? Hundreds and
hundreds of Union men have followed the Kansas Brigade to escape the clutches
of traitors. Did you ever hear this puppy Prince say a word about Maj. Dean who
was robbed and driven from his home by traitors?

Not a word of sympathy for such men. But let a slaveholder lose a nigger and
the very air resounds with cries for the return of the fugitive. ["Shame," "Shame."]
Now I'll tell you what I want of you. We'll do your fighting. We'll try and not surrender. We ask the people of Kansas to stand between us and the cowardly traitors
who stand in our rear. . . .

But the Kansas Brigade is to be dissolved because it built forts and organized
forces at Humboldt, Leroy, Neosho Falls, Verdigris, Walnut Creek, Fall River,
Turkey Creek—seven forts on your frontier, where the people, instead of being
stampeded and driven from the State can rally for your defence. . . .

What is the reason Price and Rains did not march into Kansas? Did Prince
keep off the 12,000? Did Robinson do it? . . . But they say Price and Rains had
no intention of invading Kansas—that they had made an arrangement not to
invade Kansas. With whom did our authorities make the arrangement? Not with
Gamble, for he is a Union man—it must have been with Claib. Jackson. All I can

say is that he who would hold intercourse with Jackson, is himself a traitor and deserves a rope. ["Hang him." "Hang him."]

Price marched 12,000 men from Springfield to within eight miles of Fort Scott. He intended to take it. The "peace" men all left, and a town is always in danger when the traitors run away. There were more valuable stores at Forts Scott and Lincoln, at that time, than there were at Lexington. But we get no credit for driving back the traitors because we lost 60 mules. If I am charged with those mules they ought at least to give me credit for what I have captured from the enemy. We took 150 at one haul at Morristown and it wasn't much of a day for mules either.

We are thwarted in obtaining troops because they are wanted in New Mexico. I should like to know what New Mexico is worth with Kansas lost. That New Mexican project was got up to prevent the organization of the Kansas Brigade. ["That's so."]

What has the State government done for the protection of Kansas? How was Southern Kansas saved? I called the people to the rescue. They came. I found arms belonging to Uncle Sam. I took the responsibility of opening the boxes and giving the arms to the people. Now you go to the Fort and they will tell you Lane is a thief. But Kansas would have been invaded had not those two thousand men been armed with those guns.

I am a robber because I am guilty of the terrible crime of taking arms belonging to the Government and giving them to Kansas men. I don't believe I have done a thing that Old Abe Lincoln will find fault with; the President will say, "Well done, good and faithful servant." . . .

We ask you to stand between us and the vile traitor slanderers in the rear. Position don't excuse treason. The higher the position the greater the treason. [Cheers.] I arraign before this people Charles Robinson as a traitor to his country. Last Sunday Robinson and Prince were conspiring to destroy the Kansas Brigade—seeking to do that which traitors cannot do.

The officers at this Fort have thwarted me at every step. I begged them for one piece of artillery. I could not get it. If we had had one twelve-pound howitzer, we could have whipped Price and Rains at Drywood, and thus have averted the disastrous defeat at Lexington and prevented the shedding of rivers of blood; but we could not get it. . . .

I have commanded seven armies and I have found that officers succeed when they treat soldiers as men; do that and they will fight for you. Why, my soldiers would follow me right into the middle of hell. And let me tell you that if I wanted to make a sure job of capturing the Old Fellow, I'd take the Kansas Brigade and I'd do it though he had Robinson and Prince to help him. [Terrific cheering.]

Kansas is the jewel of the West. It is all there is between the Missouri and the Rocky Mountains. It is the jewel in the cap of Freedom. In a Department with its headquarters in St. Louis Kansas is not as secure as she should be. So difficult is it to convey intelligence across Missouri that it is not safe for us to receive our orders from St. Louis. The true interests of Kansas demand that she should be in a separate Department with Fort Leavenworth as its base. [Cheers.] It is a military necessity.

The appointment of Brigadier General was offered to me and I intended to accept it when the Brigade was organized, but I could not be driven to take it. Although not a Brigadier I have been playing it all over and pretty big—betting high on small cards. [Cheers and laughter.]

For all my labor, hardship and expense I have not received one dime. Now don't you think Robinson and Prince could have afforded to let me serve my country for nothing?

If the Government will make a separate Department here, I will resign my Senatorship and accept it. This Department ought to be commanded by a Kansas man. Then we can save Kansas, restore the Cherokee country and a good deal South of it. . . .

Leavenworth Daily Conservative, October 9, 1861.

SPECIAL CORRESPONDENCE. . . .
LEAVENWORTH, Oct. 9, 1861.

DEAR PATRIOT: . . .

Pursuant to previous announcement, per blazing posters and "small bills," the man James Henry Lane, harangued a crowded audience in Stockton Hall last evening, and to the deep felt sorrow of every man in the community who has a particle of feeling for the honor and dignity of our cause and the safety of our State, again opened the personal feud between him and Robinson, and belched forth, as if from an open sepulchre, seethings of vindictive hate, and volume upon volume of the pent up corruption of his own malignant heart. For one, I see no good reason why this petty warfare should be continued. It is a shame. Already it has conduced greatly to render our cause in Kansas unsatisfactory and insufficient, and so sure as there be a God in Isreal, unless the people arise in their indignation and depose from place and power every unworthy servant who is guilty of fanning this flame of discord, of nourishing this seed of personal enmity and contention, of trifling with and jeopardizing our cause and the best interests—aye, the lives of our people—the thing will grow and grow, wax stronger and stronger, become diffused throughout regiments, companies, organizations, neighborhoods and so-cial and military circles, dividing soldier against soldier and citizen against citizen, until the State will per force of circumstances be delivered over to the dessolating hands of Price and Jackson.—Unless the matter is checked this must be the inevi-table result; and if the armies of the enemy are let loose upon Kansas, with their present insatiate thirst for revenge, if they do not leave her in pretty much the same fix that God Almighty made it, then I am much mistaken.

But Lane has a peculiar faculty for appealing to the passions of men, and artfully moulding them so as to advance his own ambitious schemes. He did not speak last night without an object. What is it, the reader will ask. It is this: he has conceived the elaborate scheme of carving from the military district, over which the true and noble Fremont has been placed, a slice of country composed of Arkansas, Indian Territory and Kansas, in which he shall reign supreme and rear a throne eventually if the thing by hook or crook should fall within the scope of human achievement. The work has been begun, and seems to be progressing to the entire satisfaction of the power behind the throne. Resolutions were engineered through the meeting, recognizing the necessity of this new district being created, and recommending and endorsing Lane as its military head. A few similarly called and conducted meetings throughout the State, and if the powers at Washington refuse, as they will of course, to grant anything of the kind, the attempt to strike the blow will as like as any way be made.

But the feature of the occasion was the charge of treason against Robinson, Prince, the commander at Ft. Leavenworth, and how many others I do not know. Lane himself embodying all the essential qualities and prerogatives of plaintiff, witness, advocate and judge.—That all parties are prepared to take every possible advantage of each other, I havn't a particle of doubt, and my private opinion is, that if the whole infernal "caboodle" of them were reduced to positions of forth corporalship in the army the country would be infinitely better off. One thing is evident, that is, that there is a conspiracy to overthrow Robinson, and, if need be, the State Government itself. When and what shall the *final* be? Ambition, official jealousy and sod-corn whisky constitute an element in our affairs which the Government has need to be more apprehensive of than rebellion itself. Be assured, they are doing a fearful—a fearful work. A great and good man hath said, "Put not your trust in Princes." Truly,

SHEPHERD.

Wabaunsee Patriot, October 12, 1861.

KANSAS "NO VERY AGREABLE COMMAND"

Hugh Walsh was territorial secretary to James Denver's governor and became acting governor when Denver returned to his position as commissioner of Indian affairs. Denver was named commander of the District of Kansas on April 2, 1862, but was sent to Indian Territory and replaced by Samuel D. Sturgis on April 6. Like many personnel matters, this reassignment after only four days had little to do with Denver's capabilities and much to do with Kansas politics. On April 4, Lincoln wrote Henry

Halleck of his dismay at Denver's appointment, noting "There is a hard pressure on me in this matter." It is widely believed that James Lane was pressuring Lincoln to arrange Kansas affairs to suit himself.

Lecompton Jany 18. 1862

Dear Governor, . . .

Since I have been gone I hear an intimation is made that you are to be transferd to Wheeling—I hope not and as Lane has had that gordian *Knot* cut & will remain in the Senate I presume it is not to be—at least I hope that no change will be made without it is your desire—I can readily conceive that a troublesome set as there is in Kansas where so many impure motives inspire every action as no very agreable command; but any change which will relax discipline, or bring into power those who seek revenge on all democrats for the outrages of the Calhoun clique, will be a wretched result, and bring on a state of discord as bad as exists in Missouri.

Whenever the government places men in power of that character in this department, and men can not rely on any thing but their own physical strength for protection there will be a limitless war in Kansas which must leave it a bloody and desolated field—

I am told that such men as Ritchy of Topeka are down on Governor Robinson for his remarks in his message about the disorders in the state in emergence of the conduct of the war last summer

Some consider the Gov in personal danger from the land pirates

The legislature yesterday had under consideration a resolution calling on General Hunter to take the State under his protection so that robery and stealing might be suppressed

Provided it passes I hope the Genl will promptly reply by stationing troops at Lawrence Topeka Oskaloosa and further south with a provost Marshall at each place who will issue the same order as Provost Marshalls' order no 3 for Leavenworth—stolen property is constantly being disposed of and brought into Lawrence and bands of Jay Hawkers or Land pirates exist at both the others to the best of my belief from good information—last year a great many people lived off of the aid furnished from the east—they have not worked as they should have done this year and want to steal from the industrious class for their winters support

They will not go into the army and ought to be made to feel the strength of a power able and willing to protect the honest and industrious citizens—

If this is not done Kansas will become a community of desperados and give the government an enormous deal of trouble—It is easier to nip things of this

kind in the bud then to cut off the branch when it is grown. . . . truly your friend
Hugh S. Walsh

James William Denver Collection, Kansas Collection, RH MS 19, Kenneth Spencer Research Library, University
of Kansas Libraries.

LANE A CHARLATAN WHOSE APPOINTMENT WOULD IMPERIL THE UNION

*Lane's holding two seemingly incompatible positions came to a head in this conflict
with Major General David Hunter, in command of the Western Department.
On January 27, 1862, Hunter announced he, not Lane, would command Lane's
expedition to Texas and Arkansas. Even knowing that Lane enjoyed the president's
good opinion, Hunter felt so strongly about Lane's unsuitability for command that
he wrote first to Secretary of War Edwin Stanton and then to President Lincoln.*

DAVID HUNTER TO EDWIN M. STANTON

Fort Leavenworth, Ks. Feby 1st 1862.

Sir: I deem it advisable to report for the information of the War Department
that Senator J. H Lane has not accepted the position of Brigadier General to
which he has been appointed by the President; but that, in the visit he paid to
me on his arrival at Leavenworth City, he stated distinctly and in terms that he
was "my visitor as a Senator of the United States and a member of the Senate
Military Committee."

It can hardly be necessary to call your attention to the anomalous and, to say
the least, perplexing position thus occupied by Senator Lane; and I find myself
compelled, in the interests of discipline and the public service, to request that some
definitive character shall be given to Senator Lane with as little delay as possible.

Previous to his arrival here, the fact of his appointment and the belief that
he had accepted it, were so widely current and credited, that many regard him
as if in the service; and I am held responsible (in the belief that he has reported
to me for duty and is under my control,) for much that I cannot endorse or
approve in his line of conduct:—while the fact that he has not accepted, but is
here as a Senator and member of the Military Committee places him beyond any
supervision of mine, and his acts are independent of my judgment.

From a variety of incidents which have transpired since his arrival, and
many applications bearing his endorsement and recommendation which have
been transmitted to me,—I am satisfied that Senator Lane feels aggrieved
and disappointed (or has resolved so to appear,) at the position to which his
acceptance of his Commission would assign him; and that his continued
presence in this Department, in his present undefined position, can only be of

detriment to the public service. The conviction is forced on me, that, dissatisfied himself, he is determined to create trouble; and my respect for the eminent and honorable body of which he is a member makes me earnestly wish to avoid that which Senator Lane would seem to be earnestly seeking.

I have therefore respectfully to request, in the interest of the public service, that Senator Lane may be called upon to accept his Commission as Brigadier General and to report for duty within a given and not remote period,—with the alternative that in case he does not accept within the time stated, it shall be regarded as a refusal and his appointment thereupon be cancelled.

Begging your early attention to this matter,

I have the honor to be, Sir,

> Very respectfully
> Your mo Obed. servt.
> D. Hunter,
> Major General
> Com.

DAVID HUNTER TO ABRAHAM LINCOLN

Fort Leavenworth, Ks. Feb'y 14th 1862.

Sir: . . .

It is due to you—due to myself—to state, that had the conduct of Senator Lane allowed me to pursue a different course,—a course more in harmony with your apparent wishes,—I would gladly have done so:—But no alternative was left.

From the hour of Senator's Lane's arrival, I had placed before me the option of practically surrendering control of the Department, or encountering the utmost hostility that an active, malignant, and unscrupulous nature could inflict. Thus circumstanced, and with my sincere esteem and friendship for you and sincere devotion to the cause of the country, I could not hesitate a moment about accepting the latter alternative as the lesser evil.

But understand me in this, and understand clearly, that the "want of harmony" to use his own phrase between Senator Lane and myself has been a thing of his own seeking,—a thing which all the evidence before me demonstrates that he had resolved upon before entering the Department. By me, he was treated with all courtesy and the respect due to his position. Had he reported for duty I would gladly have assigned him to a command not merely commensurate with his rank, in the strict military sense; but commensurate, (in so far as I could make it, without manifest detriment to the public service,) with your apparent desire for his assignment to some prominent position.

Nothing of this kind would do, however; and in my best judgment it was the determination of Senator Lane that no arrangement of a satisfactory nature, should be made. He commenced from the outset to intimate dissatisfaction in high quarters with my management of the Department affairs; he endeavoured to assume a tone of having been my only protector at Washington, never once did he talk or even hint of reporting for duty, but on all occasions used that prhrase the he wished to "coöperate" with me in conducting the Expedition,—his idea of "coöperation" clearly being that he was to command the column while I remained in Fort Leavenworth approving of his requisitions on the Quartermaster, Commissariat, and Ordnance Departments. The word "coöperation" was constantly in his mouth during our two interviews, and always in the sense given. He did not care what title he might have, provided only that he had supreme command,—this command, moreover, to embrace the Quartermaster & Commissariat Departments which were to be filled by officers of his own appointment.

To these absurd and derogatory pretensions, always advanced covertly and indirectly, but persistently and as a sine quâ to his acceptance of a command, my letter of this day's date is the only possible reply. apart from all questions personal to myself, I do not regard Senator Lane as an officer who could safely be entrusted with the command of an important Expedition. He has none of the habits of discipline necessary to the holding together of a large military organization; he is without any sense of financial or political responsibility; and, since I am compelled to say it, his sense of moral responsibility would seem relaxed to a degree rarely witnessed in persons of such eminent position. It pains me to be obliged to write what I have written and what yet remains to be said, in regard to a person whom you have apparently honoured with a share of your confidence:—but acting under a deep sense of duty to my country and sincere respect and affection for yourself,—I cannot refrain from telling you that you have been grossly deceived by one who has practised deception as the familiar art of a lifetime.

I know no man in Kansas to-night, Mr. Lincoln,—not even those very adherents of his who are gazing hungrily on the Quartermaster & Commisariat patronage they expect him to bestow,—who feels, or in ordinary conversation would even profess to feel the least confidence in the veracity of Senator James H. Lane. By friend as ennemy he is regarded as an unscrupulous trickster,—a demagogue in all the worst senses of that word,—whose promises are to be relied upon just as it may suit his convenience to keep or break them. This, in so far as I have had any, has been my own experience of his character; and it was in view of his gross misstatements of former conversations,—misstatements of which I have documentary evidence,—that I was obliged to insist upon having our official intercourse reduced to writing on both sides.

As an illustration of Senator Lane's whole character, I may briefly refer to the method adopted by him in procuring a legislative endorsement of his claims to the position of Major General. With an overwhelming majority of both Houses against his pretensions, he went to work (as I hear from good authority), representing that I was anxious to have him command the expedition, and that he could not do so unless made Major General, as I had applied for six Brigadier Generals, and there were not six junior to him in the service. "Recommend me for Major General" he said to all his bitterest opponents, "and you will at least get rid of me as Senator." To all & each of the rival aspirants for his Senatorial seat he promised the immediate & unconditional resignation of his Senatorship in case he was endorsed; & to each aspirant (it is added) made promise of all his influence & personal exertions to secure the succession. Thus & thus only it was that he obtained his legislative endorsement,—laughing at his dupes when successful & telling them that *"when made Major General he would resign but not before."*

As a further illustration of how he is regarded by citizens of the State, I may mention that Gov. Chas. Robinson has avowed his resolve to quit Kansas whenever Lane shall be entrusted with unchecked command. By the old, respectable, & honest element of the Kansas Free-state Immigration,—& of this element few have had better opportunities than myself to learn the real temper & worth,—he is, & always has been, regarded with dislike & dread. The atrocities of the Buchanan *Régime* it is true once compelled them to sustain him as a counterpoise; but their sober & upright judgment both is & has been against him almost, if not quite unanimously. It is of the scum thrown to the surface by political troubles; of the Jay-hawkers, the outlaws from all states & sections and the corruptionists—that Senator Lane is the representative & a true one.

I have written thus unreservedly and at length under a conviction of duty;—not that it is an agreable task to me to paint a charlatan in his true colours, but from my knowledge that you had been deceived and my wish that you should be deceived no longer. If I have overstepped the due limits of my position, I am willing to suffer due punishment; but I am not willing that the cause of the Union should be imperilled and it's flag disgraced by the appointment to supreme command of one whose only claim to consideration must be based on a total misapprehension of his true character.

I have the honor to be, Sir,

Very Respectfully
Your mot ob't Servt
D. Hunter
Maj. Gen.
Com

David Hunter to Edwin M. Stanton, February 1, 1862, and Hunter to Abraham Lincoln, February 14, 1862, Abraham Lincoln Papers at the Library of Congress, Manuscript Division (Washington, DC: American Memory Project, 2000–2002), http://memory.loc.gov/ammem/alhtml/malhome.html.

LEFT TO "THE MERCIES OF A VINDICTIVE AND RELENTLESS FORCE"

A Democrat, John Halderman came to Kansas in the territorial period as private secretary to the first territorial governor. Once the war broke out, he joined the First Kansas Volunteers and then the state militia.

SAINT LOUIS, MO., *November 6, 1862.*

Major-General CURTIS, *Comdg. Department of the Missouri:*

GENERAL: Herewith find communication of Governor Robinson, of Kansas, asking for authority to arm such portion of our militia as may be sufficient to protect our border against the violence of lawless bands in Missouri. I unite in this earnest appeal of the Governor. The citizens of Kansas along the eastern line of the State bordering upon that part of Missouri south of the river feel no security for life or property, and many, in despair that the Government will afford them aid, are leaving the State or moving back into the interior, abandoning crops, houses, and other improvements to the mercy of the enemy. It seems hard that the loyal people of this most loyal State, after sending their twelve regiments to the field, should thus be left with inadquate protection to the mercies of a vindictive and relentless foe. Even now, with the handful left, we do not ask for help, but ask only that we be allowed to defend ourselves, and in order to do this we have appealed to you for arms, clothing, and subsistence for our people while in the field in active service. In behalf of our State may I ask, general, for our wants and dangers your most serious consideration?

I am, general, very respectfully, your obedient servant,

JOHN A. HALDERMAN,
Major-General, Northern Division Kansas State Militia.

The War of the Rebellion: A Compilation of the Official Records of the Union and Confederate Armies, ser. 1, vol. 13 (Washington, DC: Government Printing Office, 1885), 802.

"I MUST HOLD MISSOURI RESPONSIBLE"

After Quantrill's raid on Kansas, Governor Thomas Carney angrily wrote Major General John M. Schofield, commander of the Department of Missouri, to emphasize the necessity of acting against disloyal Missourians.

Leavenworth Kansas August 24/63

Sir
    Disaster has again fallen upon our State. Lawrence is in ashes. Millions of
property have been destroyed, and worse yet, nearly two hundred lives of our
best citizens have been sacrificed. No fiends in human shape, could have acted
with more savage barbarity, than did Quantrell & his band, in their last successful
raid.
    I must hold Missouri responsible for this fearful & fiendish raid.
    No body of men large as that Commanded by Quantrell could have been
gathered together without the people resideing in western Missouri knowing
every thing about it. Such people cannot be considered loyal, and should not be
treated as loyal citizens. For while they *conceal* the movements of desperadoes
like Quantrell & his followers, they are in the worst sense of the word, their
aiders and abetters, and should be held equally guilty.
    There is no way of reaching the armed ruffians, while the civilian is permitted
to cloak him. There can be no peace in Missouri; there will be utter desolation
in Kansas—unless both are made to feel promptly the utmost rigor of military
law. The peace of both States, & the safety of the Republic, demand alike, this
resolute course of action.
    I urge upon you, therefore, the adoption of this policy, as the *only* policy,
which can save both western Missouri and Kansas; for if this policy be not
immediately adopted, the people themselves, acting upon the common principle
of self defence, will take the matter in their own hands, and avenge their own
wrongs.
    You will not misunderstand me. I do not use or intend to use any threat. I
tell you only, what our people almost to a man feel. The excitement over the
success of Quantrell is intense—intense all over the State, and I do not see
how I can hesitate to demand, or how you can refuse to grant, a Court of
enquiry by which the causes of that fatal success may be fully investigated, and
all the facts laid before the public. I go even further; I demand that, that this
Court of enquiry shall have power to investigate all matters, touching military
wrongdoing in Kansas. And I do this most earnestly to guarantee alike our
present, & future safety.
    As regard arms, we are destitute. There are none at the Fort, and none in the
State. I telegraphed the Secretary of War this fact, asking him to turn over to
me here, arms, in sufficient quanty, to meet our wants. He ordered it done, and
replied further, that anything Goverment could do to aid Kansas should be done.
This being so, will you not *express* to me arms for Cavelry & infantry, sufficient to

arm those Regiments. I enclose the Copy of the dispatch of the Secty of War to me, that you may see its purpos, & understand its spirit.

Very Respectfully
Your obt Servt
Tho. Carney Gov

To
Maj Genl JM Schofield
St Louis
MO

Thomas Carney Collection, Kansas Collection, RH MS P 299, Kenneth Spencer Research Library, University of Kansas Libraries.

"THE MERITS OF THE KANSAS PEOPLE NEED
NOT TO BE ARGUED TO ME"

In this exchange between Governor Carney and President Lincoln, the issues of regiment raising, the border war with Missouri, and the question of patronage and Kansas politics are revealed. Carney had offered the Union two regiments, but Lincoln had not yet accepted them. Both Carney and his predecessor complained that James Lane's influence resulted in a subordinate position—one no other governor had—regarding raising regiments. In mid-July 1863, Lincoln wrote Edwin Stanton that Carney should "stand on the same ground as other loyal governors," but the governor remained upset. This correspondence demonstrates both parties' frustration with the infringement of local politics on military matters.

Washington D. C. May 13th, 1864.

To the President of the United States
Sir :

Kansas has furnished more men according to her population, to crush this rebellion, than any other state in this Union. Her sons, to day, are scattered over the country, defending the old flag, while many of her peaceable citizens at home, are being murdered by lawless guerrillas. Such is the intelligence I received to day.

The Major General Commanding that Department, informed me, he needed more troops to secure protection to the State. I have tendered you two thousand troops, for one hundred days, such as you have accepted from other States, to be used as you might direct through the Commander of that Department, without other cost to the Government than the pay of Volunteers without bounty.

You referred the matter to the Secretary of War, for his consideration. I found that Officer overburdened with business of such magnitude to the Country, that he could not be seen, either upon my request or yours.

I have to ask that you will either accept or reject the proposition I made in my communication of the 12th Instant.

I hope, however, you will not allow the lives & homes of the citizens of Kansas to be jeopardized by the objections you suggested in our conversation, "that Senator Lane would probably oppose the raising of the troops, or if raised, would oppose an appropriation for their pay, in consequence of the patronage thus conferred upon the Governor of the State."

You will do me the favor to reply at your earliest convenience,

Very Respectfully
Your obt Servt
Tho Carney
Gov. of Kansas.

The within letter is, to my mind, so obviously intended as a page for a political record, as to be difficult to answer in a straight-forward business-like way. The merits of the Kansas people need not to be argued to me. They are just as good as any other loyal and patriotic people; and, as such to the best of my ability, I have always treated them and intend to treat them. It is not my recollection that I said to you Senator Lane would probably oppose raising troops in Kansas, because it would confer patronage upon you. What I did say was that he would probably oppose it because he and you were in a mood of each opposing whatever the other should propose. I did argue generally too, that, in my opinion, there is not a more foolish or demoralizing way of conducting a political rivalry, than these fierce and bitter struggles for patronage.

As to your demand that I will accept or reject your proposition to furnish troops, made to me yesterday, I have to say I took the proposition under advisement, in good faith as I believe you know, that you can withdraw it if you wish but that while it remains before me, I shall neither accept or reject it until, with reference to the public interest, I shall feel that I am ready.

Yours truly.
A. Lincoln

May 14th 1864.

~

Washington D. C. May 16th 1864

To the President of the United States
Sir:—
    Your note of 14th instant is received. I regret you do not consider the threatning attitude of affairs in Kansas, of sufficient public interest to accept at once the offer I made you, of two thousand troops, to augment the power of the Commander of the Department of Kansas.
    I did not intend to advise as to public interest outside of Kansas, though none have a deeper interest, or stronger determination to aid in crushing this rebellion than I have, nor will I allow miner matters to divert me from that purpose.
    I know you have all portions of the country to look after. In that gigantic work, you have my fullest, and most cordial coöperation.
    Kansas has been, and still is, in deep distress, and needs the fostering care of the Government, therefore, I made to you the proposition I did in my communication of the 12th instant. This care and assistance I feel the citizens of my State have a right to claim at your hands. They have been depleted of Blood & Treasur for the Common Cause. Their sufferings and Sacrifices have been great,—much greater than of any other wholly loyal State, and this, because, her Sons have gone forth to fight the battles of their Common Country, and left their homes in the care of the Government. Yet their homes have been visited by the assassin, and are again threatned by these murderous outlaws.
    It was to prevent a return of those disasters that I urged the acceptance of the troops offered; and in that spirit, and for that purpose, I again respectfully, but earnestly renew it.

Very Respectfully
Your Obt Servt
Tho. Carney
Gov of Kansas

Thomas Carney to Abraham Lincoln, May 13, 1864, and Carney to Lincoln, May 16, 1864, Abraham Lincoln Papers at the Library of Congress, Manuscript Division (Washington, DC: American Memory Project, 2000–2002), http://memory.loc.gov/ammem/alhtml/malhome.html.

FOUR

~

Kansas's Men in Blue

*I*N A LETTER to his brother on April 22, 1862, George Packard complained
that Kansas troops had few opportunities to fight. Instead, he wrote, "We have
to march around from one place to another to quell riots, enforce law, and catch
jayhawkers, while at heart we are all jayhawkers."[1] Packard's complaint captures
the frustration many soldiers felt—having joined the military to suppress the rebellion, Kansans were far from the front and often engaged in law enforcement
and antibushwhacker raids. To men eager for action and adventure, these tasks
scarcely seemed different from everyday life on the frontier.

While little regular action took place within the state itself, Kansas troops
were dispatched along the state's borders. Occasionally sent north to Nebraska,
they were more often occupied combating guerrilla activity along the border
with Missouri. In addition, Kansas troops were sent on significant expeditions
into Indian Territory to the south. Overall, Kansas's nineteen regiments and
four batteries served both near and far from home. To the south, these soldiers
served in Alabama, Arkansas, Georgia, Kentucky, Louisiana, Mississippi, and
Tennessee. They fought under Ulysses S. Grant in the Vicksburg campaign and
under William Rosecrans at Chickamauga. Kansas's troops also were dispatched
to the West: participating in the New Mexico expedition, serving in the mountains near Denver, providing escort duty for trains and railroad workers, protecting telegraph lines, building forts such as Fort Halleck in Dakota Territory,
and, of course, fighting American Indian tribes resistant to continued American
westward movement.

Ultimately, Kansas furnished 20,097 men for the Union. Although this number may seem paltry when compared to states like New York, Pennsylvania, and
Ohio, each of which furnished more than 300,000 men for the United States,
Kansas had a small population in 1860. According to that year's census, the state
had 107,206 inhabitants, of whom 58,806 were white males; of these, 32,921 were
of military age (between fifteen and forty-nine years old). As such, the ability
of the state to produce more than twenty thousand men to serve is remarkable
in and of itself. But the sacrifice these Kansans made to preserve the Union is
equally noteworthy.

Kansas had the highest mortality rate (deaths in action and from wounds) of any state in the Union. The general ratio for all states was an average of 35.10 deaths per thousand men, but Kansas had a mortality rate of 61.01. The state with the second-highest mortality rate was Massachusetts, with a rate of 47.76. Overall, Kansas suffered 8,498 casualties. Of these, 1,000 men died through combat: 796 were killed in battle while 204 later perished from the wounds they sustained. However, while war is always deadly, in this era disease commonly claimed more lives than did battle. Chaplain Hugh Fisher of the Fifth Kansas Regiment, for instance, wrote to the governor that there were "not 20 men among us who have not been sick at sometime during our stay" in Arkansas, and that to remain in the area would "disable and destroy us without gaining a victory for our armies in our country's cause."[2] Indeed, disease felled more than double the number of men killed in combat, taking 2,106 of Kansas's men. In addition, almost another 2,000 men had to be discharged because disability rendered them unfit for duty.

Although an individual's risk of death depended largely on the vagaries of war, there was one general exception: soldiers well understood that African Americans fighting in the South were at greater risk because they would likely be killed rather than held as prisoners of war. Indeed, when assessing the combat deaths of Kansas troops, this proves true for soldiers in the First Kansas Colored Infantry, which had significantly higher deaths than other Kansas troops. For instance, 4 of its officers were killed, along with 156 enlisted men. The regiment with the second-highest number of deaths was the First Kansas Infantry, which lost 11 of its officers and 86 of its enlisted men. Overall, the highest deaths from disease came from the Fifth Kansas Cavalry, which, having served in Arkansas for more than two years, lost 219 men. Finally, the regiment with the greatest number of desertions was the First Kansas Infantry, with 238 deserters. This rate of desertion is comprehensible when one considers that the First Infantry lost the second-highest number of men in combat, lost the most men to death from the wounds sustained in battle, and, with 209, had the most men discharged because of disability.

Kansas recruited sufficient men that a draft was not ordered until December 19, 1864. However, when notified of the order, Kansas governor Samuel Crawford argued that the state had not been appropriately credited for all the men it had supplied the Union. The issue of properly crediting solders was complicated. For instance, the 1860 census found only 627 African Americans in the territory, but it furnished 2,116 men for the First and Second Kansas Colored Regiments. Although most of these individuals were from Arkansas and Missouri, Kansas received credit for their service. However, the three Indian regiments Kansas raised (including one in Indian Territory) had not been properly credited. Thus, Crawford went to Washington to convince Secretary of War Edwin Stanton to reverse the draft call. He was successful, but Stanton was so lax in officially relaying the news that Crawford arrived home to discover that a number of Kansans already had been drafted and sent to St. Louis. Although ordered released, these men served in the Tenth Kansas until that regiment was mustered out, in July 1865.[3]

In addition to these troops, a number of Kansas men served in the militia. Governor Thomas Carney was especially keen to raise Home Guards to protect the border, but was denied permission by President Lincoln. Ultimately, Carney authorized 150 men to patrol the border, funded by $10,000 of his own money (later reimbursed by the state). But after the 1863 Lawrence massacre, more attention was paid to the state's security needs. By the time rumors of Sterling Price's impending invasion of Missouri and Kansas circulated, in late 1864, the state had ten thousand militia, eight thousand of whom were serving along the border.[4]

Ultimately, Kansas provided the Union with a contingent of troops that seems small when compared to other states'. Yet Kansans were on the forefront of change, raising diverse troops that included not just white men but African American and Indian men as well. Moreover, as the following documents attest, Kansans joined the fight to preserve this nation's integrity and Constitution in numbers that exceeded government requests. As with any group, the expectations and experiences of the soldiers varied considerably. Some were eager for combat and were disappointed to find themselves serving close to home. Others were appalled by the behavior of the officer corps and the morals of those with whom they served. Sent into the South, many Kansans found the seasons difficult to withstand and the leniency with which the rebels were treated confounding. Well aware that Kansas was underpopulated and lacked the men and arms necessary to defend the state, most expressed concern for those left behind. And many, meditating on the changes war wrought, likely agreed when George Packard wrote his brother that while he intended to go home after the war, it would not "be the young 'fop' that left" so many years before.[5]

KANSAS EXCEEDS ITS QUOTA

Kansas's contribution of more than 20,000 men to the Union cause is particularly impressive given that its 1860 population included only 32,921 white men of military age. Ultimately, Kansas exceeded its quota by almost 3,500 men.

Adapted from "Statement of the number of Men called for the President of the United States and the number furnished by the State of Kansas, from April 15th, 1861, to June 30th, 1865"

Date of Call	Number of Men	Period of Service	Quota for Kansas	Number of Men Kansas Furnished
April 15, 1861	15,000 militia	Three months	[None]	650
May 3, July 22, & July 25, 1861	500,000	Three years	3,235	6,953
July 2, 1862	300,000	Three years	1,771	2,936
August 4, 1862	300,000 militia	Nine months	1,771	[None]
October 17, 1863 & February 1, 1864	500,000	Three years	3,523	5,374
March 14, 1864	200,000	Three years	1,409	2,563
April 23,1864	Militia	One Hundred days	[None]	441
July 18, 1864	500,000	One, two and three years	3,729	351
December 19, 1864	300,000	One, two and three years	1,222	829
TOTALS			16,654	20,097
Surplus			3,443	

Report of the Adjutant General of the State of Kansas, vol. 1 (1861–1865) (Leavenworth, KS: Bulletin Co-operative Printing Company, 1867), xxvii.

A WISCONSIN SOLDIER MOVES THROUGH KANSAS

Aiken J. Sexton, a private from Company E of the Twelfth Wisconsin Volunteers, was one of many soldiers traveling through Kansas on the way to the war front. Sexton wrote his wife, Catherine, about conditions in the state.

Leavenworth City Kansas Feb 26/62

Dear C

. . . I did not know there was so much diferance in the wether of *Wis* and this country We have seen no winter here the coldest days I could work in my shirt sleeves the weather for three weeks back has been warm and pleaseant the frost is mostly all out of the ground and the farmers begin to make preperation for their springs work the ice is braking up in the river in two days more it will be

open. it is very muddy except the highest places and there the roads are getting
dusty; our *reg* is still quartered here except *co* F and B. They are detached from
the *reg* and sent to Kansas City distance thirty five miles our co is comfortably
situated here with plenty to eat. We draw more rations than we can eat we buy a
good many extras with our over rations. We drill now four hours a day two hours
in the forenoon and two in the afternoon the *reg* is getting pretty well perfected
in their drill We are not afraid to drill before any of them they say here we beat
anything they ever saw for the chance we have had I tell you there is military men
here military men of all rank from the highest to the lowest at the fort is stationed
a large boddy of regulars whose term of enlistment is five years they are daily
enlisting more to make up the regular army. This place is a lively one the most of
the business is Government business. yesterday there was a train of forty wagons
left here for Fort Scott loaded with pourk and flour for the army. . . .

Ever the same
A. J. Sexton

~

Fort Scott Kansas Mar 17/62

Dear Catherine
      . . . this part of Kansas is thinly settled all the settlements there is is along
the streams and they are far between it is a good farming country here the
only trouble is market they have no regular market to the nearest point to the
Mo River is one hundred miles and that is their market at present. . . . We have
considerable guard duty to do it takes twelve a day to guard the camp ground
and town if there is any extra guards wanted *co* E is the *co* they call on the
Captain spoke to the Colonel about it he said *co* E shouldrs was broad he said
they was *the* healthyest co on the ground and the largest. that is so our *co* is the
largest and the best drilled . . . there is none of our *co* in the Hospital I think our
reg is favored with good health in comparison to the *Kan Regt* they have buried
from one co four a day with the measles their doctor says they have been to free
with those fancy women which invest these Southern towns. that disease and
the measles together is pretty sure death it seems to bad to see men throw away
them selves in that way when perhaps they have Fathers and mothers *or perhaps
we* who mourn their loss if loss they might call if I were them I should consider
it no great loss. . . .

Direct Fort Scott   A J Sexton

Miscellaneous Sexton Collection, Kansas State Historical Society.

EXCERPTS FROM JOSEPH TREGO'S LETTERS

Joseph Trego came to Kansas Territory from Illinois in 1857. Settling in Sugar Mound, Trego and some compatriots constructed and operated a sawmill in town. A member of the Fifth Kansas, Trego saw action in Missouri and Arkansas. In these letters, Trego candidly assesses the officers and reveals how soldiers worried for those they had left at home.

Camp No 1 en route to M. City
Aug. 13th 1861

Dear Wife,

We have been under orders to march South, for several days but were delayed from day to day by difficulty in getting what was required. Lane has reported everything on hand and in readiness for his brigade but we did not find it so and have not been able to get a start until yesterday after dinner. . . .

It will require us to wait where we are—5 miles from Leavenworth—until the remaining can be loaded. We have 21 government wagons with us loaded with provisions, arms, uniforms and camp equipage, and when the freighting wagons are all together and drawn by six pairs of oxen, and numbering seventy five—we will be ready for another move. We will not, I think, reach Mound City before the middle of next week. The 75 wagons are loaded with provisions for Lyon's forces. . . .

Your affectionate H

~

Fort Scott Sept 5th 1861

My Dear Wife, . . .

Price has been near us for more than a week and it was believed that he would attack Fort Scott within twenty four hours at least, as his forces numbered from 7000 to 8000, and ours was less than six hundred. Such another time as they had pitching tents, and loading up company wagons. Citizens fixing up their efforts . . . wagons hustling out provisions &c has not been seen before in this country. They, the rebels, have not been yet and the houses, with all their furniture, are turned over to the use of the soldiers, . . . [we], with four soldiers as servants and a contraband wench for cook are occupying the house where Mr. Williamson was living; . . .

. . . This morning Price pulled up stakes and started for Lexington. Tonight about 300 cavalry men will stir up their camp and retake the mules if possible.

I will go back away and tell you what we have been at since we arrived here, which was at day light after marching all night, in the evening following we set out for Spring river to explore. We went as far as a little plain called Mudock, nine miles from Carthage all the rebels in that village made their escape except one who was shot in the act of loading his rifle. We *had made a long pause to listen to Zulasky sing Annie Laurie* were so near Carthage at this point, that we did not deem it safe to remain there with our little party of 140 men. . . . Our departure was accelerated by a great commotion among the dogs along the road leading toward Carthage. We have since learned that a force did come up and were in the edge of the timber within gun shot of us just after our picket was recalled for the march. . . .

~

Camp No. 3 September 12th 1861

We are on a march from Fort Lincoln to some place north in Missouri, perhaps to Lexington but I dont know, and it is quite probable that our destination is dependent on circumstances that leaves it uncertain. This is our third day out and we are now encamped in the valley northeast of Trading Post.

Gen. Lane is along. There is of Cavalry not many more than six hundred, of which Col. Montgomery has charge. . . .

Col Montgomery was too unwell to ride when we left Fort Lincoln but we heard this morning that he will be with us in a day or two. Col. Jennison is out with 36 men to-day. The army that has been camped on Dry-wood, where we had a little brush with them, is now moving northward, and we will keep somewhere near them until Lane can get his Artillery. He would have had artillery so as to be able to meet them with some show of success, but Gov. Robinson has placed every obstacle possible in his way. . . .

. . . The excitement of Camp life has ceased to be interesting except when near an enemy; the prospect of an engagement will always be attended with feelings of the livliest interest no matter how used a person may become to scenes of strife and it is only those who can maintain an approach to an equilibrium in the excitement of battle that are fit to lead. Col. Johnson was so wrought up that if he had had command at Dry-wood we would have all been killed or taken prisoners but Montgomery was sufficiently self possessed to order a retreat in time to save nearly all, tho' not quite, a few being cut off and taken prisoner.

Since we are not employed as a regular Guerilla force but are to move with the main army I conclude that we shall have no more fighting to do until a great blow shall be struck which will decide the fate of one side or the other, that is, of these two armies. . . . Since writing the foregoing we have received orders to be in readiness to ride to Butler to-night. The object is mainly, I suppose, to take in a few secessionists and a good many horses and cattle, if they can be found, to supply the army. Secessionists have furnished us all the sheep and cattle we have needed. . . .

Your Husband

~

Mound City Dec. 18th/61

My Dear Wife

. . . The withdrawal of the federal troops from Missouri has given Price's armies full possession of southwestern Missouri and at the same time the Kansas brigade was divided up until at this time there is more danger of invasion than ever has been before. On last Thursday night a party was sent up on Mine Creek who pillaged Potosi and several neighboring houses, getting all they could carry away. They killed one man and took two prisoners. We were escorting a train from Leavenworth, having gone up towards Pottowattomie to meet it. Since returning we have been on the go constantly. The Infantry had gone to Papinsville and Butler to burn those towns, also to burn every sesesh house on the way. It was but a small party and they were away so long, a day over their time, and no word from them. Montgomery became uneasy and had the Cavalry go over to meet them and ascertain if Price had cut off their retreat. We rode 40 miles and found them all right and on their way home, having done the work they were sent to do. It was a hard case as families had to be set out of doors, not however without every thing that belonged to them except their buildings.

This was done to stop, if possible, the persecution of Union men in Missouri who have since the federal troops left, been robbed and driven from their homes. More than at any former time. Just at this time it is impossible to know what shape affairs will take here, but if the *new* Generals will return to the border the forces that have been ordered away, and add to them enough to be able to make anything of a show of defence for the country and the Gov. stores that are now here then there will be no danger of invasion. At this time there is 15 to one against us if Price should undertake the job. . . .

Goodbye your loving husband

~

Camp Defiance Dec. 28th 1861

My Dear Little Wife

It is impossible for me to express the disappointment I have felt in not being able to meet you at Leavenworth at the time I designated. Just about at that time we were very apprehensive that that the Southern army would invade Kansas, which they could have done if they had attempted it at the right time, of course I did not wish to have you coming here while that danger existed. . . .

29th Last evening while I was writing and had progressed so far, our company returned from a trip twenty miles into Missouri wither they had gone to *attend* a secesh ball. They missed the road on their way down last night, which made them too late for the dance, the company having dispersed. They however scoured the neighborhood and took in some prisoners one of whom is an officer in the Southern army who had come home to remain awhile. They brought in several teams loaded with bacon, dried fruit, apples, lard, butter, honey &c but had no fight. . . . Col. Montgomery has an old Dibley tent, smoky and cheerless, in which he receives all the yahoos from Missouri who are anxious to see him, and there is generally a tent full of them, who will lay around him by the hour, talking about border Ruffian times when they supposed that Montgomery was an 'awful man' but they had gone right, far enough to vote for Lincoln, and for that they were driven from Missouri: If they had been worth as much as a good cigar they would have defended themselves at home, instead of running at the first approach of danger. Why the Col. permits such men to occupy so much of his time is known only to himself. . . .

Your impatient Husband

. . . Heavens! what a miserable out the officers of this Brigade have made in the matter of pay. There are lots of men whose families are in a more destitute condition than were the poor of last winter and they cannot get a cent for them. . . . The men are getting very much discouraged but not so much as they might, and those who have been neglectful of their duty as to cause so very much of suffering on the part of soldiers' families should and may be they are, ashamed of themselves to say the least. . . .

~

Helena Sept. 7th 1862

My Dear Wife

. . . I am sick. Lt. M. is sick, lots of the men are yet sick. the regiment is badly managed. Major Walker improves backward as he goes up, showing that he is much better as a Captain than acting the part of a Col, as he has been trying to do since Lt. Col. Jenkins went home to see his family. We have always been in bad odor in this army. The Missouri Republic hates all Kansas troops and the bulk of this army read and admire the Republic. Walker is likely to increase this distaste at Head Quarters. We are not now surprised that Robison should send Walker here. He was our only hope for the salvation of the Regiment. That hope is gone and we are gloomy. I cant make up my mind to leave the boys and yet I believe that to remain in this regiment and in this army so much dissatisfied, and the debilitating effects of this climate operating upon me I shall never get well. . . .

With much love to you and children, I am your H

〜

Fort Smith Ark. Nov. 23^d 1863,

My Dear little Wife

. . . Our scouts captured about a dozen bushwhackers on the way down. Genl McNeil is keeping them here to have them ready to hang to telegraph poles when ever the wires may get cut agreeably to the orders lately issued and which you have probably seen in the papers. Genl Blunt is here and likely to remain until he shall be reinstated in his command. I hear from those who have a right to know, that McNeil himself wishes Blunt reinstated. They are on very friendly terms and have had several big drinks at which McNeil got gloriously drunk. Haskell who never drinks nor is present at any of their carousels, and for which many of the drinking fraternity dislike him, says that Blunt *never gets drunk,* and has always been ready for duty, which he attends to very promptly, though he does certainly imbibe largely. Capt Haskell shows himself a high toned gentleman who dispises vulgarity, and also very practical and precise in his business requirements, which makes him unpopular with many of the officers here who I must say are generally a disgrace to our army. I therefore place much confidence in what he says in matters of fact or of opinion. He says of Blunt, "he is a good officer, understanding and attending to the details of business, and equally competent as a Genl when a fight is on hand, but as a man he is grossly immoral." I can see for myself that the appointment of McNeil to this command has not bettered matters in any particular.

There have been misrepresentations with regard to Genl Blunt's operations, as we hear there have been with regard to Haskell's bringing a large stock of goods to this place on his own private account, of which there is not one word of truth. . . .

〜

Little Rock Ark.

May 16th 1864

My Dear Wife

I was highly gratified last evening with receiving yours of the 2d; . . . but before I got through with your letter, I felt pained and am now so chagrined that I scarcely have patience to write, but I must, to tell you how unfortunate it was for you that you seemed to be under the necessity of giving accommodations to those officers of the 14th Regt. All that you named, but one, are strangers to me. I have no doubt but that they are gentlemen, and I have no particular objection to your having them in your house if you like, would prefer however that you did not have to do the extra work which it will necessitate. It ought to be needles for me to tell you that a man may be a villian and yet *very* amiable and corteous, that is absolutely essential for them to be successful in their impositions. But where, my loving little wife, is your intuitive perception of depravity that you used to exhibit when such men as old Dr. Underhill was near enough for you to feel the contamination of the very atmosphere with which he was surrounded. *Know* that Col. M is one of the most depraved of men, who will stoop—if it is stooping for him—to intercourse with negro wenches, on the march, as he did do last fall on the way to Ft. Smith, and such wenches as they were too.

Can you wonder that I am excited when I learn that such a man as he has gained access to my fire-side. If you love me you will send him from the house as soon as possible, *never* to return. I will write you again in a few days

From your Husband

Joseph Harrington Trego Papers, Collection 523, Kansas State Historical Society.

A DOUGLAS DEMOCRAT PLEDGES HIMSELF TO LINCOLN

Regiments were filled both by Kansas residents and by those from other states. Born in Switzerland and raised in Ohio, Christian H. Isely lived in St. Joseph, Missouri, near the Kansas border, when the war broke out. Appalled by secessionist sentiment in Missouri, he crossed the border and joined the Second Kansas Cavalry. The Isely family has collected Isely's correspondence with his wife, Eliza Dubach Isely, as Uncommon Writings by Common Folk.

Willow-Dale Doniphan Co Kansas. May 6th 1861

His Excelency

The President of the U. S. of N. America

Mr. Abraham Lincoln

The addressed greeting:

Dear and noble Sir!

. . . With a bleeding heart do I think of the dangers that are surrounding our heretofore so happy and prosperous Land and Nation. With every comming day the danger seems to in crease; the rebels are getting more numberous and active, and the traitors more bold and despert. And I think duty requires every true hearted citizen to cluster closely around the heart of our Nation—around the head of our worthy and honorable President—and show to the world, and especialy should it be made known to all those whose hearts are filled with treachery againts our Dear, dear-beloved Land that we the friends of the "Union" are Unanimous! that we are as "One Man." . . .

We as a Nation have long lived as the most happy, the most prosperous, and the best governed, on earth; under the "Star Spangled Banner." Now why should we not be true to that Banner which waved gracefuly over us, and under which we have so long lived securely and savely? Could there be any crime more abomanable on earth, than our indifference to those beautiful Stars and Stripes, in a period so critical like this, when we see that its existence is about to be extinguished and destroyed? No. Never, as long as our hearts shall beat, and as long as there is blood in our veins, and as long as a muskel moves within us, shall we be true to our Banner—true to our Constitution—true to our Country and Goverment. . . . Such is the general feeling and voice of the people of Kansas— And such let the motto be of every true hearted "Union Man" and then we have nothing to fear, but every thing to gain. . . .

. . . I am a citizen of St. Joseph, Mo., member of the O. L. Presbyterian church, and many are the prayers that have ascended to the throne of grace allready in my beloved church. But every thing is in confusion since fort Sumter is taken. The secessionists are very numberous and despert and a Union man has for a while been affraid to express himself openly. On the 20 of April the excitement was to its highest pitch; they hoisted secession flags and made secession speeches. To prevent the sheding of blood the Union men withdrew and interfered not in the least. But I could not look at there ruinous action—my heart was sore and aching with pain and grief. I have a small house in St. Joe and the worst of [it] is I owe some money on it yet, and to a secessionist at that, but I left every thing commiting it to the care of God, and came over here to Kansas.

. . . And now I came over here to join a company of Union men soldiers, to fight for my country if it is needed. I know that I am not among traitors in Kansas, but if [in] Missouri I could not say so. My Father lives in Ohio but was originaly from the Alpine Switzerlan. I have been a Douglass Democrat and voted for him last fall. But I will now fight for Mr. Lincoln and the admistration if is necessary. And remain by subscribing my self as your humble Friend and obedient servant.

Chr. H. Isely

～

Camp near Ft. Scott Kansas
Wednesday July the 1st 1863

Mrs. Eliza Isely . . .

Thursday, July 2nd / 63.

. . . The rebels are radical in their cause of the distruction of our once happy
Union and if we want to counter-ballance their ruinous efforts, we must do it by
radical measures; concervatism weighs nothing against them. And to be radical
now is to stand firm by our Government & Administration although either
may also be wrong in some inferior points it is nevertheless our Duty now to
stand by them as truely Loyal Patriots ought to do. or we must admit that our
Government is wrong and the rebel Government is right. they surely cannot
be both right or both wrong and I take it for granted that our Government &
Abraham Lincoln is right and the rebel conspiricy & Jeff. Davis wrong. I give
my hearty support to the former. . . . Many cry about the violation of our Laws
and the constitution by Pres. Lincoln. they are poor short sighted people that
continually induldulge in such arguments. if they would look at it in a propper
light they could plainly see that the same Law that governed us in time of Peace
& security, can no more govern us now in time of civil war, than a sick person
can digest the same kind of food as he was accustomed to do when he was
well! Would it then not be more than cruel to force the same kind of diet on
a poor sick person that he used to relish when well? and then cause his death
under the most excruciating pains? Would it not be wiser to prepare his diet and
his medicine as the nature of the advancing disease requires it, till it is finally
subdued and the patient saved? So it is now with our bleeding country as the evil
progresses so it assumes a new and different aspect and new Laws have to be
made to meet and check the malady, till it is removed and the country saved once
more. That this *will* be done I have not the remotest doubt.

Hence I claim that Abe Lincoln needs and deserves all the support that
posibly can be rendered him by all the truely Loyol & Patriotic hearts, and it is
also your Duty to take a firm stand in his and our countrys behalf. . . . There is
one thing yet however that I wish to mention; it is this: The people of our Nation
is evidently devided in Five different classes. The first imbraces all the good
people, all true Christians, and all true patriots. they are all Loyal to the Federal
Government and give it their undevided Love & hearty support. They pray, weep
& fight for. The second class are all those that come out boldly yet manfully to
fight against us in a fair warfare & fair manner. The third Class are those that
continually find fault with our Government yet are to cowardly to join the seecsh
army. The Fourth class are all those that pretend to fight in a sneaking manner
like the Brushwhackers against any soldiers. And the Fifth Class are all those

that sneake about at home and try to injure our cause all they can while they try to make all the money they can off of the Government. Now to which class all should belong is more then self evident. . . .

> . . . From your own Loving & devoted Husband
>
> Chr H. Isely . . .

Isely Family Papers, Special Collections and University Archives, Wichita State University Libraries.

"THE CAUSE OF THE WAR MUST BE REMOVED":
THE LETTERS OF SAMUEL AYERS

When the Seventh Kansas Volunteer Cavalry was organized, in 1861, Samuel Ayers joined as chaplain. Initially ordered to New Mexico, the Seventh was diverted to Mississippi and Tennessee instead. These letters reflect Ayers's strong antislavery views and his dismay over the leniency with which Confederates were treated. They also provide an account of the Lawrence massacre of August 1863. Poor health forced Ayers to return to Kansas, where he served as post surgeon.

Lawrence Kansas April 5th/62

Friend Langdon, Dear Sir

. . . From our late victories some may conclude our war is nearly closed—I wood it was so if peace can be restored on a bassis which will seem a permanent peace. But rather than peace should be closed on any other principal I would rather as much as I desire a secession of arms the war would continue even for years. I think however if propper measures are instituted the war may be brought to a perminent close in a year from now if not before. To accomplish this it is my opinion that the cause of the war must be removed before any thing perminent can be accomplished unless provisions are made by Congress for its speady removal. . . .

Yours Affectionately

Hon L Langdon   Samuel Ayers

~

In Camp at Union City Ten
June 12th/62

Friend Langdon

. . . I am movcing on still further south and more into the heart of seceshindom. From what I can learn there are but few truly loyal men in these parts and those who are loyal at heart are so defenceless they dare not say a word in vindication of the Union

In fact the secesh are not afraid to come out and boldly announce their secesh sentiments to our soldiers as we march a long and in one instance as Gen Mitchel and his body guard were passing a schoolhouse the teacher and schollers came out and hurrard for Jef Davis and at the same time they passed unrebuked. There is something connected with the movements of our commanders I do not neither can I fully understand as reguards their treatment of rebbells. They act as though they were afraid they would be injoured in person or property. Say the the secesh are erring bretherin and must be treated as such such were the orders as I am informed given by Gen Quimba to a detachment which was sent from Columbus to Mosco and that if any our interfear and in any respect with their person or property they should be sevearly dealt with. Now as it reguards jayhawking I am and ever have been an opposer of the practice. Yet I can but wonder at the sensativeness of our leaders on this point. If a Union man is robed by a secessionist it matters but little—it is a natural consequence but the property of a secessionist must be held sacred. For soldiers to take the propperty of rebells and appropriate to their individual use I believe to be wrong further than is necessary for their immediate comfort but I do not think it wrong for the government to appropriate through their agents the property of active secessionist to the liquidation of the expence of the war for they are the party who have caused the war and accruing expences arising there from. Yet even this I think should be conducted on proper principles and in such a way as to give the government the full benifit of thos means. When however the property of a secessionist is tuched they will come forward and ask do you believe in living up to the requirements of the constitution? Claiming notwithstanding they have ignored it. . .

Hon L Langdon

Yours Affectionately
Samuel Ayers

~

Moneka Linn Co Kansas Feb 18th/63

Friend Langdon . . .

From what I can learn I think the Kansas 7th are not taken to Vicksburgh but are left with some 3 or 4 other Cavalry Regiments to protect the Rail Roads in the vicinity of Memphus Corinth and Jackson Tenn—Nelson sais in his last letter that Gen Price was following them up as they fell back from Miss. Whether he will force them into a fight I cannot say—I am very sure however of one thing and that is this—if the Kansas 7th can have any thing like a fair show they will not run backward for they hate this crawfish work. . . .

You may think it strang when I say that though we have of late obtained several important advantages over the enemy yet I view our affairs as criticle as at any former period. These views however do not arise from any distrust of our army or the officers who command it but from the traitors in our midst hear in the free states. The southern rebel I view as an honerable man beside our northan foe. For they manlike come out boldly and show their true colors whilst their northan sympathizers try to hide them selves behind their professions of loyalty and friendship for their country—Of all the low mean and contemptable beings in the world such men are the most base and vile for they have not the manhood to come out as men should and publicly avough their real sentiments but secretly in the dark do all they can to supplant that government that for years has fostered them protected their rights and secured to them every advantage that a good and wholsom government could secure to any nation.

Why it is that rebellion is treated so mildly in the north to me is supprising For one I can see but little difrence between a northern and a southern rebel. If any difrence dose exist and either recieve any levity I think the southern rebel is the one who ought to recieve it for as stated above they are the more honorable of the two

But the term honor when applyed to rebellion either north or south is I think very impropperly used. . . . War a broad is bad enough but when it comes into our neighborhood it is much more distressing—those who have not seen its devastating effects cannot fully realize its horors. I hope and pray the time may soon come when it can be said the last rebel is conquered and our country is free—that peace justice and liberty prevail and all unholy oppression is forever done a way—when it shall nomore be said that whilst we bost of our free institutions we are the supporters of the barbarous system of Affrican slavery. No when it shall be said our war is closed but it likewise be said with us as a nation slavery is ended—then may we look for and confidently expect the blessings of the God of nations on our institutions our Agricultural and machanical persuits as well as our commercial and Universal prosperity attend us on our onward movements. . . .

Yours truly
Samuel Ayers

Hon L Langdon

⁓

Moneka Kansas June 1ˢᵗ/63

Friend Langdon . . .

The most we have to complain of is the operations and deprodations of the
Bushwhackers and the *Red Legs.* They pay us a visit occasionally and levy a tax
to the ammount of one or more horses—Sometimes plunder houses—run off
cattle—kill a few men and burn some houses—. . . Along our Missouri border we
have to be on the watch for gurrilla parties who ever and anon mak a raid into
our state doing the work of their master; but as a general thing do not extend
their ravages many miles from the line

. . . Our Gov is now making arangements to organize the militia along our
border counties to defend our settlements. I hope some eficent measures will be
adopted to protect our border—Most of the Kansas troops are at a distance from
home leaving us quite unprotected—To me it seams no more than right that
enough of our men should be left to protect our homes—It appears hard that
men should not be permitted to defend their own families and firesides but in
many instances such is the fact. . . .

                                                    Yours Affectionately
Hon L Langdon   Samuel Ayers

                                ∼

August 24, 1863

Friend Langdon
Dear sir . . .

. . . the events of last month to our nation are repleat with interest and
ought to beget grate and unfained thankfulness in our hearts to God for his
intoposition in our behalf. Never, or but seldom has it fallen to the lot of a nation
to record as many grate and important Victories in the space of one month as
has been the priviledge of ours during the past.

The surrender of Vicksburg of its self was sufficient to produce a universal
thrill of pleasure in the heart of every loyal citizen, but when we ad the repulse
of Price Marmaduke & Homes at Helena, Lee's defeat at Gettysburg, the
surrender of Port Hudson—the retreat of Braggs army in connection with
Morgans capture and several other smaler advantages secured by our armies
make a page in our history that must and will command the gratitude of every
true American citizen. . . . What is to be the future of Kansas is more than I
can divine at present. Dark clouds at present are hanging over us yet I would
not dispair. From all I can learn Gen Blunt is placed in rather a critical position

having only some 3000 or 3500 men to oppose to Steel who has from 12000 to 15000—Blunt has requested reinforcements but Gen Scofield refuses them and order him to fall back. If Blunt complies with said orders it throws the Indian country open to the raviges of the enimy—Again if he falls back from Ft Gibson there will be no place where he can make a stand untill he gets to Fort Scott which is a very weak post and hard to defend and if this point is past our southeastern border is left open to the ravages of the foe—Take it along our Missouri border we are subject to almost constant raids from the Bushwhackers over the line who rob our citizens burn thier houses and murder prominent men.

Last Friday or it may be it was Thursday the troops stationed at the Trading Post were ordered to Kansas City The following night a company of secesh came in and robed som 12 or 14 families and burnt some houses of the number I am not informed. But the most distressing event which has occourred in Kansas since the commencement of the war and in fact since the settlement of the state took place last Thursday night or friday morning. A company as near as I can assertain numbering near 300 men or I may say demons entered Lawrence killing all they could see in the streets and burning the buildings on each sid of Massachusetts St (the main business St in the town) without regard to the removal of the inmates of the houses. In the Eldgrage House I am informed that 15 women and children were burned to death and at last accounts 130 bodies had been found of persons killed or burnt to death. Many of them were taken from the ruins of burnt buildings

What acts could be more barberous more inhuman To kill in battle appears bad enough—But to set fire to a town and then shoot down all that attempted to make their escape from the flames is an act of barbarity but seldom if ever eaqueled by the most savage tribes. And thes are the men your—I will say our copperhead citzens wish to aid and abet and on whom they wish to bestow their sympathies

How long we shall be called to endure such outrage I cannot say—but hope for the honor of our country and the cause of humanity that we may never hear of an other such an event. The people of Kansas have become used to almost all kinds of abuse and outrage but this last act I think is the climax. It has been reported that when these inhuman monsters had finished their work of destruction and murder at Lawrence they started south on the main road leading toward Osawatomie and Paola burning every farm house for the distance of eleven miles. But for the truth of this statement I cannot vouch reports are so conflicting . . .

Oct 27th. . . . The destruction of life and property at Lawrence was full greater than represented above. Considerable over 200,000 dollars in cash was taken at the loss of property is estimated at over two millions. Over 150 bodies have been found and burried and still the work of interment is going on—you undoubtedly will get the perticulars through the press before you get this.—The burning of farm houses to Brooklin from Lawrence as stated above is correct and was only stopt by Gen Lane rallying some 20 or 30 men and persewing them giving them battle and following them on their retreat. . . .

Quite a number of the vilins had been killed and their dead bodies left along the road most of whom had quite an ammount of green back in their pockits one had $10,000 It is to be hoped not one of them will escape. . . .

Affectionately yours

Hon L Langdon   Samuel Ayers

Samuel Ayers Papers, Kansas State Historical Society.

THE FIRST KANSAS COLORED INFANTRY AT ISLAND MOUND, MISSOURI

James Lane began recruiting a regiment of African Americans without authorization in August 1862. Largely formed of escaped slaves from Missouri and Arkansas, the First Kansas Colored Infantry was mustered into federal service on January 13, 1863. It was the first regiment of African Americans organized in the North after three regiments had been formed in the South. Despite their unofficial status, the First Kansas Colored Infantry saw combat in August 1862, becoming the first African American troops to do so. Major Richard G. Ward describes the skirmish at Island Mound, where a detachment of 225 drove off 500 Confederates.

OCTOBER 29, 1862.—Skirmish at Island Mound, Mo.
Report of Maj. Richard G. Ward, First Kansas Colored Infantry

DEAR SIR: . . .

. . . I started from Camp William A. Phillips Sunday, October [26], with 160 men and 6 officers, joining Capt. H. C. Seaman and command, comprising some sixty-four men (colored) and a small party of white scouts, and moved by the way of Mound City and Camp Defiance to the Dickey's Crossing of the Osage, in Bates County, Mo., at which point we arrived Monday afternoon. Shortly after crossing the stream we were made aware of the presence of the enemy in force by their scouts and by information from citizens, who stated that Cockrell, Campbell, Hancock, and Turman had concentrated their forces on Osage Island, and that their combined force amounted to some 700 or 800 men, all splendidly mounted. We immediately took possession of old man Toothman's house (a noted rebel guerrilla) and commenced skirmishing with the enemy's scouts and pickets, we trying to draw them off the island and the enemy trying to draw us to the bushes. Tuesday we were engaged all day in desultory skirmishes, but the wind was so high were unable to injure them with our sharpshooters, they taking good care to keep a respectful distance. At night, after a consultation with Captain Seaman, we concluded to send runners to Kansas for a force of cavalry sufficient to aid us in dislodging the enemy. Accordingly we sent three, one to you at Fort Lincoln, one to Fort Scott, and one to Paola. Wednesday morning I detached Captains Armstrong and Crew, with a force of some sixty men, to engage the attention of the enemy, while Captain Seaman, Captain Thrasher, of his command, and Lieutenant Huddleston, with a force of some fifty men, foraging, as we were entirely out of food with the exception of beef and parched corn. Captain Armstrong found a force of the enemy some two miles from camp, and immediately threw out his skirmishers, under command of Orderly Sergeant Smithers, of Company B, who immediately moved forward to the attack and drove the enemy from position to position until they had been driven some four miles from camp, the enemy shouting to the boys to "come on, you d—d niggers," and the boys politely requesting them to wait for them, as they were not mounted. We succeeded in placing seven men *hors de combat,* with no loss on our side, and the boys felt highly elated on their return at their success.

While at dinner the enemy made a dash at our pickets and ran them into camp and then drew off. Suspecting that they were concentrating troops behind the mound south of us, we threw out a small party of skirmishers to feel toward them and ascertain their force and retake our picket ground. The boys soon drove the enemy over the hill, and the firing becoming very sharp, I ordered Lieut. Joseph Gardner to take a force of some twenty men and proceed to rally the skirmishers and return to camp, while I placed Captain Armstrong's force (consisting of detachments from Companies A, B, E, H, and G) under arms. I here found that Captain Crew and Lieutenant Huddleston had left the camp and had gone toward where our skirmishers were engaged. Becoming uneasy at the prolonged absence of Gardner and the skirmishers, I marched Armstrong's force toward the firing and placed them behind the bluffs, and went forward myself to reconnoiter the position of affairs. I found a detachment of the enemy posted on a mound immediately south of me and some of our scouts occupying a mound west of me, on the right. I sent Adjutant Hinton to that point to ascertain where our force (Gardner's) was. He returned with the information that they were at a house some 800 yards south of the mound and were making preparations to return, feeling confident that the enemy would attempt to cut them off. I ordered Armstrong to move by the right flank and gain a position in rear of the mound, and dispatched a messenger to camp to inform Captain Seaman of the position of affairs and requesting him to place other forces under arms and to be ready to move immediately. No sooner had this happened than the enemy charged with a yell toward Gardner's little band of twenty-five men. The boys took the double-quick over the mound in order to gain a small ravine on the

north side, but while they were on the north slope the enemy came upon them.
Nothing dismayed, the little band turned upon their foes, and as their guns
cracked many a riderless [horse] swung off to one side. The enemy cried out
to the men to surrender, but they told them never. I have witnessed some hard
fights, but I never saw a braver sight than that handful of brave men fighting 117
men who were all around and in amongst them. Not one surrendered or gave up
a weapon.

    At this juncture Armstrong came into the [fight] like a lion, yelling to his men
to follow him, and cursing them for not going faster when they were already on
the keen jump. He formed them in line within 150 yards and poured in a volley.
The enemy charged down the slope and were met by a volley from Captain
Thrasher's command, who had just been posted by Seaman. They swung to the
right in order to outflank Armstrong and gain his rear. I immediately ordered
a detachment of men under Lieutenants Dickerson and Minor across the open
angle between Thrasher's and Armstrong's, which was executed with promptness.
The enemy finding themselves foiled, wheeled their force and dashed up the hill.
The brave Armstrong saw them through the smoke (they, the enemy, having
set the prairie on fire), charged his brave lads through the fire, and gave them a
terrible volley in the flank as they dashed by. This ended the fight, although they
had re enforcements arriving, estimated by some of our best judges to be from 300
to 400 strong. They did not wish "anymore in theirs." They had tested the niggers
and had received an answer to the often mooted question of "will they fight."
Here commenced the most painful duty of the day—the removal of the killed and
wounded. On that slope lay 8 of our dead and 10 wounded, among the former the
brave, lamented, and accomplished Captain Crew. He fell as a brave man should
fall, facing the foe, encouraging his men never to yield, and casting defiance at the
enemy. Three of them rode up to him and demanded him to surrender, saying
that they would take him to their camp. He told them never. They said that they
would shoot him then. "Shoot and be d—d," was the reply of the heroic soldier,
and set them the example by running backward and discharging his revolver
at them, but almost immediately fell, pierced through the heart, groin, and
abdomen. Among the wounded was Lieutenant Gardner. He fell shot in the thigh
and knee by a heavy load of buckshot. While in this situation, unable to move,
one of the cowardly demons dismounted, and making the remark that he would
finish the d—d son of a b—h, placed his revolver to his head and fired. The ball,
almost by a miracle, did not kill him; striking his skull and glancing around his
head, came out on the other side. He will recover. It is hard to make distinctions
where every man did his whole duty, and I hereby return my thanks to every
man and officer of the expedition for their splendid behavior. . . . Accompanying
this you will find a list of killed and wounded, heroes all, who deserve the lasting

gratitude of all the friends of the cause and race.* Thursday the enemy fled and nothing of interest occurred until you arrived and took the command.

I have the honor to be, sir, respectfully, your most obedient servant,

R. G. WARD,
Captain Company B.

Col. J. M. WILLIAMS,
Commanding First Regiment Kansas Colored Volunteers.

*Nominal list (omitted) shows 1 officer and 7 men killed, 1 officer and 10 men wounded.

The War of the Rebellion: A Compilation of the Official Records of the Union and Confederate Armies, ser. 1, vol. 53 (Washington, DC: Government Printing Office, 1902), 455–58.

TO BE KEPT HERE "WILL DISABLE AND DESTROY US"

Pastor of the First Methodist Episcopal Church in Leavenworth before the war, Hugh D. Fisher joined the Fifth Kansas Regiment as chaplain. Organized in 1861, they initially served largely in Missouri but left Rolla to join the Army of the Southwest in Helena, Arkansas, in June 1862. From then until the winter, the Fifth Kansas saw heavy skirmishes. After the war, Fisher published a memoir entitled The Gun and the Gospel: Early Kansas and Chaplain Fisher.[6]

Helena Arkansas
December 30th 1862

Hon Thos Carney
Governor of Kansas.
Sir

After a free conversation with several of the officers of the 5th Kansas Regiment I address these lines to you, hoping they will meet your hearty aprobation, and recieve your immediate attention.

Our Regiment has been at this point since the 14th July, at which time we numbered 856. Now we only number 705 a Decreace of 151 by Death & Discharge. 85 or 90 of the number have Died of Deseases incident to this climate, and at least 150 more are partialy or permanently Disabled by Desease. There are not 20 men among us who have not been sick at sometime During our stay here. Many of these are very liable to be cut down by spring sickness, and indeed another season here will probably result in the Death of Scores of our Galliant comrads. Our Men are well Mounted and Officered but to be kept in this "Cheapominie [?] of the Missippi", will disable and Destroy us without gaining a Victory for our armies in Our countrys cause. We pant for a possibility to do something for our country. But in our present reduced condittion it is next to impossible.

Therefore we most respectfully ask you as Govenor of our youthful but Patrotic State, to ask Genl Curtis that we may be imediately returned to Kansas to fill up our Regiment, and recruit our health, so as to take part either with Genl Blunt, or in any other field which may be open for our Company.

Knowing your humanity as well as love of country we appeal to you; governor, in the most respectful terms for the sake of Mercy. Use your influence to have us Ordered Home. . . .

Permitt me to subscribe myself *Yours.*

H. D. Fisher

H. D. Fisher Papers, Collection 343, Kansas State Historical Society.

PROUD TO BE IN THE WEST'S ARMY

A native of Ohio, Harrison Kelley moved to Kansas in 1858, when he was twenty-two years old, settling in Ottumwa, Coffey County, along the Neosho River. When war broke out, he enlisted in the Fifth Kansas Cavalry, rising to captain of Company B and serving in Missouri, Mississippi, and Arkansas. Kelley was elected to the House of Representatives in 1888.

Little Rock Ark
Sunday Eve Sept 13/63

Sister Artie

We have driven the "Arkansaw traveler" generally known as "Old Pap Price" from his favorite and pleasant retreat and as you see by heading of this, the capital of another confederate state is occupied, and that permanantly by the feds; and the old "traveler" and his ten thousand friends including two hundred he let out of the penitentiary as he was leaving town the latter no doubt constituting the most respectable portion of his army, are in *inglorious* and hasty retreat toward the "last ditch" He and other rebels Generals have held high carnival here for the last two years, and the citizens of this Loyal City have been held during that time in complete subjection and forced to contribute to their support. I presume no portion of our army have been met with greater expressions of joy than we were hailed with by the citizens of Little Rock. Of course we were pleased as well as surprised to meet friends again. Long strides are now being taken towards the end of the rebellion in the transmississippi department We consider this army commanded by the gallant and soldierly Gen Steel as invincible and able to whip all the forces the Rebs have west of the Mississippi. Tis four weeks since we left Helena and our march was made in the hottest part of the season and drove the rebels all the way and *routed* them here, and the best time for making a fall campaign in this climate is just commencing so I see nothing to prevent our making a triumphal march through Louisanna and Texas during the next two months, but the tardiness of military operations may keep us back, and I would not be surprised if they did to a certain extent, but hope for the best. One week ago to day at eight O clock in the morning the rebel Generals Marmaduke and Walker fought a duel on a sand bar opposite this city, resulting in the death of the latter. They fought with revolvers at fifteen paces and exchanged the third shot before he was killed. Marmaduke was uninjured. We fought them both at Helena the 4th and Marmaduke accused Walker of showing cowardice on that occasion resulting in a chalenge by the latter and finally in his death. *So* one after another of the rebel leaders are passing away *mostly* by their own hands. A Rebel Gen killed in a duel on Sabbath morn by a brother Gen! A fit terminus of a traitor's life! May the end of all the leaders of this rebellion be as inglorious.— . . .

Please accept love from your brother

Harrison.

~

Pine Bluff Ark
Sept 30th 1863

Dear Carrie—

. . . You say its strange Western Officers have not the same privileges those of the Army of the potomac have. I am proud to say I am a soldier in the Wests army privilage or no privilage. I am very positive that the Western army could have drive the rebel army out of Virginia ere this. . . .

Oct 1st . . . There has been a great influx of negroes to our Regt since coming into this town. We are now overtaking many of the slaves that were run out of Mo for safety. Planters have given up the idea of running them any farther They say it is no use, the yanks will get them any way. If I am not badly mistaken the rebellion on this side of the Mississippi is played to a hole, and the hole is caving in. Tis amusing and instructive to contemplate the folly of the rebel authorities in their efforts to sustain their Slaveocracy. The hand of Providence has always been visable to me since the commencement of this war in direct thrusts at Slavery, but by no act has the final destruction of the whoe system been made so sure as by the order of Davis for raising colored troops, but I must close as I will miss mailing my letter,

Yours,

Harrison.

Harrison Kelley Letters, Collection 408, Kansas State Historical Society.

JOHN A. MARTIN REPORTS ON THE BATTLE OF CHICKAMAUGA

John A. Martin joined the Eighth Kansas Volunteer Infantry and was put in command on February 8, 1862; he was promoted to full colonel in 1863. The Eighth Kansas fought in Georgia, Kentucky, and Tennessee. In this report, Martin details his troops' contribution to the battle of Chickamauga. Over September 19 and 20, the Confederates forced the Union to fall back to Chattanooga, inflicting over sixteen thousand casualties.

HDQRS. THIRD BRIG., FIRST DIV., 20TH ARMY CORPS,

Chattanooga, September 28, 1863.

CAPTAIN: . . .

On the 28th of August the brigade was ordered to march from Stevenson, Ala., and at 5 p.m. started, reaching the banks of the Tennessee River at 11 p.m. We bivouacked for the night, and at daylight next morning were ordered to cross the river in pontoon barges and occupy the other side. . . . As soon as the opposite bank was reached the regiments were rapidly formed, the Twenty-fifth and Thirty-fifth Illinois left on the bank to protect the shore, while Colonel Heg advanced the Eighth Kansas and Fifteenth Wisconsin across the bottom to the foot of Sand Mountain, keeping a strong line of skirmishers in front. Reaching the mountains, the Fifteenth was left at the foot and the Eighth Kansas advanced up the mountain road, occupying the summit at 10 a.m. The Fifteenth Wisconsin was ordered up at about 3 p.m., and at dusk the two regiments advanced about 3 miles across the mountain and camped, remaining in this position until the 2d instant. The Twenty-fifth and Thirty-fifth came up on the evening of the 30th. Frequent scouts were sent out from the brigade during the time we occupied the mountain; one under Lieutenant-Colonel Abernathy, Eighth Kansas, penetrating to near Trenton, Ga., discovering the enemy in force.

On the 2d we marched 16 miles to Will's Valley; 4th, marched 5 miles to Winston's; 9th, ascended mountain and marched across 14 miles, bivouacking at the entrance of Lafourche [Neal's?] Gap; 10th, marched south along summit of mountain and descended into the valley through Henderson's Gap, bivouacking near Alpine; 14th, crossed back over mountain to Lord's farm; 15th, marched back to Winston's; 16th, marched over mountain to Stevens' Gap; 17th, descended into valley and bivouacked near Lee's Spring; 18th, marched 4 miles north on Chattanooga road.

On the 19th instant we marched at 8 o'clock, and at 11.30 o'clock reached a point near General Rosecrans' headquarters. The brigade filed through the woods to the right, and after marching about a mile was rapidly formed in line of battle, the Fifteenth Wisconsin, Eighth Kansas, and Thirty-fifth Illinois being in line, and the Twenty-fifth Illinois, a reserve directly in their rear. The brigade then moved three-quarters of a mile to the right, then by the left flank forward. We had not advanced more than a hundred yards when the enemy, concealed in the timber and behind fallen logs, opened a destructive fire on us. The men replied with promptness and effect, and pushed forward vigorously. The roar of musketry at this time was deafening.

The Twenty-fifth Illinois was ordered forward and came gallantly into line. The stream of wounded to the rear was almost unparalleled. Still the brigade held its ground, cheered on by the gallant, but unfortunate, Colonel Heg, who was everywhere present, careless of danger. The enemy was constantly re-enforced, and at last flanked us on the left, pouring a destructive fire down our line. We had then held the ground three-quarters of an hour. Colonel Heg gave the order to fall back, and the men slowly retreated, taking shelter behind the trees, firing at the advancing enemy, and stubbornly contesting every inch of the ground. Fifty yards to the rear they were again formed and again advanced, almost gaining their original ground, but were again compelled by overwhelming numbers to fall back. Again and again they formed and advanced, only to be driven back. Almost half of the brigade was killed or wounded. Colonel Heg was mortally wounded; but the remnants of the brigade, falling back to a fence a short distance in the rear, held the enemy in check until re-enforcements came up and relieved them, when they fell back across an open field, taking position in the edge of a forest behind a log barricade. What remained of the brigade I reformed here, with the assistance of Captain Morrison, assistant adjutant-general of the division, and again advanced across the field, taking our old position behind the fence, and remaining there until nearly dusk, when the ammunition of the men was exhausted, and we withdrew to the barricade in the edge of the woods again. Just at dark we were withdrawn by order of General Davis, and went into bivouac near the battle-field.

During the night of the 19th the brigade changed its location, crossing the Chattanooga road, and occupying a strong position on a ridge in the woods to the north. Our ammunition was replenished to 60 rounds. At noon we received an order to support General Sheridan on the right. We advanced across the road again and formed in line of battle, and then advanced to near a small barricade in the woods, fronting an open field. Finding the barricade already occupied by our troops, the brigade was moved by the right flank to the rear of General Carlin's brigade, and was ordered to lie down in a small ravine.

This order had hardly been executed when I received an order to move back by the left flank and take position on the left of General Carlin's brigade, the troops that occupied the ground having been moved away to the left. I directed the movement, passing General Carlin and moving by the right flank forward to the barricade. The three regiments on the right of the brigade reached their position, but the Thirty-fifth Illinois, the regiment on the left of the line, had not reached its position, when the enemy rose up from the tall weeds in front and advanced on us four columns deep, pouring in a destructive fire. The left flank of the brigade was entirely exposed, as the troops that had occupied that position had moved so far to the left as to be out of sight, and we were soon flanked and exposed to a destructive enfilading fire. The enemy in front was terribly punished as he came up. Our men fired coolly from behind the barricade and with terrible effect, the closed ranks and heavy columns of the enemy making their loss very heavy. The brigade held the position until the enemy had mounted the barricade, when, flanked on the left and overpowered by numbers in front, the men fell back in confusion, partially rallying about 200 yards in rear, but, finding all support gone and the line on the left in disorder, breaking again.

On the brow of the hill in the woods across the road they were again rallied, formed in line, and left the field by order in the rear of Sheridan's division, which had rallied at the same point.

I inclose herewith a list of killed, wounded, and missing of the brigade during the two days' engagement. By far the larger number were lost the first day; our loss on the 20th being light. On the second day we had hardly 600 men left in the brigade when we were thrown into the fight. These were opposed by at least a full division of the enemy's army. The list accompanying shows the loss to be fully 60 per cent. of those engaged, and amply attests the courage, stubborness, and determination with which the troops fought.

Where all behaved so gallantly it would be invidious to mention individuals as particularly conspicuous for their actions. The vacant ranks, eloquent with heroic memories of the dead and wounded, speak for our absent comrades; the living, who fought by their sides through the terrible storm of two days' conflict, have again established the invincible courage of the defenders of the Union.

The effective fighting force of the brigade, when it went into the engagement of the 19th, was as follows:

Command	Commissioned Officers Present	Enlisted Men Present	Aggregate
25th Illinois Volunteer Infantry	17	320	337
15th Wisconsin Volunteer Infantry	19	157	176
8th Kansas Volunteer Infantry	24	382	406
35th Illinois Volunteer Infantry	18	281	299
Total	78	1,140	1,218

The loss of the brigade during the two days' engagement was as follows, viz:

Command	Comd. Officers Killed	Comd. Officers Wounded	Comd. Officers Missing	Enlisted Men Killed	Enlisted Men Wounded	Enlisted Men Missing	Aggregate
25th Ill.	–	11	1	10	160	23	205
15th Wisc.	2	6	4	3	47	49	111
8th Kansas	3	8		30	154	25	220
35th Ill.	3	5		14	125	13	160
Total	8	30	5	57	486	110	696

Since the battles on the 19th and 20th the brigade has been re-enforced by a number of returned convalescents and by two companies of the Fifteenth Wisconsin Volunteers, which joined us on the 21st from detached service at Island No. 10. Many of the men slightly wounded have bravely returned to duty, considerably augmenting our force.

I am, captain, very respectfully, your most obedient servant,

JNO. A. MARTIN,
Colonel, Commanding Third Brigade.
Capt. T. W. MORRISON,
Asst. Adjt. Gen., First Div., Twentieth Army Corps.

The War of the Rebellion: A Compilation of the Official Records of the Union and Confederate Armies, ser. 1, vol. 30 (Washington: Government Printing Office, 1890), 528–31.

Members of the Eighth Kansas Volunteer Infantry at Lookout Mountain in Tennessee.
Reproduced by permission from the Kansas State Historical Society.

A MAGNIFICENT EFFORT, "BUT AT WHAT A SACRIFICE!"

When he joined the army, John A. Martin, who would be elected governor of Kansas in 1884, left his newspaper, the Atchison Champion, *in the care of John J. Ingalls. During the war, Ingalls was judge advocate on General George Deitzler's staff in the Kansas State Militia; after the war, he was a senator from 1873 to 1891. In this letter, Martin offers a more candid view of the situation in Tennessee than he had in his official report.*

Chattanooga, Tenn.,
Oct. 18th, '63

Dear Ingalls:— . . .

About the Battle, I presume you have already read more than I could write or say. Whether it was a defeat or victory depends pretty much on what was desired to be accomplished by the campaign. If this was to end by the taking of Chattanooga, it was a great victory for us, for with an army of only 35,000 men we held the rebel army of 120,000 at bay for two days, and we yet have Chattanooga—we damaged them as much as they did us, captured as many prisoners (not including wounded) as they did, took from them half as many pieces of artillery as they took from us, brought all our transportation off safe; and hold Chattanooga, so strongly fortified that they cannot take it with 200,000 men. There was bad Generalship on our side (not on "Old Rosy's part, but by some of his subordinate commanders) and our Right, the second day, was simply *crushed* by overpowering numbers. Our little Division, reduced by the first day's fight to less than 1200 men, was confronted the second day by at least *two full divisions* of the enemy's army, and both its flanks were left exposed by some one who moved the troops on our left away. McCook & Crittenden were under the cloud, but whether the errors of that day are attributable to them or not, I cannot say. Certainly it didn't look well to see them in Chattanooga on the evening of the 20th, when their thrice decimated Corps were yet fighting at the front, eight miles from this town.

Our Regiment fought magnificently. No more sublime courage was ever witnessed. There was hardly a straggler from it, found in the rear. It has received the highest praise from the Division Commander, Genl. Davis, for its action. But at what a sacrifice!—the whole Regiment does not now look larger than two of our Companies used to. . . .

We are in no danger here unless the rebels succeed in cutting off our communications and starving us out. But a great army ought to be massed here. We should be enabled to assume the offensive in a month, and drive the rebels from our front. The d—d silly expeditions the Government seems to be

constantly getting up to *occupy territory*, should be denounced by the press of
the country in the strongest terms. Annihilate the rebel army, and the territory
will need no army of occupation—it will come back itself. Destroy Bragg's and
Lee's armies and the war is practically ended—there will be nothing more but
guerilla warfare, which only cavalry can put down. Such nonsense as Sabine
Pass Expeditions, Blunt's Arkansas and Indian Country campaigns, &c, certainly
ought, by this time, to be exploded humbugs. In the name of reason what do we
want with the Indian Country or Texas now, or why take men there, where they
can accomplish no practical good, and let our forces in Tennessee and Virginia
constantly confront armies superior to them in numbers.

> Respects to all friends.
> Yours truly,
> Jno A. Martin

John J. Ingalls Papers, Collection 177, Kansas State Historical Society.

THE BATTLE OF POISON SPRING, ARKANSAS

*In his report, Colonel James M. Williams relates the defeat at Poison Spring,
Arkansas, where Confederate troops captured the supply train he escorted. During
this battle members of the First Kansas Colored Infantry were killed rather than
taken as prisoners of war. This regiment, mustered into federal service in January
1863 and out in October 1865, suffered the most casualties of any Kansas regiment.*

CAMDEN, ARK., *April 24, 1864.*

CAPTAIN: . . . In obedience to verbal orders received from Brigadier-General
Thayer, I left Camden, Ark., on the 17th instant with the following force, viz: 500
of the First Kansas Colored Volunteers, commanded by Major Ward; 50 of the
Sixth Kansas Cavalry, commanded by Lieutenant Henderson; 75 of the Second
Kansas Cavalry, commanded by Lieutenant Mitchell; 70 of the Fourteenth
Kansas cavalry, commanded by Lieutenant Utt; one section of the Second
Indiana Battery, commanded by Lieutenant Haines; in all, 695 men and two guns,
with a forage train of 198 wagons.

I proceeded westerly on the Washington road a distance of 18 miles, where
I halted the train and dispatched parts of it in different directions to load, 100
wagons, with a large part of the command under Major Ward, being sent 6
miles beyond the camp. These wagons returned to camp at midnight, nearly all
loaded with corn. At sunrise on the 18th, the command started on the return,
loading the balance of the train as it proceeded. There being but few wagon
loads of corn to be found at any one place, I was obliged to detach portions of
the command in different directions to load the wagons, until nearly my whole

available force was so employed. At a point known as Cross-Roads, 4 miles east
from my camping-ground, I met a re-enforcement of the following force, viz:
Eighteenth Iowa Infantry, 375 men, Captain Duncan; Sixth Kansas Cavalry, 25
men, Lieutenant Phillips; Second Kansas Cavalry, 45 men, Lieutenant Ross;
Fourteenth Kansas Cavalry, 20 men, Lieutenant Smith, and two mountain
howitzers from the Sixth Kansas Cavalry, Lieutenant Walker; in all, 465
men and two howitzers, which, added to my former force, made my whole
command consist of 875 infantry, 285 cavalry, and four guns. But the excessive
fatigue of the preceding day, coming as it did at the close of a toilsome march
of twenty-four days without halting, had so worn upon the infantry that fully
100 of the First Kansas (colored) were rendered unfit for duty. Many of the
cavalry had, in violation of orders, straggled from their commands, so that at
this time my effective force did not exceed 1,000 men.

   At a point 1 mile east of this my advance came upon a picket of the enemy,
which was driven back for 1 mile, when a line of the enemy's skirmishers
presented itself. Here I halted the train, formed a line of the small force I then
had in advance, and ordered that portion of the First Kansas Colored Volunteers
which had previously been guarding the rear of the train to the front, and gave
orders for the train to be parked as closely as the nature of the ground would
permit. I also opened a fire upon the enemy's line. . . No response was elicited
save a brisk fire from the enemy's skirmishers. Meanwhile the remainder
of the First Kansas Colored Volunteers had come to the front, as also those
detachments of cavalry which formed part of the original escort, which I formed
in line, facing to the front, with detachment Fourteenth Kansas Cavalry on my
left, and detachments Second and Sixth Kansas Cavalry on the right flank. I also
sent orders to Captain Duncan, commanding Eighteenth Iowa Volunteers, to so
dispose of his regiment and the cavalry and howitzers which came out with him
as to protect the rear of the train, and to keep a sharp lookout for a movement
upon his rear and right flank. Meanwhile a movement of the enemy's infantry
toward my right flank had been observed through the thick brush, which covered
the surface of the country in that direction. Seeing this, I ordered forward the
cavalry on my right, under Lieutenants Mitchell and Henderson, with orders
to press the enemy's line, force it if possible, and at all events to ascertain his
position and strength, fearing, as I did, that the silence of the enemy in front was
but for the purpose of drawing me on into the open ground which lay in my
front. At this juncture a rebel soldier rode into my lines and inquired for Colonel
De Morse. From him I learned that General Price was in command of the rebel
force, and that Colonel De Morse was in command of a force on my right. The
cavalry had advanced but 400 yards, when a brisk fire of musketry was opened
upon them from the brush, which they returned with true gallantry, but were

forced to fall back. In this skirmish many of the cavalry were unhorsed, and Lieutenant Henderson fell, wounded in the abdomen, while gallantly urging his men forward. In the mean time I formed five companies of the First Kansas Colored Volunteers with one piece of artillery on my right flank, and ordered up to their assistance four companies of the Eighteenth Iowa. Soon my orderly returned from the rear with a message from Captain Duncan, stating that he was so closely pressed in the rear by the enemy's infantry and artillery that the men could not be spared.

At this moment the enemy opened upon me with two batteries, one of six pieces in front, and one of three pieces on my right flank, pouring in an incessant and well-directed cross-fire of shot and shell. At the same time he advanced his infantry both in front and on my right flank. From the force of the enemy, now for the first time made visible, I saw that I could not hope to defeat him; but still I resolved to defend the train to the last, hoping that re-enforcements would come up from Camden. I suffered them to approach within 100 yards of my lines, when I opened upon them with musketry charged with buck and ball, and after a contest of fifteen minutes' duration compelled them to fall back. Two fresh regiments, however, coming up, they again rallied and advanced against my lines, this time with colors flying and continuous cheering, so loud as to drown even the roar of the musketry. Again I suffered them to approach even nearer than before, and opened upon them with buck and ball, their artillery still pouring in a cross-fire of shot and shell over the heads of their infantry, and mine replying with vigor and effect; and for another quarter of an hour the fight raged with desperate fury, and the noise and din of battle of this almost hand-to-hand conflict was the loudest and most terrific it has ever been my lot to listen to. Again were they forced to fall back, and twice during this contest were their colors brought to the ground, but as often raised.

During these contests fully one-half of my infantry engaged were either killed or wounded. Three companies were left without an officer, and seeing the enemy again re-enforced with fresh troops it became evident that I could hold my line but littler longer. I directed Major Ward to hold that line until I could ride back and form the Eighteenth Iowa in proper form to support the retreat of this advanced line. Meanwhile, so many of the gunners having been shot from around their pieces as to leave too few men to serve the guns, I ordered them to retire to the rear of the train and report to the commanding officer there. Just as I was starting for the line of the Eighteenth Iowa my horse was shot, and caused a delay long enough to obtain and mount another one, which done, I rode to the rear and formed a line of battle facing the direction in which the enemy was advancing. Again did the enemy hurl his columns against the remnant of men which formed my front and right flank, and again were they met as gallantly as before. But my decimated ranks were unable to resist the overpowering force hurled against my line, and after a check had been given their advance, seeing that our line was completely flanked on both sides, Major Ward gave the order to retire, which was done in good order, forming and checking the enemy twice before reaching the rear of the train. With the assistance of Major Ward and other officers I succeeded in forming a portion of First Colored Regiment in rear of the Eighteenth Iowa, and when the enemy approached this line they gallantly advanced to the line of the Eighteenth Iowa, and with them poured in their fire. The Eighteenth Iowa maintained their line manfully, and stoutly contested the ground until nearly surrounded, when they retired, and, forming again, checked the advancing foe, and still held their ground until again nearly surrounded, when they again retired across a ravine which was impassable for artillery, and I gave orders for the pieces to be spiked and abandoned. After crossing this ravine I succeeded in forming a portion of the cavalry, which I kept in line in order to give the infantry time to reach the swamp which lay in our front, which they succeeded in doing, and by this means nearly all except the badly wounded were enabled to reach camp. Many wounded men belonging to the First Kansas Colored Volunteers fell into the hands of the enemy, and I have the most positive assurances from eye-witnesses that they were murdered on the spot. The action was commenced at 10 a.m. and terminated at 2 p.m. I was forced to abandon everything to the enemy, and they thereby became possessed of this large train, two 6-pounder guns, and two 12-pounder mountain howitzers. With what force could be collected I made my way to this post, where I arrived at 11 p.m. of the same day.

At no time during the engagement, such was the nature of the ground and the size of the train, was I able to employ more than 500 men and two guns to repel the assaults of the enemy, whose force I estimate at 10,000 men and twelve guns, from the statements of prisoners. The columns of assault which were thrown against my front and right flank consisted of five regiments of infantry and one of cavalry, supported by a strong force which moved upon my left flank and rear. I have named this engagement the action of Poison Spring, from a spring of that name in the vicinity.

My loss during this engagement is as follows: Killed, 92; wounded, 97; missing, 106. Many of those reported missing are supposed to be killed. Others are supposed to be wounded and prisoners. The loss of the enemy is not known, but in my opinion it will much exceed our own.

The conduct of all the troops under my command, officers and men, was characterized by true soldierly bearing, and in no case was a line broken except when assaulted by an overwhelming force, and then falling back only when so ordered. The gallant dead, officers and men, all evinced the most heroic spirit, and died the death of true soldiers.

Very respectfully,

J. M. WILLIAMS,

Col. First Kansas Colored Vols., Comdg. Escort.

Capt. WILLIAM S. WHITTEN,

Assistant Adjutant-General.

Revised list of troops engaged and casualties in the action at Poison Spring, Ark., April 18, 1864.

Troops Engaged	Officers and men	Killed and missing	Wounded
1st Kansas Colored Volunteers	438	a 117	65
18th Iowa Infantry Volunteers	383	59	21
2d Kansas Cavalry	122	15	6
6th Kansas Cavalry	77	1	1
14th Kansas Cavalry	92	9	. . . . .
2d Indiana Battery (two guns)	33	1	4
6th Kansas Cavalry (detachment, two howitzers)	25	2	. . . . .
Total	1,170	204	97

a Killed.

Captured by the enemy: Second Indiana Battery, 2 10-pounder field guns; Sixth Kansas Cavalry, 2 12-pounder mountain howitzers; quartermaster's stores, 198 teams and wagons.

The War of the Rebellion: A Compilation of the Official Records of the Union and Confederate Armies, ser. 1, vol. 34 (Washington, DC: Government Printing Office, 1891), 743–46.

THE DIARY AND LETTERS OF WEBSTER MOSES

Webster W. Moses served in Company D of the Seventh Kansas Cavalry. On January 1, 1864, four-fifths of the regiment reenlisted as veteran volunteers in Memphis, Tennessee. After a thirty-day furlough, they were reequipped in St. Louis before returning to Memphis. The Seventh Kansas Cavalry served in Tennessee and Mississippi before returning to St. Louis and participating in the Missouri campaign.

In his diary, Moses indicted some soldiers for their immoral behavior, yet he must have known that his observations were not for public consumption because he papered over those entries dealing with the sad fate of Mary French with a note that it was "not to be opened at present." In his correspondence with Nancy Mowry, who became his wife, the couple discussed a wide range of topics, from Missouri society to President Lincoln's assassination.

EXCERPT, DIARY OF W W MOSES

January 1865

23rd. . . Mary French Lient Henry's mistress arived from St Louis. and he spends most of his time with her alass how corrupt and demoralized is our armey becomeing.

Miss Mary French, when we came to Franklin she was a very respectable young girl aged about 16 years her mother was a prostitute her father in the Union armey. 1st Sergt William Henry (now 1st Lient) by promises of marriage (although indirectly promised) succeeded in seduceing her and for about a month slept with her every night while William Sheldon slept with her mother. Mr French came home and took his children to St Louis Mo Mrs French was left behind a public whore. the 18th of Jan Mary French came here from St Louis Mo to see her intended husband Lient Henry. alass she is unaware what disgrace and disappointment are in store. she fondly hopes some day to be his wife. she knows not that Henry has a family at home. She will soon be added to the no of prostitutes that throng our cities and towns and hang round the camps of our soldiers. Alass how has this war corrupted the morals distroyed the healths and blighted the fond hopes and joys of our land. Virtue is indeed scarce a wonder few have passed through the army without yielding to the tempter God help me to still live right and shield me from all sin

W W Moses co D 7th Kan Cav
Franklin Mo Jan 24th 1865

CORRESPONDENCE WITH NANCY MOWRY MOSES

Camp 7th Kan Cav Memphis Tenn
10 oclock P.M. June 16th 1864

My Dear Nancy, . . .

Gen Sturgis defeat was the most discracefull affair that has ever happend here the colored soldiers fought like tigers some say better than the whites.

I must close but will write again as soon as I can, it may be not for ten or twelve days or untill we return . . .

W W Moses
Co D 7 Kan Cavalry
Memphis Tenn

Wyanet Bureau Illinois
June 20th 1864

Dear Webster

. . . I am sorry to hear of our loss at Corinth. we had heard nothing of it untill we get your letter. I sincerely hope that it may not prove as bad as reported we will hear all about it in A few days when we get the papers. I expect it seems more like Soldiering to you now that you have got horses and arms and have began to scout again. I know that you are exposed to more hardships and dangers now than when you was in St Louis

God grant that they may all be passed through in safety.

we are all well at present. . . .

Nancy Mowry.

Webster W Moses

~

Wyanet Bureau Illinois
June 26th 1864

Dear Webster . . .

we have had A full account of Gen Sturgis defeat which is even worse I think than you wrote. I am glad to here that he has been put out of office. when O when will this war seace and peace again be ours to enjoy to me it seems as though there had been enough blood shed to atone for the sins of A Nation. . . .

Nancy Mowry

~

Wyanet Bureau Ill
July 7 1864

Dear Webster . . .

I am glad to hear that you are liveing well although it is at the expence of the Rebels. Grant did not succeed in gaining Richmond by the fourth but if he gains that and Petersburge this summer we need not complain of him. he is A good General if all of our Officers had done as well as he has I think that this war would be nearer its close than it is now. it seems cruel and barbarous to shoot prisoners, but I suppose that as long as they shoot our prisoner we must theirs. O cruel war, cruel in every form as long as they stand and fight it does

vary well or as well as war will admit, but to shoot A helpless prisoner is noting
less than murder. . . .

Nancy Mowry.

~

Camp 7th Kan Cav Wolf River Bottom New Germantown Tenn
Saturday Eve Sept 3rd 1864

Dear Nancy:
 . . . to day is the anniversary of our mustering with the U. S. Servace, three
years ago yesterday we left our pleasant homes. three years have we marched
and fought. how little did we realize then the events that would transpire within
three short years. but they are passed and gone with all their hardships and
pleasurers
    In a fiew days some of the Co "D" will be leaveing us for their Northern
Homes. I almost wish sometimes that I could go with them, then as I read of the
copperheads and Traitors at Home I wish that I could enlist a hundred times to
fight them. We are in hopes that the north will come out all right yet
    The Boys are going home as soon as the proper papers can be made out, it
will be several days yet. They are all anxious to be off as I know you at home are
anxious to see them. . . .
    The health of the Regt is good now, they are haveing the Yellow Fever some
in Memphis. We expect to go south soon instead of going to Missouria. . . .
    Three long years have passed since we commenced our correspondence, yet
how quickly passed Your letters are to me what the Oasis is in the Desert . . .
    Write often to yours affectionately and truly

W. W. Moses.

~

Camp 7th Kan Cav Vols
Rolla Mo Nov 17th 1864

My Dear Nancy
    . . . . our expedition after Price has closed. we have returned to this place and
are now waiting for transpotation to St. Louis where we expect to be in a fiew
days. You have proberly seen an account of the success we have had in driving
Price out of Mo. in the papers. we marched from Jeff City to Callifornia then to
Lexington to Independence where the 13th Mo Cav and the 7th Kansas mad[e] a
Sabre charge and captured two pieces of artillery and drove Price toward Kansas

City when Gen's Blunt and Curtis met him and drove him south the next day the 7th Kansas had another skirmish with the enemy but there being onely Gen McNeal's Brigade present we had to fall back. we attacked Price in the Flank and could see the whole Rebel armey pass by the next day we followed the rebs to the Osage river

Gen Prices force was about 20,000 ours about the same most of it Mo and Kansas Militia. the next day we crossed the Osage and came on to a large prarrie where both armeys were in full view of each other

The Rebs made a stand and we came up formed a line of battle and charged with Sabres captureing General's Marmaduke and Cabell and 600 prisoners 8 pieces of artillery &c &c. we followed them 48 miles that day and the onely thing that saved their whole army was our horses gave out and we had to stop could we have had fresh horses Prices armey would be now in St Louis Prisoners

We pursuid as far as Newtonia when Gen McNeals Brigade went to Spring field then back to Cassville then to Rolla where we arrived the 13th all well the 7th Kansas lost not a man killed or wounded many of our horses gave out and we now have but about 150 horses here. It has been a hard campain for horses and men some of the tim my horse was not unsaddled for four days. While parched corn and fresh beef was our living Hard Tack was a luxury when we arrived here, our healths are all very good and as soon as we get horses again we will be ready for some other field. we some expect to go south again.

Gen Curtis and Blunt are still after Price and have sent back many Prisoners. Prices intention was to invade Kansas but he onely went about one mile in Kansas . . .

$$\sim$$

Hd Quarters Moselle Bridge
December 29th 1864

My own Dear Nancy:

. . . Shermans victory was complete while Hoods armey is nearly chrushed indeed the Rebs seen to be giving way in all directions Peace must come soon and Glory to see it.

We are knowing fine times here this winter. our duties are very light. the citizens all loyal or pretend to be and our neighbors kind I would like to remain here untill I am discharged. A few days ago I was at a social gathering near hear. . . .

In my life I have seen a great many public gatherings of all descriptions but none equal to this It was an exact type of Mo society after dancing several sets Supper was announced the supper was very good then *ladies* and *gentlemen* all had a smoke, either cigars or pipe, then dancing most of the time untill 12 midnight when the Whiskey was passed round when most of the *Ladies* and *Gentlemen* took a drink then another smoke indeed some were smooking most of the time which in decent society would be very dissagreeable.

I returned to the camp completely disgusted with Mo society. . .

W. W. Moses.

Address Franklin MO

∼

Wyanet Bureau Co Illinois
April 23rd 1865

My Dear Absent Husband,

What shall I write to you, My Webster? shall I write of the slow weary days that have passed since the news of the terrible death of our beloved *President*. I do not know what to say. for awhile it seemed as though A dark and impenetrable cloud had settled over us all.

where A little while ago all was gladness and joy in honor of our recent victorys now is silence and sorrow and I hope in many places *prayer* what A privalige is the Christains who when trials come has A Friend to whom they can go for comfort and strength. and Oh! what A trial that was, how we all needed the consolation which can come from but one Source. let us ever remember that *God* still rules & reigns, let us look to *Him* in every time of need. . . .

I have an idea that if Co 'D' could be seen now it would be slightly changed in apearance from what it was when you spoke of it the 10th yet I do not think it can be vary long untill peace is declared although there has been such A great change at the head of affairs lately. and I think perhaps you *will* be at home by the fourth yet. What A joyous Selabration it would be if our Soldiers should all return before that time. but how much *more* joyous had Lincoln lived to see that time. . . .

Your loving Wife
Nancy M. Moses . . .

Webster Moses Collection, Kansas State Historical Society.

THE DRAFT: "SOME ONE IS TO BLAME"

As in many states, the draft was controversial in Kansas. The confusion over who was in charge of recruiting turned into recriminations once it was feared that conscription would begin in the state.

THE DRAFT

People are fearing and complaining of the proposed draft, in Kansas. Citizens believe that our State has furnished its full quota and that a draft now is unjust. They believe that if we could have the proper credit for the men raised here, we should not be subject to the draft and that some one is to blame because that proper credit is not given on the Rolls at the War Department.

Now that is just what we believe, and it just what we have always predicted would be the result of the unprecedented and irregular action of War Department with this State—an action making Kansas an exception to all States in the business of recruiting. In other States, the Governors do the business—here the Senator—Jim Lane—has done it, and when he has not done it, then his particular friend, Gen. Blunt has done it.

We all remember when the 2d Kansas was here prepared to be mustered in, Jim Lane and his friend, Gen. Blunt, manifested in every way their dissatisfaction with that organization and in every way they could, tried to discourage it. They were mad because Mitchell was to be the Colonel, they were mad because Blair would be Lieut. Colonel, mad because they could not control all the offices in the regiment and give them to the partizans of Jim Lane. Still, the military reputation since acquired by these officers has vindicated their appointment and it has also shown that Lane's action at that time was criminal and unpatriotic. He did what he could to discourage enlistments and prevented thousands from enlisting all over the State; for at a time when the whole community were ripe for enlistment, he introduced partizan politics into it, delayed it, that he might go to Washington and manage in some way to get full control of the matter.

While he was doing that the patriotic ferver of the people was dying out.

The War Department made him a Recruiting Commissioner for Kansas, Nebraska, &c., &c. He commenced his labors; he appointed his friend recruiting sergeant to traverse Kansas, Nebraska, Colarado and all the region north to the British line, west to Utah, and south to the uttermost limits of the Indian country. Such sergeants the county has rarely seen, and the State, when the draft comes, will hope never to see again. As they were appointed because they hated the State government, or to hire them to hate it, of course they cared not how its credit stood on the recruiting rolls of the War Department. The Governor protested against this irregularity, predicted its result, and so did we. We were threatened with a "doing up of our office" by Gen. Blunt, who actually issued an order for the arrest of Gov. Robinson, which however, he did not dare to execute.

Recruits were raised, companies and regiments organized and sent to the field, with officers appointed by Lane. Those officers had no commissions and it was the especial pride of many of them "not to have a commission soiled by the hands of Charley Robinson." The paymaster came round. The officers and men wanted their pay, but the paymaster could not pay them without they had their commissions. What could they do? Jim Lane who had appointed them, asked them to denounce the Governor as a coward and a traitor; and they had been fools enough to do it. They did not believe that he would be fool enough to commission a man who had done so. Thus they stood without pay and without commissions, hoping Jim Lane could work them out of their difficulty by his influence at the War Office.

Of course all this work without pay discouraged enlistments. Officers and men had to feed their families and must have money to do it. They could do neither. Worst of all, the men thus raised, nearly all of whom are from Kansas, were credited not to our State, but to the District over which Jim Lane presided as Recruiting Commissioner.

In all these actions the people can see what obstacles have been placed in the way of enlistment and a proper credit for the men enlisted. Lane is behind it all; and should we have a draft he is responsible for it.

Gov. Carney has written to the War Department concerning the matter. As early as last June that Department wrote to him that we had an excess of over 4,000 men at that time. Since then we have raised in new regiments, for old regiments and of veterans, 4,000 more. He is calling the attention of the War Office to these particulars and requesting of it to correct their lists so that we shall not be unjustly subjected to the draft.

While he is doing this for our people, Provost Marshall Clark, Lane's chief fugleman, is traversing the State bawling fraud, writing to the P. M. General of the U. S. that the Governor is not a man of truth and is of doubtful loyalty.

Lawrence Journal, reprinted in the *Council Grove Press*, April 16, 1864.

THE DIARIES OF DAVID R. BRADEN

David R. Braden kept a diary of his military activities from 1864 to 1866. Braden was a private in the Ninth Kansas Volunteer Cavalry before being mustered as a fourth duty sergeant in February 1865. Initially the Ninth was assigned to Missouri to pursue William Quantrill but were ordered south to Arkansas in April 1864.

JAN THE 1ST 1864
JOURNAL OF THE EVENTS OF LIFE COMMENCING JAN 1ST
CAMP COLD WATER GROVE

. . . During this time I have enlisted in the Army I wase along when Quantrel was driven from Lawrence It wase the first time that I seen a man shot it wase about the first time that I wase on a scout that amounted to any thing we wer out 10 days got back to camp on the 2nd day of September

And after that time we scouted nearly all of the time but dident acomplish any thing much until Shelby made his raid up through Mo then we wer out 24 days seen some prety hard times We have moved camp twice from the Trading Post (the place whare I enlisted) to Petosi and from there to Cold Water Grove Kansas since we have been at this place we have not scouted very much I enlisted in the army on the 20th day of July 1863 . . .

January 26th 1864 . . .

La[s]t night Jacob Wilson of company E stayed with he had formily been a bush whacker and I believe he deserves killing he acknowledged that he had robed Union familys and I think that he wase one of the Devils that help rob Father in July I felt very much like shooting him. . . .

Thigs are all quiet in camp to day I see one of Cooks boys to day and have a long talk with him about their troubles and my own since this war came up he gives me quite a history of this Jacob Wilson which staid all night with us he said that he wase a long when Steane robed Charley Haddsell at Parkervill in Mo which he denied to me I feel sorry that I dident shoot him when I had a chance for I feel confident now that he is one of the Devils that robed me . . .

February 8th . . .
Midnight.

I wase aroused by the Bugle and wase informed that about 300 Rebels had crossed into Kansas 4 miles north of Auberry and that they wer strikeing for Olathie. We wer ordered to saddele up evry man that wase able to goe it wase not long until I wase on Frank again and ready for another scout left camp at 1. oclock and struck for Aubery Arived there about 3. oclock in Morning When we got there we founde to oure astonishment that the report was false that it had been a company of the 15th Kansas that had went down from Olathie on a scout into Mo and that they had made the citizens think they wer bush whackers. . . .

[August] 31st

. . . We are stil at the same place we wer when the Month comenced I am getting very tired of this place and of the way the thing is a runing in this part of the United States It looks to me like a regular swindling machine for a fiew lowlifed shoulderstraps Swindling bothe Govr and the soldier of his just dues such as his rations of sustenance We muster to day for pay 2 months due. . . .

8ᵗʰ November

. . . I am on Fatieuge duty today. I suppose that today is the day that tells the
tail between olde *Abe & Mc* anxious am I to hear the result of it for I think that
the destiny of our nation depends upon the result If olde Abe is elected it wil
show to the world that we are wiling to support olde Abe in the war and that we
are wiling to try it 4 years longer . . .

[November] 19ᵗʰ Noon Another Mail arrives . . . bringing me the sad inteligence
of the way Price youced them when he wase in Kansas It was a painful job for
me to read it but reveng "Ile" have if ever I get able to scout again. . . .

1ˢᵗ December

. . . I think the commanders of this department are like what olde Abe said
about McClellen "heavy on the review and when thats done all is done" I am
beggining to think that olde Abe has forgotten us poor fellows down in this
corner of the world or he would of removed old Steele ear this but the way is to
be patient and wait results. . . .

25ᵗʰ December

Old Christmas is on us once again. It finds me at the negroes quarters of
the Plantation under charg of Maj Chase. And Oh what a difference there is to
compare my situation this morning and this one year ago, but such is the soldiers
fate. Many and varied are the changes and scenes of this one short year. Today I
make the negroe quarters my abode. my living is one hard tack and a fiew bacon
rines which my charitable neig[h]bors "the negroes," give to me. . . .

January 1ˢᵗ A. D. 1865.
Camp 9ᵗʰ K.V.C. Deuvalls Bluf

Once again New Years day has made her appearance and claims a leaf in this,
The book of time and life. And let one take a moment or two in thought and oh
how short it appears. And what have I done, to tel the exact truth "Nothing." I
have of course served my country to the best of my ability, but nothing can I see
that I have accomplished. . . .

[January, 1865]. . . . Had some little excitment last night an old "John Henry" tried
to run through the lines but he found "what Shaler terms as wooden men on
post." Awake and ready to give him one of *old Abes Cathartic Pills for rebs.* . . .

[March] 4ᵗʰ

Today is a day which all true Americans wil look uppon with joy. This Day
shows to the world that the United States are stil a unit, and are determined to

fight "this Accursed Rebelion to the last, that they intend war to extermination or subjection to the laws of the United States. "That we as a Nation are willing to support the old Rail Splitter." And I think this day wil be as heavy a blow to the C. S. A. as any victory we ever gained I think if old Grant dont meet with any back set that the 1st of April wil see him in the great city *Richmond*. . . .

10th April, 1865

Great is the Rejoiceing in camp to day. For the reason that the Steamer Comercial brings the news that Richmond is fallen. I think it is a most to good to be true, but I hope it may.

13th [April, 1865]

Today the news of the fall of Richmond is confirmed. And the way the folks around these parts are rejoiceing is not verry slow The Artilery are having fine times to day they are a making the earth quake. . . .

May 1st 1865
Camp 9th K. V. C.
Devalls Bluff Ark

. . . . Great is the Rejoiceing in the camps at the prospect of speedy peace & the same as to the sad fate of oure late beloved President ("only Great is the sorrow,") . . .

May 4, 1865

Aroused from my slumbers this morning by the booming of Artilery—Today is a day of mourning for our late beloved President, A. Lincoln. Minet guns are being fired all day and camps dressed in mourning. The feelings of the soldier are much hurt to hear of that for if anyone knows how to appreciate the goodness of *Abe* it him, but such work as this only makes it that much harder on the Rebels for the soldiers after hearing of the like of that becomes more determined . . .

May 23, 1865

Today they muster out a portion of oure company under provisions of an order from the War Department, but I am one of the unlucky ones, so my bondage is not to an end. Yesterday the 22nd the noted Guerila chief *"Rabern"* surendered his command to our Regt. . . .

June 1st 1865

. . . I am getting verry anxious to get to goe home more so than ever before since I have be a soldiering for the reason that I think the object is accomplished for which I enlisted that is the rebellion of oure country crushed out. But I think that a fiew days will see us on oure way home. Today we recieve the news of old Smiths surrender which I think will send us to oure homes . . .

June 7, 1865

. . . There is conciderable of excitement in camp to day. The officers term it a mutany, but I look at in a diferent way. They try to make the boys take their arms again "Them that have been mustered out They send 49 of them down to the Stockade They talk that they have an order for so doing but Dont show it.

June 9, 1865

. . . I am wanting out of the service worse at this time than ever before for I think that the war is over and that Uncle Sam needs us no longer. But I think if oure officers can accomplish what they would like they would keep us every one til the last day in the morning—"at least one would judge so from their actions" The boys that wer sent to the Stockade Day before yesterday are returned to camp to day. They take their armes again as they think it the easyest way they can get out of it. Not that they are convinced that they (The officers) have any wright to make them do so. . . .

June 29, 1865

Once again I arise and goe forth and lo what am to hear and see. why that 30 of C. Co. took with a leaving some time last night, and are no whares to be found this morning. It is supposed they have gone to Kans. The officers appear to be conciderably beaten over it. They order the rest of Co C to get readey and goe after them, but they come to the conclusion that we are too willing to goe, and dont let us goe— . . .

July 17, 1865

Today we are mustered out of Uncle Sams Service. And once again I concider myself a free boy. Fully satisfied to goe home contented with soldiering for a living

David R. Braden Diaries [transcripts], Kansas State Historical Society.

FIVE

Warfare along the Kansas-Missouri Border

*I*N DECEMBER 1859, during a tour of Kansas Territory, Abraham Lincoln spoke at Leavenworth and offered the following advice to his fellow Republicans: "Leave your Missouri neighbors alone. Have nothing whatever to do with their slaves. Have nothing whatever to do with the white people, save in a friendly way. Drop past differences, and so conduct yourselves that if you cannot be at peace with them, the fault shall be wholly theirs."[1] Kansans proved unable to heed such sage council because the differences Lincoln so easily dismissed had not been consigned to the past within the territory. Kansas's early history had been a violent one, shaped by a border infested with both antislavery jayhawkers and proslavery border ruffians who inflicted depredations on residents of both Kansas and Missouri. Yet tension between opposing factions during the territorial period had been aggravated by the fact that ideology was often a convenient disguise for general lawlessness. Never truly terminated, this hostility naturally continued during the Civil War and saw the rise of a new group, the Red Legs, who formed during the war ostensibly to protect the border. These jayhawkers wore red leather leggings and attacked Missourians and Kansans suspected of being proslavery or pro-Southern.

In general, however, poor relations along the border were exacerbated by memories of the recent past; indeed, the situation seemed to be a continuation of the violence of the 1850s, especially since some of those committing atrocities were well known from the territorial period. Senator James H. Lane had threatened to invade Kansas in 1856 with an "Army of the North" to save it from slavery; five years later, his brigade repeated the threat. Similarly, James Montgomery and Charles Jennison were two of Kansas's best-known territorial jayhawkers and both were in charge of regiments during the war. In January 1861, Montgomery wrote that he was "not in favor of invading the slave states so long as they keep themselves at home. But if they cross the line to interfere with us, as Missouri is now threatening to do, then I would consider the war begun." Montgomery's lack of patience was directly tied to what he termed his "late experience."[2] Men like these were considered "practical abolitionists"; that is, they advocated direct action to end slavery and welcomed the Civil War as it would allow greater activity on this front.[3]

With the organization of the Confederate States of America, Kansans understandably kept a nervous eye on the state's borders. Several skirmishes with Confederate forces were fought along the state's eastern border in the first year of the war. When Missouri governor Claiborne Jackson called on troops to repel the "invasion" of his state by federal troops commanded by Brigadier General Nathaniel Lyon, Kansas governor Charles Robinson interpreted Jackson's proclamation as a declaration of war against his state. On June 17, 1861, he called on citizens to prepare for a Missouri attack. Almost immediately Montgomery and Jennison began liberating slaves and plundering along the Kansas-Missouri border. They were joined by a number of Unionist Missourians displeased with the secessionist activity in their state.[4]

The first major battle of the border region would be fought at Wilson's Creek, near Springfield, Missouri, in August 1861. This battle was the first of former Missouri governor Sterling Price's efforts to capture the state for the Confederacy. Among the Union forces battling to retain Missouri in the Union were the First and Second Kansas Infantry regiments. This first engagement was costly: 23 percent of all engaged at Wilson's Creek became casualties, one of whom was Lyon, the first Union general to die in battle during the Civil War.[5]

In the aftermath of Wilson's Creek, military engagements were often more informal but were nonetheless devastating to this border region. By September 1861, James Lane had formed Lane's Brigade, consisting of approximately twelve hundred men of the Third, Fourth, and Fifth Kansas regiments. For the next three months, these troops contributed to a cycle of retaliatory raids which would culminate in the Lawrence massacre. The most notorious of these raids was the assault on Osceola, Missouri. On September 23, 1861, Lane's Brigade pushed out Confederates who had fired on them on the outskirts of town, but hearing rumors that some remained hidden in the town center, orders were given to burn them out. Soon after, the soldiers found a warehouse full of whiskey, and what was not consumed was set afire. By the end of the raid, the business district and almost every house had been burned and the brigade had taken the $4,000 in the local bank and almost every moveable commodity to be found, ranging from food and gunpowder to a piano and church paraphernalia.[6] Lane claimed Osceola to be revenge for a sack of Humboldt two weeks earlier while Missourians cited Osceola to justify the 1863 attack on Lawrence.

The activities of both official Kansas regiments and unsanctioned groups along the border created considerable consternation among Union generals. Major General Henry Halleck, for one, insisted that these men be reined in lest they push Missouri into the Confederacy. Even Confederate general Ben McCulloch believed Lane's activities hurt the Union's cause. Among the most notorious regiments was the Seventh Kansas, which included men from Kansas, Missouri, and Illinois who had responded to Charles Jennison's call to join Jennison's Jayhawkers. The Seventh Kansas was known for its lack of discipline and for the famous Company K, filled with fanatical abolitionists led by Ohio's John Brown, Jr. This regiment soon was sent south to remove them from the field of temptation. Ultimately, the border activities were so detrimental that General John Schofield argued Kansans had to be kept out of Missouri and recommended the two states be placed in the same department to facilitate keeping each state's troops separated from the others'.[7]

Kansans living near the Missouri border were upset by various raids but most reserved their greatest fear for William Clarke Quantrill's group. Born in Ohio, Quantrill journeyed to Kansas and became involved in jayhawking, but by December 1860 he had switched sides, allegedly to avenge the death of his brother. Thereafter, Quantrill moved into Missouri, gathered a band of like-minded guerrillas, occasionally numbering more than three hundred, and proceeded to wreak havoc on border residents. His first notable action was the attack on Olathe in September 1862, but his campaign against Kansas culminated in the Lawrence massacre of 1863.[8]

On August 21, 1863, Quantrill led approximately 450 men into Lawrence at dawn. The raid was systematic: they shot every man they saw; trampled twenty-two recruits of the Fourteenth Kansas encamped in town, killing seventeen of them; and proceeded to burn everything. By the time they left, 164 men and boys had been killed and large portions of the town had been torched and the business district along Massachusetts Street destroyed. Lawrence was chosen because of its abolitionist reputation but, during the war, it also acted as a conduit for goods illegally obtained from Missouri. The town served as the headquarters for the Red Legs and openly held public auctions of stolen goods. Although it came at a high cost, Kansas was finally sent desperately needed arms. General John Schofield of the Department of Missouri (which then included Kansas) sent three thousand stand of arms, while Secretary of War Edwin Stanton sent five thousand more. Although they lacked uniforms and were distinguished only by a red badge pinned to their hats, the state was able to equip its militia for the first time.[9]

Despite many skirmishes, Kansas did not see organized warfare within its borders until the fall of 1864. On September 19 General Price led Confederate forces into Missouri once again, intending to rally its citizens to the Confederate cause and to seize supplies in St. Louis. After several skirmishes, Union forces pushed Price away from Missouri's interior toward Kansas City. Engagements were fought along the Kansas-Missouri border, including the battles of the Little Blue, Byram's Ford, Lexington, and Westport, where on October 23, a Union victory forced Price to retreat southward.

Kansans had followed reports on Price's Missouri Expedition (also known as Price's Raid) with great concern. On October 8, Governor Thomas Carney called out the Kansas State Militia and General Samuel Curtis, in command of the Department of Kansas, merged his forces with these militia regiments to form the Army of the Border. Together with General Alfred Pleasanton's cavalry division from the Department of Missouri, more than 22,000 men participated in the pursuit of Price in Kansas. Kansas troops first engaged the enemy at the October 19 battle at Lexington and four days later, they fought Price's troops in their home state. The battle near the Marais des Cygnes River, also known as the battle of Trading Post, began on October 25 with Pleasonton's early morning artillery bombardment, after which Union troops attacked the rebel line. Although outnumbered, they were victorious and forced a Confederate withdrawal.

A second engagement occurred later that same day six miles to the south of Trading Post at Mine Creek. Here Confederate troops, unable to cross the ford, had formed a line on the north side of Mine Creek. This engagement resulted in the capture of six hundred Confederates, including two brigadier generals, John Marmaduke and William Cabel. The battle of Mine Creek was the largest battle fought in the state, involving some ten thousand troops, and federal forces earned a decisive victory: the Confederacy suffered twelve hundred casualties, the Union only one hundred. After Mine Creek, Price fled back into Missouri, where he was unable to cross a second river and was forced into his third engagement of the day. At the battle of Marmiton, Price was again defeated, and his expulsion from Kansas on October 25 was the beginning of the end for his expedition. Three days later, he was routed at Newtonia and finally retreated across the Arkansas River on November 8. His retreat ended the last significant threat of a Confederate invasion of Kansas.

Ultimately, the border skirmishes led to two notorious orders issued by the commander of the District of the Border, Thomas Ewing. With only about twenty-five hundred men in his district to combat the bushwhackers and their activities, Ewing resorted to removal. Order No. 10 was issued on August 18, 1863, a few days before the Lawrence massacre, while Order No. 11 was issued after the massacre, on August 25. Order No. 10 was limited, but families of the worst guerrillas suspected of providing material aid to the bushwhackers were ordered out of the district and out of Missouri. Order No. 11 went further, as Ewing ordered all Missourians living in Jackson, Cass, and Bates counties and part of Vernon County to leave their homes by September 9, 1863. Those who could prove their loyalty to the commanding officer of the nearest military station were permitted to go to any military station in the District of the Border or to any part of Kansas except along the eastern border with Missouri. Ewing's orders were effective and the depopulation of the area helped insure the safety of Kansas's eastern border—with the bushwhackers driven into the interior of Missouri and into smaller bands, they never raided a Kansas town again.[10]

"EXTERMINATION IS OUR MOTTO"

*Like George Packard, who arrived in 1857 from Maine, many Kansans came from
New England in the territorial period. In 1862, Packard's regiment was sent to Fort
Union, New Mexico, but soon after were ordered south. Ultimately, Packard served
in Missouri, Indian Territory, and Arkansas.*

Salina, Kansas July 14, 1861

My Dear Mother,—. . .

The Indians are all quiet and manifest a disposition to behave themselves
during the war. I wish I could say the same for the Missourians but cannot. C.
Jackson the Governor is in South Kansas with an army but it is rumored that he
is in a position that he can't get back to Mo. for the Kansas boys are hard to whip
and Jackson has got to break the lines of the Kansas boys before he can get back.
I hope he will be caught army and all.

We are talking some of taking part of our company below, that is those that
can well leave, men without families like myself. We are of no earthly use to
the country as we are and why not go. I don't believe in being idle neither do I
believe in being rash, but if duty calls I go. . . .

Yours truly,
from your son,
George W. Packard

⁓

Osowottomie Ks Feb 25, 1862

Dear Brother,—. . .

I think the prospects are good for a speedy termination of the war, althow
at an immense expense of blood and tears. There is but little prospect of our
regiment getting disbanded and but little show of our getting into a fight.
You need not fear for my safety for I don't believe I shall ever get a chance at
the rebels. . . . O how I long to have this rebellion crushed out. How I long to
hear that the last gun has been fired and the last saber returned to its scabbard.
When the bugle and fife and drum shall cease to call to arms the thousands
of volunteers that are now engaged in the defense of their country and their
country's honor, still I cannot say that I want peace until the last slave is
liberated and the stars and stripes shall float over a land where all can look to it
for protection. . . .

From your brother,
George W. Packard

~

Troy, Kansas, April 22, 1862

Dear Brother Zibeon,

. . . We don't get much fighting here to do so we have to march around from one place to another to quell riots, enforce law, and catch jayhawkers, while at heart we are all jayhawkers.

Our company was transferred from the 8th to the 2nd, then from the 2nd to the 7th in which we now find ourselves today as at "A". . . .

I have not been out of the service but three days since I joined. I wish I was out for I think that the west has no use for so many soldiers. Three or four regiments are about to cross the plains for New Mexico. The poor fellows don't like it and are deserting every day. It would be a hard trip but I should like it first rate for adventure don't bother me at all and the more danger the more it suits me. . . .

Yours truly,
Geo. W. Packard

~

Fort Riley, Kansas Aug. 20, 1862

Dear Mother, . . .

The border is again infested with the bushwhackers who kill in the dark, murder, destroy and rob the country of everything they can carry off. I hope that when the union army moves through Mo. again it will be a war of extermination. About two thirds of the inhabitants of Mo. ought to be killed like wolves or as any other venomous wild animals. And so it is throughout the South. If half of the present inhabitants were destroyed it would be of no loss to the world but a benefit rather. It is rough but I am satisfied that it would be for the best. But a good many of our best men are doomed to get killed in doing the good. . . .

My best love to you all
Yours truly,
Geo. W. Packard

~

Paola Kansas
May 7 1863

Dear Bro. Zibeon, . . .
Our reg. is stationed along the line to protect our settlements from the
bushwhackers. Murder, robbery, and plunder seem to be the order of the day.
But the 7th Kansas is a terror to them. We are all well mounted and when we
we get on their trail our Galigers patent rifles and Colts Dragoon revolvers are
apt to talk in a thundering tone to them. You can hardly imagine the amount of
travelling I have done through the brush in Arkansas and Mo. for them. . .

Yours truly,
Geo. W. Packard
(Write soon)

Paola, Kansas June 27, 1863

Dear Mother, . . .
I have been at work most of the time for weeks scouting after bushwhackers.
About two weeks ago a party of about fifty men belonging to our regiment were
surprised by a gang of double their number of bushwhackers. They were in a
lane when attacked and were followed up through the lane for about one mile,
when our men formed a line of battle and the bushwhackers fled, falling back
through the lane shooting through the head all the wounded soldiers (14 in all).
Not one of the fourteen but what were shot in the head. Six more were badly
wounded but hid from them.
Our party of about the same number went through the lane about three
hours ahead of them on our way to Kansas City, five miles distance. On hearing
of the disaster we were on the field on double-quick. We hunted the country
over, picked up the killed and wounded all that night. The next morning we
struck a trail and followed it through the brush so thick that one could hardly
get along, until about noon we saw horses ahead, dismounting we crept on our
hands and feet until we were almost mong them when we found there were only
five of them with all of the horses and plunder they had taken the day before.
We dispatched four of them and the fifth escaped, but without arms. . . .
Our Co. has never been surprised by them for the fact that we are always on
the alert, we never move without an advance man has his gun ready for use. We

have adopted their rule, is to take no prisoners, leave no wounded men. There is no other way to fight bushwhackers. Extermination is our motto. We hunt them like wolves and are fast ridding the country of them . . .

Yours truly,
Geo. W. Packard

George Packard Letters [transcribed by Georgiana Brune], Kansas State Historical Society.

LIFE AND DEATH ON THE BORDER

In this letter to her parents-in-law, Martha W. Vansickle relates the death of her husband John. The couple had married in 1858 and settled in Bourbon County, near Xenia, where John farmed and ran a dry goods store. John joined the Third Regiment of the First Kansas Brigade in 1862 and was killed the following year while arresting a gang of thieves. As this letter demonstrates, life on the Kansas border was rife with danger even when it was not an active battlefield.

Xenia Kans July 21 / 63

Dear Father and Mother

. . . I will give you the particulars of Johns death as well as I can there is a gang of theives liveing about 6 miles from us and 4 nights before he was killed 2 of them came to Xenia and robbed a store and the day after the store was robbed he went with 5 or 6 other men to hunt for the goods and found them in their possesion they took the goods and arrested the 2 theives and brought them to Xenia then they was kept there till about eleven oclock at night and then 6 or 7 men started with them to take them to Paola to turn them over to the military autorities John told them that was no time to start with prisoners and he came home.

the next evening 2 of the set come along inquiring after them John told them all he knew about them and these 2 said if the others were not killed it would be all right but if they was hurt they would take a dozen mens lives to pay for them. the night they started to take them to Paola the men that was with them let them get away before they had got 2 miles from town and the man that the store belonged to that was robbed fired 3 shots at one of them in the dark and one ball took effect in his thigh close to his body but it did not disable him very much for he got home the next day and the day before John was killed one of our neighbors went with another man down to where the thieves lives to help him hunt for a stolen horse and they made their brags that before a week they would be enoug of them to come and burn Xenia and kill every man that had taken part against them. the night before John was killed there was men riding all night to notifiy the men all to meet the next morning to come to a conclusion what to do it was a general turn out of the citizens they thought the best way was to go rite on and take them before they had time to gather any more force when they got there they could not find any of the gang except the two that robbed the store the wounded one was not able to get away but the other one run into a brush thicket in bottom of a hollow that is close to the house. and hid there and John was put in command and he ordered a charge into the thicket and himself and Lieut Ford and one other man started but the balence of them was afraid that the brush was full of men and all of them kept out of danger.

the way it happened that he shot somany of them before he was killed he was hid so completely that they could not see him and he could see them as they were crossing a little opening in the thicket John an Ford was stooped forward looking through the brush when they was shot they fell only about 12 feet apart John had his revolver in his hand when he fell and after he fell took his other hand and studied his right and fired one shot but no one knows whether the shot took effect or not the thief was wounded in two places when the soldiers come for there was dry blood about 2 bullet holes if I knew that John shot took effect in him it would some satisfaction to me but I dont know nor never will . . .

I will close I remain yours very affectionately

M. W. Vansickles

John Henry Vansickle Collection, Kansas Collection, RH MS P170, Kenneth Spencer Research Library, University of Kansas Libraries.

THE LAWRENCE MASSACRE

On August 21, 1863, Lieutenant Colonel William C. Quantrill led Confederate sympathizers on a raid on Lawrence, Kansas. One of those caught in the raid was George Edwin Young. In this letter to his father in Massachusetts, Young vividly describes his close encounter with Quantrill's raiders.

Minneola Augst 23 1863

My Dear Father

I sent you a paper yesterday day with some account of the burning of Lawrence I wase there at the time and came very near being killed, all the Business part of the town is burnt also a great many of the best [?] our one hundred forty killed. they gave no quarter shot every man that they could get a shot at, I got into town the night before with my mowing machine four horses wagons & c.c. on my way to Lecompton where I had taken a job of mowing and stoped at the Johnson House, just as I wase getting up in the morning some one run by the House crying that Bush Whaker wase coming into town and the next thing I herd wase the firing of guns, and it wase not ten minutes before they had full possesion of the town, in fact the place wase taken by surprise and they had every thing there own way, they first shot every body that they could find in the streets and then put a guard over the Hotel, and a great many private Houses, at same time robbing the stores, banks of all money *and* goods that they could take away with them and then sett fire to all the stores on Massachesets St, and killing every man that came out of the burning buildings. they gave no quarter, they came to the Johnson House and after orderig out all the women and children, commenced shooting the men as they let them out of the House, they took me and four others up between two buildings, on Massachusets St and then commenced firing at us three wase shot right side of me, (on one side of us wase a new Building only partly finished) I run as they fired at me and got into the celler of the new building. I then thought they had got me shure, as they saw me go into the building and wase after me. I did not have much time to consider what to do. as I wase looking around to see what next wase to be done I Saw a small draine whole in the celler just large enough for me to lay down in I got into the drane as my last chance and as luck would have it there wase two body laying near by which I covered myself with. I had not been covered up a Second before two men came in looking after me, they passed through with out finding my hiding place. I wase in there over an hour, and I could all the time hear them shooting people in the street, I wase there all the time the Buildings were burning on Massachusetts St. the only thing that saved me wase that the Building wase new and lumber green so that it would no burn very fast. buildings on both sides of me wase burnt to the ground, as soon as I got out I went around to the Johnson House stable and found it standing found three of my Horses running in the street near by. My mowing machine wagon & cc all safe, and my other Horse came home to Paola during the next day with part of a harness on him, they robed me of my Watch abt two hundred & fifty Dollars in money that I had in my pockets, abt 200 dollars worth of goods burnt and abt Eight hundred Dollars from the bank. I dont expect to get one cent from the Bank, . . .—as soon as I got a Horse and saddle pistol, & cc I started with Gen Lane and party after the Bush Wakers after riding our horses fifteen mils we came up with there rear guard and had three or four little fights with them killing two or three of them I went with the party forty mils when my horse gave out dead Lame, and I had to return if my horse had shoes on I would have gone on, with the party. the last account ten had been killed horses and goods have been picked up all along the road. I am going to Lawrence to day and will send you full account as soon as I can get them. One hundred & eighteen wase buried saturday, and large numbers yet in the burnt buildings. I saw M McCrackin and others from Leavenworth making arrangements for poor that wase suffering for food.

Yours in Haste. . .

The Ruins of Lawrence, Kansas, from *Harper's Weekly*. *Courtesy of American Memory, Library of Congress.*

"A NIGHT OF TERROR"

Duncan Allison was killed in the Lawrence massacre and, in the following account, his widow, Isadora Augusta Johnson Allison, remembers the Sunday following Quantrill's raid. After a mass funeral, Lawrence residents were terrified anew, so petrified that William Quantrill had returned that they spent the night in James Lane's cornfield.

A NIGHT OF TERROR.

The Sunday following the Quantrill Raid of Aug. 21st 1863 had been a trying one to the people of Lawrence.

It had been a hot day, as August days are expected to be, but the heat had been increased by the fires which still smouldered from the burned buildings all over the town, and the odor of fire and smoke filled the air.

A general funeral service had been held at the old Congregational Church, which has been torn down long ago, and the sermon was preached by the Rev. Richard Cordley, then the honored pastor of Plymouth Church. The building was crowded.

Weping friends, widows and orphans, fathers and mothers, brothers and sisters, had gathered for the only funeral service that was held for the 185 murdered men and boys, whose remains—many of them burned beyond recognition—had been hastily buried in boxes or rohghly made coffins two days before. Every one was in a state of exhaustion and illy prepared for the night of terror and excitement that followed. . . .

The neighbors, who had been in and out all day, had gone to their homes and we were alone and in quiet.

The husband and wife sat on the door step talking in low tones of the trying scenes of the day. Through the open door of are adjoining room I could see the old mother of my friend bending over the pages of her well worn Bible, from which she sought strength and comfort. She was a Scotch woman of strong character—one not easily turned from doing what she thought right, and full of courage and endurance.

All was so still that it was almost oppressive: one could hear the soft breathing of the children on the bed. Perhaps I slept, but all at once, I became conscious of the clattering of horse's hoofs in the distance. Nearer and nearer they came and then a sentence seemed to fall on my ear, without my understanding. I heard my friend exclaim, "Did you hear that?" Before her husband could reply the rider was flying past, and into our ears came the startling words: "Fly, fly for your lives, Quantrill is coming, killing and burning everything as he goes"!

All was confusion in a moment. The husband of my friend was determined to go out and see where the enemy was and help defend the town, but my friend clung to him and pleaded pitcously for him to stay with her and the baby. As he had neither arms nor ammunition he could do nothing else. "Come, let us go" my friend said to me. "Go! go where?" "To the corn field of course," she replied.

Taking my baby in my arms, I started out in my thin lawn dress and thin soled slippers. Catching up a small single blanket, my friend threw it over my shoulders and drew it around the sleeping child so that it helped me to carry her. Mr L_ took their child while my friend snatched up a few clothes for the children and the old mother gathered some of her valuables and we started for a place of safety. We had gone but a few steps when the old lady stopped, crying, "I have forgotten my mother's teaspoons." and started back. Her daughter said: "Never mind the spoons, Mother, we have no time to get them." But when the old lady replied in reproachful tones: "Your Grandmother's spoons that I brought from Scotland with me must be saved," she let he[r] go, saying, "We'll wait for you at the Lykins' corner," and hurried on.

While waiting for her we could see in the starlight, men, women and children flitting in every direction carrying bundles of clothing and valuables. We waited some minutes before the old lady came up, breathless with her exertion, carrying the precious spoons in her hand. We had to climb a high board fence and Mr L_ had helped his wife and me with our babies over safely, but the Mother, thinking to make up for lost time, climbed up by herself and, as she was getting down on the other side, fell heavily to the ground and her silver was scattered in every direction. We felt about until we found all but one of the treasured teaspoons, the loss of which was always a sore trial to the dear old soul who was so determined to save them.

When she attempted to get up from where she had fallen she sank back, exclaiming: "Oh, my foot, I have sprained my ankle and cannot step."

She begged us to leave her and save ourselves, but giving the baby to my friend, Mr L_ picked her up and tried to carry her, but she was too large for even as strong a man as Mr L_ was to carry far. So he had to put her down and support her while she walked as best she could. Fortunately, we were near our haven of safety, and we proceeded more slowly.

We had gone but a few steps when we were called to "Halt," in frightened trembling tones and we recognized in the dim light one of our towns men who was trying to be brave as he marched back and forth guarding the home of his lady-love who was ill from the scenes of the Friday before, and unable to seek refuge in the corn field, which was just in the rear of the house.

It is, perhaps, easy to be courageous in battle, with soldiers all around you, guns and ammunition to use but, alone, in darkness with a rusty old rifle that would not "go off" if fired or, if it did, might go the wrong way, is quite a different thing. We told him who we were and receiving the news that the corn field was full of people, we hurried on and soon were within its sheltering protection.

This cornfield was made famous as the place of refuge for hundreds of people the day of the Raid. Even Gen. James H. Lane had not disdained its shelter. It was his own corn field of one hundred acres, just in the rear of his house on Mississippi street. The corn was of the tallest of Kansas growth and was tall above the head of the tallest man and, once within its borders, one was safe from the enemy.

We did not go far into the cornfield, but stopped when we were three or four rows from the edge.

We made a bed of the bundles of clothing and a large woolen shawl for the old lady and sat down in trembling silence to wait for the morning.

We could hear low whispers from different directions, or the cry of a child which was quickly hushed. Occasionally some new comer would stumble past in the darkness. The night wore on—We looked anxiously for the first streak of day light. The air had grown quite chilly and the childred needed the few wraps we had. The old lady was suffering intensely and could hardly repress an occasional groan. Finally we decided to make our way towards my home, which was also on the edge of the corn field, and if the house was still standing, try to get into it.

It was a work of time to make our way over the rough ploughed ground. Little clods of earth and pebbles would get into the low slippers making walking a torture—and when I lost my slippers I did not try to find them. Finally we reached a place where we could see that my house was there, and leaving my baby with the others and covering my light dress with the dark shawl I crawled on hands and knees through the yard and around to the front door.

After all these years, I can still feel the terror that filled my heart as I rose to my feet to unlock the door, and looked around almost expecting to see the street full of bush-whackers. I got the door open and was into the empty house, which was never to be my home again. Th[r]ough the parlor, into the sitting room, out into the dining room and through the kitchen, I reached the back door, how, I never knew, and was back with those I had left, as they thought, a long time before. . . . We started a fire in the cook stove and prepared a little breakfast.

As we sat at the table we could see our neighbors and friends come to the edge of the corn field and look out fearfully, then finally venture forth with their little bundles of valuables and go to their homes. But it was well towards noon before the corn fields had yielded up its last timid occupant and it was several days before it was learned why we had passed such a fearful night. For there was no enemy near. Quantrill and his men were hiding in the mountains and caves of Missouri and the crazy horseman who carried such terror in his mad ride was a good farmer living a few miles east of Laurence. He had seen a big fire caused by the accidental burning of some hay stacks near the town of Eudora and had hastily concluded it was Quantrill returning to complete his muderous work. Quantrill had carried off or destroyed all the arms and ammunition and the people had nothing to defend themselves with or perhaps they might have acted differently. As it was, all sought safety in flight to the ravines, the woods and corn fields. The dear old lady did not put her foot to the floor for three months, but when telling of the experiences of that awful night she would say triumphantly, "But I saved my mother's teaspoons."

Isadora August (Johnson) Allison Collection, Kansas Collection, RH MS P241, Kenneth Spencer Research Library, University of Kansas Libraries.

"DEATH, SUDDEN AND MOST UNEXPECTED"

Born in Vermont, Oscar Learnard moved to Ohio, where he worked as an attorney. He went to Kansas, where he helped found Burlington and became a district judge. When war came, Learnard joined the First Kansas Volunteers, resigning his commission in 1863 and joining the state militia the following year. In these excerpts from two letters to his wife, Mary S. Eldridge, Learnard recounts Quantrill's raid.

Lawrence, Kansas.
Sept. 3rd 1863.

Dear Mary—

On Sunday I attempted to write you but succeeded so badly that I seriously doubt if I made myself in any measure intelligible. I have not, and cannot write you the details of the terrible calamity which has fallen upon our poor, ill-fated Lawrence Tongue cannot tell, pen cannot discribe the terrors of that fatal morning, which brought death, sudden and most unexpected to two hundred citizens, distruction to One hundred and eighty-five Houses, and untold miseries upon an entire community—I can, even now, hardly realize the fearful truth

The Block in which was the Hotel, is entirely destroyed on Mass-Street with the exception of the Miller Block, in which is your Uncle Tom's store.

The Block opposite both on Mass and New Hampshire streets is entirely burned, not a single building standing

Every thing on the street, further down was burned excepting Pease's meat market and [?] store.

The private houses burned, were scatered all over town and are not so noticable unless you visit the different localities where they were—Fraziers, Ross's, Uncle Ed.'s & Brooks were in that part of town beside many more

Both of Thomas' houses were saved, also Ludington's—

Notwithstanding all this the few that are left are generally moving toward reconstructing their homes & business— . . .

Mr⁵ Jenkins is in one of the Kimbal's houses, and I am boarding there for the present. They lost every thing, but are in good spirits— . . .

I send *Love* without limit

O. E. L

∽

Lawrence, Kansas,

September 15ᵗʰ 1863

My Dear Mary— . . .

I know that at the distance you are from the *presence* of the great catastrophe which has fallen upon devoted Lawrence, with all the terrible doubts and fears which beset you, it is difficult to so familiarize yourself with it as to relieve in any considerable degree its horrors.

And yet we here—even those who have suffered most in loss of property and friends are beginning to buoy up their griefs and nerve themselves for the great Future which awaits their coming. Most are cheerful, and all hopeful.

Many have, of course, left, some never to return, but their places and the places of the *Dead* will be filled by others and Lawrence will continue her onward march.

Of course life and in many cases, property can never be recovered, and yet
I apprehend that a few years will hardly retain a trace of the ravages of today,
excepting the long line of "Tomb Stones," engraved August 21ˢᵗ 1863, . . .

Affectionately

O. E. Learnard . . .

Oscar Eugene Learnard Collection, Kansas Collection, RH MS D113 V4, Kenneth Spencer Research Library,
University of Kansas Libraries.

"THE OLD BORDER HATRED":
OFFICIAL REPORT ON THE LAWRENCE MASSACRE

*In this letter to Colonel Edward D. Townsend, Major General John Schofield,
commander of the Department of Missouri, assesses the Lawrence massacre and
General Order 11 (General Thomas Ewing's August 25, 1863, order depopulating four
Missouri counties bordering Kansas). Awarded the Medal of Honor for heroism at
the battle of Wilson's Creek, in 1861, Schofield became secretary of war in 1868 and
rose to commanding general of the United States Army.*

Hd. Qrs. Dept. of the Missouri.

St Louis 1863.

Colonel.

I have the honor to forward herewith for the information of the Gen-in-Chief,
Brig-Gen. Ewing's report of the burning of Lawrence, Kansas and massacre of
its inhabitants, and of the operations of his troops in the pursuit & punishment
of the rebels and assassins who committed the attrocious deed.

Immediately after his return from the pursuit of Quantrell on the 25ᵗʰ of
August, General Ewing issued an order depopulating certain counties and
destroying all forage and subsistence therein. The reasons which led him to
adopt this severe measure are given in his report.

The people of Kansas were very naturally, intensely excited over the
destruction of one of their fairest towns and the murder of a large number of its
unarmed citizens, and many of them called loudly for vengence, not only upon
the perpetrators of the horrible crime, but also upon all the people residing in
the Western counties of Missouri, and were assumed to be more or less guilty of
aiding the criminals.

It would be greatly unjust to the people of Kansas in general to say that they
shared in this desire for indiscriminate vengence.

But there were not wanting unprincipled leaders to fan the flame of
popular excitement and goad the people to madness, in the hope of thereby
accomplishing their own selfish ends.

On the 26th. of August a mass meeting was held in the city of Leavenworth at which it was resolved that the people should meet at Paola on the 8th. of September, armed and supplied for a campaign of fifteen days, for the purpose of entering Missouri to search for their stolen property, and retaliate upon the people of Missouri for the outrages committed in Kansas.

This meeting was addressed by some of the leading men of Kansas in the most violent and inflamitory manner, and the temper of these leaders, and of their followers, was such that there seemed to be great danger of an indiscriminate slaughter of the people in Western Missouri, or, of a collission with the troops under General Ewing in their efforts to prevent it.

Under these circumstances, I determined to visit Kansas and Western Missouri, for the purpose of settling the difficulty, if possible, and also, for the purpose of gaining more accurate information of the condition of the border Counties of Missouri, and thus making myself able to judge of the wisdom and necessity of the severe measures which had been adopted by General Ewing.

I arrived at Leavenworth City on the 2d of September and obtained an interview with the Governor of the State, and other prominent citizens. I found the Governor and his supporters opposed to all unauthorized movements on the part of the people of Kansas, and willing to co-operate with me in restoring quiet, and in providing for future security.

I then sought and obtained an interview with the Hon. J. H. Lane, United State Senator, who was the recognized leader of those engaged in the Paola movements.

Mr Lane explained to me his views of the necessity, as he believed, of making a large portion of Western Missouri a *desert waste,* in order that Kansas might be secure against future invasion. He proposed to tender to the District Commander the services of all the armed citizens of Kansas to aid in executing this policy. This I informed him was impossible.

That what-ever measures of this kind it might be necessary to adopt, must be executed by U. S. troops. That irresponsible citizens could not be entrusted with the discharge of such duties.

He then insisted that the people who might assemble at Paola should be permitted to enter Missouri "in search of stolen property" and desired to place them under my command, he, Gen. Lane pledging himself that they should strictly confine themselves to such search, abstaining entirely from all unlawful acts.

Gen. Lane professed entire confidence in his ability to control absolutely the enraged citizens who might volunteer in such an enterprise! I assured Mr Lane that nothing would afford me greater pleasure than to do all in my power to assist the outraged and despoiled people to recover their property as well as to punish their despoilers. But that the search proposed would be fruitless, because all the valuable property which had not already been recovered from those of the robbers who had been slain, had been carried by the others far beyond the border counties, and that I had not the slightest faith in his ability to control a mass of people who might choose to assemble under a call which promised the finest possible opportunity for plunder. Genl Lane desired me to consider the matter fully and inform him as soon as possible of my decision, saying if I decided not to allow the people the "right" which they claimed he would appeal to the President.

It was not difficult to discover that so absurd a proposition as that of Mr Lane could not have been made in good faith, not had I much difficulty in detecting the true object which was proposed to be accomplished. Which was to obtain if possible my consent to accept the services of all who might meet at Paola and take them into Missouri under my command, when I of course would be held responsible for the murder and robbery which must necessarily ensue.

I soon became satisfied that, notwithstanding Mr Lane's assertion to the contrary, he had no thought of trying to carry out his scheme in opposition to my orders, and that the vast majority of the people of Kansas were entirely opposed to any such movement. On the 4th of Sept. I published an order, a copy of which is enclosed, prohibiting armed men, not in the military service, from passing from one state into the other, and sent a sufficient force along the state line to enforce the order against any who might be disposed to disobey it. The people quietly acquiesced. The Paola meeting, which had promised to be of gigantic proportions, dwindled down to a few hundred people, who spent a rainy day in listening to speeches and passing resolutions relative to the Senator from Kansas and the Commander of the Dept. of the Missouri.

I enclose a copy of correspondence with Gov. Carney showing the measures which have been adopted to place the state in a condition to protect itself against such raids as that made against Lawrence. These measures together with those which are being carried out in Western Mo., will I believe, place beyond possibility any such disasters in future.

Not the least of the objects of my visit to the "Border" was to see for myself the condition of the border counties and determine what modification, if any ought to be made in the policy which Genl Ewing had adopted. I spent several days in visiting various points in the counties affected by Genl Ewing's order, and in conversing with the people of all shades of politics who are most deeply affected by the measures adopted. I became fully satisfied that the order depopulating certain counties, with the exception of specified districts, was wise & necessary. That portion of the order which directed the destruction of property, I did not approve, and it was modified accordingly.

The evil which exists upon the border of Kansas and Missouri is somewhat different in kind and far greater in degree, than in other parts of Missouri. It is the old border hatred intensified by the rebellion & by the murders, robberies & arson which have characterized the irregular warfare carried on during the early periods of the rebellion, not only by the rebels but by our own troops and people.

The effect of this has been to render it impossible for any man who openly avowed & maintained his loyalty to the Government to live in the border counties of Missouri outside of military posts. A large majority of the people remaining were open rebels, while the remainder were compelled to abstain from any words or acts in opposition to the rebellion at the peril of their lives.

All were practically enemies of the Government & friends of the rebel guerillas

The latter found no difficulty in supplying their commissariat wherever they went, and, what was of vastly greater importance to them, they obtained prompt & accurate information of every movement of our troops which no citizen was so bold as to give us information in regard to the Guerrillas. In a country remarkably well adapted by nature for guerrilla warfare, with all the inhabitants practically the friends of the gurillas, it has been found impossible to rid the country of such enemies At no time during the war have these countries been free from them. No remedy short of destroying the source of their great advantage over our troops could cure the evil.

I did not approve of the destruction of property at first contemplated by Genl Ewing for two reasons; viz:—I believe the end can be accomplished without it, and it can not be done in a reasonable time so effectually as to very much embarras the guerrillas.

The country is full of Hogs and Cattle running in the Woods:, and of Potatoes in the ground, and corn in the field which can not be destroyed or moved in a reasonable time

I hope the time is not far distant when the loyal people can return in safety to their homes and when those vacated by rebels, will be purchased and settled by people who are willing to live in peace with their neighbors on both sids of the line.

The measure which has been adopted seems a very harsh one, but after the fullest examination and consideration of which I am capable, I am satisfied it is wise and humane It was not adopted hastily as a consequence of the Lawrence massacre.

The subject had long been discussed between Genl Ewing and myself, and its necessity recognized as at least probable. I had determined to adopt the milder policy of removing all families known to be connected; with, or in sympathy with the guerrillas and had commenced its execution before the raid upon Lawrence. The utter impossibility of deciding who were guilty, and who innocent, and the great danger of retaliation by the guerrillas upon those who should remain, were the chief reasons for adopting the present policy. In executing it a liberal test of loyalty is adopted. Persons who come to the military posts and claim protection as loyal citizens are not turned away without perfectly satisfactory evidence of disloyalty. It is the first opportunity which those people have had since the war began, of openly proclaiming their attachment to the Union without fear of rebel vengeance

It is possible that Genl Ewing might have done more than he did do to guard against such a calamity as that at Lawrence, but I believe he is entitled to great credit for the energy, wisdom and zeal displayed while in command of that District The force at his command was larger, it is true than in other portions of the Dept. Yet it was small for the service required; necessarily so, as will be readily understood when it is considered how much my troops have been reduced by reinforcements sent to Genl Grant, Rosecrans, Steele & Blunt and how much the Territory to be occupied has been increased by our advance into Arkansas and the Indian Country

I am Colonel
Very Respectfully
Your obt Servt.
(Signed) J. M. Schofield
Maj Genl. . .

John M. Schofield to Edward D. Townsend, September 14, 1863, Abraham Lincoln Papers at the Library of Congress, Manuscript Division (Washington, DC: American Memory Project, 2000–2002), http://memory.loc.gov/ammem/alhtml/malhome.html.

"I SHALL NOT LEAVE LAWRENCE UNTILL IT IS DESTROYED THE THIRD TIME"

Jennie and Elizabeth S. C. Earl had relocated to Lawrence from back east. A few weeks after the raid on their town, Elizabeth reassured her family in Connecticut that they had survived the Lawrence massacre. The sisters had also survived the 1856 sack of Lawrence and, in these two letters, Elizabeth demonstrates resilience in refusing to be driven from her home.

Lawrence Sep 22, 1863

Dear Brother . . .

My Dear Brother you know nothing of the Horrors of this war, nor neather did I, untill the 21ˢᵗ day of August, our town was surprised about day light, by 300 men headed by Quandrel, who murderd every man that came in their way, most of our people were in bed, and the rebels would knock at the door and when the men opened the door, they would shoot them down, and then rush in, and set fire to the house, threatning death to the women, if they stird, and by that way the House would get to burning so fast, that it would be impossable to got the bodys of their Husbands out, so that they would have to burn up, many men were shot, and then thrown onto Houses that were burning, O it is heart rending to write about it, but I have seen what I hope I may never see again, untill it is to see those men that came here burnt at the stake, and then I should feel that we had had our revenge in some degree

Ralph Lase was shot and burnt up, his Widow remains in Lawrence for the present, almost all of the women have left the place, becaus the desolation is so great that they cannot remain, I see our beautifull town in ruins as it is at the present time, is enough to stir the heart of those demons to pity and remorse I shall not leave Lawrence untill it is destroyed the third time. I have been here through one invasion, one massacre, and when it is visited once more, then I will think about leaving. I was not molested, my House being out from town, and not on the road that they came and went on, I was up and from my door, saw all of the devastation, as soon as they were out of town I went down and what a sight met my eyes. I cannot describe it makes me sick at heart to think of it.

The women were not insulted as much as has been repersented, some few were abused, but as a general thing the Rebbels had some thing else to do besides insult the women The people that are left are trying to do business and to make every thing look as beautifull as circumstances will permit

Pleas answer soon
Farewell
From your sister
ESC. . .

~

Lawrence Sep 22 1863

Dear Mother

I am alive, but have had my nerves so unstrung, by the late Massacres, of our citizens, that I have not written to you, to let you know that I had escaped unhurt, you have heard all about Quantrels comeing into Lawrence before this, but Mother, you cannot imagine the distress, and suffering, of our women and children, by the suden death of their Husbands and Fathers, 100 and 80 widows and over 2,00 orphans were made in one day, and in two hours time, I have written to Tommy, some of the particulars, and you can read his letter, which will soon be writeing the same to you, I dont like to think of it, any more than I can help, for it unfits me for any thing else.

I at the present time, am takeing charge, of the City Hotel, the only one
that is left in Lawrence, the Old Gentleman was shot, and his Wife, has gone East
with her two Daughters, and I am to take charge of the House untill they return,
that is if my health will permit, I shall try and stay, for some one must remain,
I cheer up those that are obliged to stay, many women have left, Horrorfide
and will never return, others have left, thinking by so doing, they can throw off
the feelings, which has come over them, by the late Massacre, of their friends
Husbands and brothers. . . .

From your Daughter
ESC . . .

Jennie and Elizabeth S. C. Earl Collection, Kansas Collection, RH MS P285, Kenneth Spencer Research Library,
University of Kansas Libraries.

A YOUNG SIGNAL CORPSMAN SEES BUSHWHACKERS FOR THE FIRST TIME

*A native of Providence, Rhode Island, Lewis A. Waterman enlisted on April 29,
1864, when he was only sixteen, to serve in the United States Signal Corps. After
training in Georgetown, D.C., Waterman was sent to Fort Leavenworth in June. As
this letter to his brother-in-law Lewis Williams Anthony attests, young Waterman
was eager for his assignment.*

June 17th / 64
Arrow Rock Missouri River

Dear Lewis

You perhaps think it strange that I left camp so suddenly. Two days before we
started (which was June 5) Orders came to camp to have 110 men ready to start
within a day or two 53 of them were to go to Fort Leavenworth Kansas. The
Sergent who was to take us there had his choice of the whole And as good luck
would have it I was chosen among the rest You had better believe I was tickled.
Every man of the 110 wanted to go but they couldnt 53 was all that was wanted.

The Sergent had such confidence in his men that he lets them do as they please
We had no guard placed over them any of the way they went where they pleased
and he looked out that we fared well. We started Tuesday June 7th and got to St
Louis on the 10 We went over to Scholfield's Barracks staid there 2 nights and a day
we then went on board the boat Sunshine to go up the Missouri River to St. L on
Sunday staid there until Tuesday afternoon about 2 o'clk when when we started

The Capt expected to get there about Saturday night it is now night and we
have got just half way which is 250 miles they are fixing the boiler when we leave
here we will go into the Gurilla country or Bush Wackers as they are call about

here. Nothig more or less than Robers and cut throats they murder every person they catch old and young black and white, blind or lame. If one is caught he is shot with no trial at all as they cant share the rope long enough to hang him. You have no idea how mad the soldiers in Missouri are with them Last night guard was put on the boat and every man slept on his arms which was Colts Navy Revolvers and Saber loaded and caped the saber in particular.

The Bush Wackers are thicker than hops have spin all over the country. There are two who are suspected on this boat now we have fellows a watching them. They said they were going to Leavenworth and we are not going to let them get off this side of that place. We will probably be fired on tonight if we start from here to night

The boys are eager to have them board us. When I get to the Fort I will write all the particulars of my journey . . .

Yours Aff
Lewis Waterman
Direct your letters Signal Corps
Ft Leavenworth
Kansas

Lewis A. Waterman Collection, Kansas Collection, RH MS 515, Kenneth Spencer Research Library, University of Kansas Libraries.

JAMES LANE ON STERLING PRICE'S 1864 RAID

In his account, Lane describes the effort to repulse Confederate General Sterling Price's last attempt to invade Missouri. The main battle was fought on October 25, 1864, when Union troops overtook Confederates unable to transport their wagons across Mine Creek. Although outnumbered, U.S. troops captured six hundred men, including two of Price's generals, brigadiers general John S. Marmaduke and William L. Cabell, thus forcing Price out of Kansas.

*JAMES H. LANE
PRICE RAID
THE PART TAKEN BY LANE IN THE RAID—
WRITTEN BY LANE HIMSELF*

[1864]

In compliance with your request that I report to you the part I took in the recent campaign against Maj Genl Sterling Price & what facts came under my observation during that campaign as volunteer Aid de Camp upon your Staff I have the honor to submit the following:

On my arrival at Fort Leavenworth from Washington City via St Louis I found you absorbed in preparations to resist the invasion of Kansas by the rebel army under Genl Price which was then marching through the state of Mo. intact gathering stength day by day as it approached our border.

The Military force of the Dept having been rapidly concentrated in the Eastern portion of the State comprising volunteers and militia all under the immediate command of Maj Genl Blunt I reported to you at Olathe on the 10ᵗʰ of Oct & entered at once upon duty From the 10ᵗʰ to the 14ᵗʰ I was employed with others of your Staff under your personal direction in selecting positions & making despositions of troops along the border and on the Blue visiting for that purpose Wyandot, Kasas City, Independence & Hickmans Mill

At this point Genl Curtis directed Genl Blunt with the Brigades of Col Moonlight & Col Jennison to move Eastward until he found the enemy and to learn his exact position & line of march which had hitherto, from all information obtainable in any quarter been but mere conjecture, with instructions to harrass & impede him in every possible manner: at the same time ordering me to accompany the Expedition while he returned to Wyandotte to Superintend the further organization of his Army

Acting upon the information recd of the capture of Sedalia by the Enemy and supposing him marching upon Warrrensbugh Genl Blunt moved in that direction leaving Hickmans Mill after dark & making a march of 30 miles the night of the 15ᵗʰ to Pleasant Hill. Between P. H. & Holden we met two or three hundred Mo Militia falling back from Warrensbugh who joined our force & were engaged in the further operations of our detachment.

At Holden recvg definite information that the column which had destroyed Sedalia had moved north towards Lexington Genl Blunt at once determined to move direct to Lexington with the hope of reaching it in advance of the Enemy with a view of saving the Govt property. Arriving here we found the town evacuated by our troops who had taken away the greater part of the public property & the bushwhackers under Poole in possession of the place. Col Moonlight was ordered to charge which he did gallantly driving out the Enemy killing & wounding some & taking several prisoners.

Genl B. established HdQrs in the town and made such disposition of his force as would best defend the several approaches to the place & awaited the approach of the Enemy whose advance was then but a few miles distant

At 1 ock P.M. of the 19ᵗʰ the Head of Price's column struck our force under Col Jennison on the Waverly road

Col Moonlight was orderd to move at once to the scene of action Genl B & myself peceding him. The two Brigades thus consolidated were disposed across the road from Lexington to Independence.

By the stubborn fighting & skillful management of the troops Genl Blunt held the enemy for five hours falling back slowly at night down the Kansas City road not however until almost surrounded & enveloped by the vastly superior number of Price's advancing columns which pressed us closely for several miles to the Little Blue

On the morning of the 20th we took up a position on the north back of the Little Blue determined to dispute the passage of that stream with all the force while I was dispatched to Genl Curtis then at Independence to inform him of the position of affairs I found Gen C. at Ind. having formed his forces on the Big Blue and being engaged in fortifying the fords on this stream determined to make his final stand at that line. He then order all of Genl B. force back to this position except Col Mo Brgd which was left with order to burn the Bridge & delay the Enemy as long as possible at the little Blue.

On the morning of the 21st information reached us around 9 ock that the efforts to burn the Bridge on the Lill Blue had failed that the Enemy was forcing the passage of the river & were engaging Col Moonlight—.

Col [?] Brg & Col Fords Brigd including McLane's battery were at once ordered forwarded under Genl Blunt, Genl Curtis following quickly after & superintending movements on the field. The engagement here was severe & desperate the troops fighting with courage & dauntlessness creditable to veterans. The commanding Genl assisted by Genl Blunt who seemed everywhere present the bravest 7th was constantly under fire directing movements & inspiring by his own example his greatly inferior force till flanked & threatened with annihilation he fell back from ridge to ridge fighting at Independence until dark. When he crossed the Big Blue establishing HdQd for the night on the north bank on the road leading to Kansas City the Enemy meanwhile going into camp at Independence

On the morning of the 22nd the Enemy commenced demonstrations at the different fords along the stream but were stubbornly resisted at all points. His superior numbers having enabled him at length to force a crossing at Byrons ford but his advanse was sharply resisted back in the vicinity of Westport where night coming on our main force was withdrawn to Kansas City & placed in line of Battle leaving a suffict force in the neghborhood of Westport for observation

During the night we learned from prisoners & other sources that Price with his Eastern army estimated at 35000 was upon us intent upon the capture of Kansas City Leavenworth & the devastation of our State & that Pleasanton with his cavalry was close at hand

At daylight all the troops were moved forward to Westport & put in line of battle where Col Moonlight & a portion of the Militia was engaging the Enemy. The fight soon opned along the whole line & while unabated the welcome sound of Genl Pleasantin artillery was heard thundering in the rear of the Enemy which was soon followed by a Courier from Genl Pleasanton himself confirming our hopes & reassuring us of present help. Immediately on recpt of this intelligence Genl Curtis ordered a charge along the whole line in which all participate from Comdg Genl to soldiers the volunteers & Militia charging with great impetuosity amid cheers & shouts

The Enemy at first resisting with desperate determination soon began to wane, gave away slowly & doggedly but at length broken by the resistlessness of our troops & terror striken from the sound of artillery in their rear, turned their forces southward & fled precipitately.

The Enemy beaten, disheartend & flying the pursuit was taken up Genl Blunts Div in front was continued for 15 miles to Santa Fe where night ended the day's operations. During the pursuit about ten miles from the battlefield of the morning Genls Curtis, Pleasanton & Blunt met for the first time.

The following morning the pursuit was resumed by the combined force of Curtis & Pleasanton except McNeils Brigade which came up during the march Genl Blunt still in the advance assumd comd of the whole force Genl Curtis having at West Point the pursuit still continuing the order of march was changed, owing to the exaustion of Genl Blunts men that portion which had fought at Lexington not having food for days and Genl Pleasantons Div was placed in the advance Genl Blunt having meanwhile detached Col Moonlights Brgd to operate on the right & for the protection of Olathe Paola Mound City & Fort Scott on the Kansas border. On the order the march was continued during the night to the Trading Post where our column came up with the Enemy about 1 ock in the morning.

He at once took up his flight leaving behind him wagons, provsions & plunder of every description & was boldly pursued by our advance to Mine Run where he made a stand and was beaten with the loss of one piece of artillery At the Osage he made another stand & was again beaten losing seven guns &, many persons among whom were Marmaduke & Cabell he was beaten near Fort Scott. At this point Genl Pleasanton deeming rest & sleep necessary to his command withdrew to Fort Scott & from there returned to St. Louis. On the following morning Genl Curtis resumed the pursuit and at night camped at Haughain and on the next day the 27th his force reached Rousse's Point about 2 oclk PM where being relieved from further duty I left the army & returned home

The foregoing is a brief resume of what I saw and participated during these eventful days.

James Henry Lane Collection, Kansas Collection, RH MS 28, Kenneth Spencer Research Library, University of Kansas Libraries.

SIX

Kansans and Antislavery

$\mathcal{K}$ANSAS ENTERED THE Union with its antislavery reputation firmly established by the Bleeding Kansas ideological struggle of the 1850s. For many of the state's activists, war had long been expected and indeed was welcomed. In 1862, for instance, E. B. Whitman wrote that had it not been for "our successful struggle in Kansas the nation would never have been in the throes of deliverance from the monster slavery, as she is to day."[1] As a result, it should come as no surprise that some Kansans were at the forefront of both "liberating" slaves and recruiting African Americans for service in the Union army.

The effort to free slaves began informally—as in the territorial period, Kansans crossed the border to rescue Missouri slaves. By September 1861, the provisional governor of Missouri, Hamilton R. Gamble, had warned President Lincoln that something had to be done about this antislavery activity. Moreover, Gamble was worried that Kansans were arming African Americans to cross into Missouri and commit depredations. With a rumored Southern force seventy thousand strong forming in Arkansas to invade his state, Gamble did not want to have to be "diverting a portion of my force from this necessary object to the slaying of negro invaders and their associates."[2] Gamble was right to be concerned. Although there would be no Negro invasion, Kansas's citizens were spiriting some of Missouri's slave population into their state. By November 1861, Lane's Brigade had "scores of Negroes in ranks as teamsters, cooks, even soldiers." In November, two of the brigade's chaplains, H. H. Moore and H. D. Fisher, escorted "a black brigade of 160 wagons filled with Negroes into Kansas."[3]

Senator James H. Lane wanted to persuade Lincoln to accept the African American troops he was raising in Kansas. Although he had been explicitly told by both the president and Secretary of War Edwin Stanton that the United States would not accept any such troops, Lane persisted. By August 1862, the First Kansas Colored Infantry Regiment had been organized at Fort Scott, Kansas. But the lack of enthusiasm in the White House was mirrored by potential recruits. In part, their reluctance to enlist was due to Lane's poor offer: the $10 per month offered was less than that given to white soldiers, while the certificates of freedom extended to African Americans were particularly worthless, as residence in Kansas meant these men were already free. To fill the regiment, an attempt was even made to kidnap slaves from across the eastern border, but these men were recovered by the Missouri militia.[4] Most of the recruits who formed the First Kansas Colored Infantry were not from the state, and many had been coerced into enlisting.

Commanded by Colonel James M. Williams, the First Kansas Colored Infantry was largely made up of fugitive slaves from Arkansas and Missouri. Even though they had not yet been mustered into service, this regiment was the first black unit to engage the enemy. In October 1862, they fought a skirmish at Island Mound, Missouri, against a unit of Confederate guerrillas that resulted in the first combat deaths of black soldiers in the Civil War. A detachment of 225 faced 500 and, in driving off the Confederates, 10 members of the First Kansas were killed and another 12 were wounded. A few weeks later, on January 13, 1863, the regiment was formally mustered into federal service. Although Benjamin Butler had formed three regiments of black soldiers for the Union, they had been recruited in New Orleans. Thus, the First Kansas Colored Infantry was the first black regiment recruited in the North.

The First Kansas Colored Infantry served in Missouri, Indian Territory, and Arkansas. It became the Seventy-ninth U.S. Colored Troops on December 13, 1864. The state also raised the Second Kansas Colored Infantry as well as an independent battery.[5] The Second Kansas Colored Infantry served mainly in Arkansas; in December 1864 it became the Eighty-third U.S. Colored Troops. Like many black troops throughout the Union army, service carried a particular risk—that Confederates would not respect their uniforms and would refuse to take them as prisoners of war. During the battle of Poison Spring, Arkansas, in April 1864, of the 438 men and officers who joined the battle, the First Kansas Colored Infantry lost 117, and another 65 were wounded in the engagement. As its commander, James Williams, reported, "many wounded belonging to the First Kansas Colored Volunteers fell into the hands of the enemy, and I have the most positive assurances from eye-witnesses that they were murdered on the spot."[6] The Second Kansas Colored Infantry was especially affected by this outcome at Poison Spring, yelling "Remember Poison Spring!" when they attacked a battery at Jenkins Ferry soon after, on April 30, an engagement that resulted in high Confederate losses.[7]

Of course, while the service of troops like the First and Second Kansas Colored Infantry regiments contributed considerably to the country's reassessment of the humanity of African Americans, many others were reluctant to embrace these men as soldiers or to extend them civil rights. Encamped near Atlanta in late July 1864, Andrew Harris, for example, expressed horror over the possibility that his state would give blacks the vote. If that came to pass, Harris wrote, it would be better to simply abandon Kansas to African Americans than to coexist with them.[8]

However, others in Kansas proved more accepting of African Americans. During the territorial period, Kansas had had approximately five hundred slaves, but those numbers began to dwindle after 1858 when it became clear that Kansas would enter the Union as a free state. By 1860, the census revealed only two slaves and 625 free persons in Kansas. Those numbers quickly began to change as contrabands flooded the state. By 1862 the Kansas Emancipation League had been formed to provide succor for the new population.[9] This early embrace of refugees would help when the true exodus out of the South and into Kansas began in the aftermath of the war.

THE FUGITIVE SLAVE LAW IN KANSAS

Reluctant to enforce the Fugitive Slave Law, the unpopular 1850 law that obligated Americans to render aid to capture escaped slaves, Kansas's first U.S. marshal, James L. McDowell, wrote U.S. attorney general Edward Bates for clarification. McDowell likely believed that a new Republican administration and the outbreak of war would affect enforcement of the law, especially since Kansas was a likely destination for many escaped slaves; however, Bates informed him otherwise.

July 23 1861.

J. L. McDowell Esq
US Marshal, Kansas
Sir,

Your letter of the 11th of July, rec[d] 19th (under the frank of Senator Lane, of Kansas) asks advice upon the question whether or no you should give your official services in the execution of the *Fugitive slave law.*

It is the President's constitutional duty to "take care that *the laws* be faithfully executed." That means *all* the laws. He has no right to discriminate—no right to execute the laws he likes and leave unexecuted those he dislikes. And, of course, you & I, his subordinates, can have no wider latitude of discretion than he has.

Missouri is a state *in the Union.* The insurrectionary disorder in Missouri are but individual crimes, and do not change the legal *status* yeto [yet to] date nor change its rights & obligations as a member of the Union.

A refusal, by a ministeriel officer, to execute *any* law, which properly belongs to his office, is official misdeameanor, of which, I do not doubt, the President would take notice

Very respectfully
Edw. Bates

James L. McDowell Papers, Collection 425, Kansas State Historical Society.

"FIRST REMOVE THE CAUSE OF THE DISEASE, THEN CURE" IT

The insistence by the editor of the Wabaunsee Patriot *that slavery was to blame for the war comes as no surprise given the antecedents of the town. Wabaunsee Township had been established in 1854, but was transformed by the arrival of the Connecticut Kansas Colony in 1856. These antislavery settlers are better known as the "Beecher Bible & Rifle Colony," so called because they left New England particularly well provisioned for the struggle in the territory. Reverend Henry Ward Beecher led fundraising efforts to ensure they carried not just hymnbooks and Bibles to Kansas, but Sharps rifles as well. Named after Chief Wabaunsee of the Pottawatomie tribe, the town is located in central Kansas, between the Pottawatomie Reservation and Fort Riley.*

THE ISSUE.

The great question . . . is the propriety, expediency, or more properly speaking, the manifest DUTY, morally as well as politically, of the Government and the people who are sustaining it, to at once make the present contest a direct conflict and war with slavery. It is a question which we do not deny has from the first been agitated to some extent, but not until Gen. Fremont issued his proclamation giving freedom to the slaves of rebel masters in Missouri, and the nullification or modification manifesto of the President had followed upon its heels into the newspaper press of the country; not until then, we say, had its solution become of such universal interest as now. It is discussed publicly and privately, in the various prints of the day, upon the rostrum, in the family circle, in the soldiers' camp, in the field and by the way-side. It is the all-pervading topic and few there be but manifest a certain degree of disappointment, coupled with feelings of regret, mortification and even indignation, at the uncalled for action of the President. The unanimous voice of the press, with the N. Y. Herald in the lead, was in support of Gen. Fremont and his initiatery blows against the enemy's coat of mail, slavery, and the public mind was beginning to breathe freer since the long dreaded attack upon the monster had been made, and contrary to the grave forewarnings of political wiseacres, he had not wrathfully belched forth utter annihilation to the people of the North.

. . . We have deliberately and candidly "looked on this side then on that," and have arrived at the conclusion that there is no hope in our government, or in the cause of the people who sustain it, except it be written in letters of living gold, upon their flags, their banners and their heart of hearts—*The overthrow of Slavery and Rebellion!* First remove the cause of the disease, then cure the disease itself.

. . . Every school-boy can give a ready and correct answer, as to the legitimate cause of the present trouble in the Nation, and common sense will teach the inquirer that so long as the cause remains, bitter, relentless, never-ending outbreaks, similar to the present, will necessarily follow. What sense, then, is there in caviling about it, or in shrinking from grasping the monster by the horns at once, and done with him forever? Let us make this a conflict with Slavery and Rebellion—"one and inseperable"—thus giving to the war finality and morality of character, the former consideration as potent in enlisting our own "men of the North" in the fight, as the latter is certain to win the sympathy and support of every civilized nation—two *very essential* features, and two which, unfortunately, our cause undeniably fails to reflect at the present time.

Wabaunsee Patriot, September 28, 1861.

FLEEING INTO KANSAS

The influx of so many refugees into Kansas required that funds be raised for their support. Eastern philanthropists like George L. Stearns, who had supported antislavery efforts in territorial Kansas, were natural targets for fund-raising efforts.

Lawrence Kansas Nov 19th 1861

George L Stearns Esq
Dear Sir
Contrabands in large numbers are fleeing from Missouri into Kansas and especially into Lawrence 131 came into Lawrence in ten days, yesterday 27 had arrived at 4 P. M. Thus far they have been taken care of; as the farmers needed help and hundreds if not thousands are now employed in harvesting who will soon be out of employment; and then they will gather into town for us to feed and clothe. No doubt a part of the farmers will provide for, those now at work for them, during the winter; but all will not do it; then as to the newcomers; there is not an intelligent slave in Mo, but knows where Lawrence is; and we shall have them here by thousands, and unless our friends from the east assist there will be starvation and death among them. There will be much suffering in all events. As you have heretofore shewn your self much interested in behalf of this oppressed class of our fellow men will you not lay this matter before the friends of humanity at the East and ask them to send us funds to relieve their wants . . .

Respectfully
Yours
John B Wood

P. S. I was not out last eve in consequence of indisposition but since writing the above I learn that 86 came into town in one drove last evening

J. B. W.

George L. Stearns Papers, Collection 507, Kansas State Historical Society.

THE *FORT SCOTT BULLETIN* ON CONTRABANDS

Fort Scott was home to the First Kansas Colored Volunteer Infantry, but the decision to enlist African Americans was not, as the first editorial from the Fort Scott Bulletin *reveals, necessarily welcomed. Yet the second entry, from a member of the First Kansas, indicates that the South was losing its grip on slavery as the war continued.*

July 26, 1862

Recruiting under the new call for 300,000 troops goes on briskly. The different States are offering large bounties to volunteers, and the ranks are filling up rapidly. 30,000 are reported ready for the field. While white men are so ready to fight for their country, why will abolitionists continue to insult our brave soldiers by their efforts to place them side by side with negroes. If slaves of rebel masters can be used to build roads or dig entrenchments, we say all right, go ahead; but we never will agree to their being armed and employed as soldiers.

An effort is being made in Leavenworth to raise a regiment of negroes. There are contrabands enough in Fort Scott to fill up two companies; you can have them as soon as you choose; the sooner the better. We advise those interested to keep their black regiment away from the Kansas troops now in the field. We know whereof we speak, when we say that, with one exception, there is not a Kansas regiment from which they would have as much to fear as from the rebels.

September 13, 1862

From the First Kansas, August 27th

THE CONTRABAND EXODUS.

It is gratifying to observe that a very large proportion of the passengers going North are of the *colored persuasion.* Scores of grinning contrabands may be seen on every upward-bound train. The North Star is no longer looked for as the guide to the land of freedom—the panting fugitives steal their way to the nearest military post, and inquire for the man that gives "passes," and then fly as fast as steam can carry them, to perform the labor necessarily abandoned by the brave men of the North who have enlisted to fight for the old flag.

Until recently their masters, or more frequently their mistresses would follow them into camp, and in some instances they succeeded in getting the poor slaves to return to bondage, Col. Deitzler, commanding the Post, considers it his duty to enforce "General Orders No. 3," rather than lie in the guard house half the time for disobedience of orders. But since the passage of the confiscation and emancipation laws, there is less hunting for runaway negroes.—Whenever a loyal citizen—*i.e.:* one that has taken the oath—comes and asks permission to look for his "boy," the Colonel refers him, kindly and courteously, to the law of Congress which provides that "any military or naval officer who attempts to decide whether a negro is free or slave, or returns one to his pretended owner, shall be cashiered." The conviction is fast forcing itself into the minds of all classes in this community, that the "peculiar institution" is about played out. And it is so. A large number of chattles "vamose the ranche," and those who remain refuse to work.—Slaves are very uncertain and unprofitable "property." It needs no law of Congress nor proclamation by the President to abolish slavery—the good work of tearing up by the roots the "sum of all villainies," which will make all the States all free, and restore prosperity and *permanent* peace to the nation, goes bravely on, and as rapidly as is desirable. If the fanatical abolitionists of the North would cease their unreasonable howling for the abolition of slavery at one fell swoop, by Congressional or Presidential action, and shoulder a musket, and assist us in driving the traitors into the Gulf, the country would give them more credit for honesty and sincerity. The slaves are virtually freed as fast as we push the federal troops southward. It is one of the inevitable results of this war.

Fort Scott Bulletin, July 26 and September 13, 1862.

First Lieutenant William Dominick Matthews, Independent Battery, U.S. Colored Light Artillery. *Reproduced by permission from the Kansas State Historical Society.*

A SUBSCRIPTION TO AID COLORED VOLUNTEERS

The following appeal by Charles H. Langston addresses the poverty of recently escaped freedmen. The grandfather of the poet Langston Hughes, Charles Langston came to Leavenworth in April 1862 to work with the contrabands. Langston had been born free in Virginia to Captain Ralph Quarles, a white man, and a part-Indian slave whom his father had manumitted.

TO THE PEOPLE OF THE DISTRICT OF THE TWELFTH REGIMENT.—To facilitate enlistments in the 12th Regiment Kansas Volunteers, and procure the prompt filling up of the Regiment, one thing is absolutely essential,—some provision ought to be made for the families of those who volunteer. Most of the colored people of Kansas are necessarily poor. They have but lately come out of slavery. The colored men are anxious to go into the service of their country. Like white men they are also anxious to see their families provided for. Many colored men whom I have asked to enlist, told me they would enter the service at once, but that with daily labor provided their wives and children with daily bread, and as soon as they go into the army their families must suffer. A few dollars from our generous and wealthy white fellow citizens will remove this difficulty, and be the means of getting many good men into the army.

I want to see every able-bodied colored man aiding to put down this slave holders rebellion. I therefore appeal to the loyal people of this district to provide for the necessities of their families while they fighting the battles of their country.

CHAS. H. LANGSTON.

Aug. 25th.

Leavenworth Daily Conservative, August 27, 1862.

"IN THE THROES OF DELIVERANCE FROM THE MONSTER SLAVERY"

Having come to Kansas as an agent for the National Kansas Committee, E. B. Whitman saw a clear connection between the struggle to make Kansas a free state in the 1850s and the struggle against the proslavery Confederacy.

Lawrence Sept 7 1862

Geo L Stearns Esq
My dear Sir . . .

I am sorry to feel that Kansas is not developing itself as the paradise we were wont proclaim it. Last year, as if to make up for the previous year of excessive dryness, the rains decended and the floods came and many of our crops were ruined in the planting, tho, on the whole the harvest was considered plentiful, more perhaps from the amount of land sown and planted than from the abundance of the yield. This year we are again suffering from long continued drought and multitudes of insects. The early spring was wet enough, hence our crops had a good start and winter wheat yielded a plentiful harvest, but of all other crops except sugarcane there is likely to be an almost entire failure in many parts, except the corn which as a general thing will average from 1/3 to 1/2 a crop. Roots of all kinds are an entire failure and so of all winter vegetables except beans.

The uncertainty of the climate is what is discouraging us. Perhaps there may be something to which the climate is better adapted than the products we are now seeking to make. Wool growing, wine making, sugar making cotton and silk growing may some or all of them succeed better than our present staples, but then before these or most of them can flourish the population of the country must undergo an almost entire change. The man born and bred to raise corn and pork can never turn his hand successfully to grape raising or sugar making.

But with all this apparent disappointment in the country and its adaptations, do not understand me as saying or thinking that the outlay and efforts we made in settling Kansas and maintaining the institutions of freedom here as abundantly repaid in the harvest we and the nation are to day reaping. But for our successful struggle in Kansas the nation would never have been in the throes of deliverance from the monster slavery, as she is to day, instead of it the chains would have been revetted for another century at least, not only upon the blacks of the South but upon the whites of the North. We may finish in the agony but better so than the living death that was being prepared for us, But I do not so expect, when Pharroh shall let my people go, as "Thus saith the Lord"—then the day of deliverance will begin to dawn. The experiment of using the escaped slaves, at least, not only at the spade but with the musket will I am confident be tried *here in Kansas* under some form or other. Already we have organized or nearly so, ten companies of "Contrabands" and it is expected that two entire regiments will soon be in the field. In addition to our white force of about ten thousand already in the field, we shall make out under the new levy three regiments more of whites.

Of Kansas with a voting population of less than twenty thousand shall send an army of fifteen thousands, what state will do more than that. Old men and young are alike rushing to the field. In two companies just now completed in Lawrence, the ages range from *thirteen* to *seventy*. Many men beyond the age of drafting are now right around me arranging their affairs, by putting two families into one house so as to join the Army.

Of the four male members of my family two of us will go. One old gentleman who has enlisted states that he has four sons and eight grandsons? now in the army. The North and West must either bow their neck, and the

necks of their posterity to the galling chains a degrading servitude—or maintain
the integrity of this Union under a Free government—Such is the aspect of
the question to us North Kind remembrances to the members of your family I
remain as ever very truly yours

E. B. Whitman

George L. Stearns Letters, Collection 507, Kansas State Historical Society.

EMANCIPATION: DOING RIGHT

The unprecedented liberation of more than three million slaves (almost another
million residing in areas not under rebellion would remain enslaved) by the
upcoming Emancipation Proclamation drew the attention of many newspapers,
including the Oskaloosa Independent.

December 27, 1862

EMANCIPATION.

As our pen traces the word, the President is performing the act. It is the New Year's
Day of the world, and more than that to the poor slave—it is to him a NEW LIFE.

The President is reported to have said that "he could not if he would, and
would not if he could" withhold the proclamation. That sounds like him. It is the
voice of a man who has risen to the lofty position of a firm resolve to DO RIGHT.
God bless him, and bless the words he shall utter, and the poor oppressed ones to
whom they shall go forth as the sound of Jubilee, as the voice of hope, and the
beginning of manhood.

It is seldom Heaven gives to one man the privilege of becoming immortal by
such direct means. Abraham Lincoln will live forever in the memory of man.

There is no telling the blessings that will flow from emancipation. The prospect
is illimitable. It lifts the incubus from this otherwise happy land—that dire load
which has been sinking the country down, until this accursed rebellion has been
ozed out of the pressure and sent its slime and fetid breath even the fair plains of
the sunny climes where the curse has rested as a blight and mildew more deadly
than that of the Upas of the east. . . .

It is vain to believe that the slaves are in ignorance of the forthcoming word of
LIBERTY. They know it well. They have known it from the beginning; and it will not
find them unprepared.

They have been waiting the hour of deliverance with expectation on tip-toe;
and through all the South there are signs which will follow.

We do not apprehend that there will be the horrible condition of things which
some have predicted. We think that there will be no rapine and murder, unless

the slaveholders and not the slaves inaugurate such a state of affairs. The slaves if not punished on suspicion by their masters and overseers, will quietly await the coming of our armies. But if the owners commence the work of persecution by whipping or shooting slaves they may suspect of a desire for freedom, there is no telling what will be the sad result.

Should the slaves, raised up on expectation, be crowded down more oppressively than before, as is too often the case, there will, in all human probability, be scenes of terror and crime from the contemplation of which the mind turns with sadness.

We expect quiet conduct on the part of the slaves; but we do not believe they will be kept down by force on the part of their masters. May all work together for good.

Oskaloosa Independent, December 27, 1862.

THE BATTLE OF HONEY SPRINGS

Major General James G. Blunt, the only Kansan to earn that rank in the Civil War, reported this engagement in Indian Territory, about twenty miles from Fort Gibson. Coming two weeks after victories at Gettysburg and Vicksburg, this battle resulted in Union control of Indian Territory north of the Arkansas River. Blunt commanded three thousand men, including American Indian and African American troops. It was a decisive victory, as his three thousand Indian Home Guard, Kansas, Colorado, and Wisconsin troops suffered fewer than one hundred casualties while the Confederates, led by Brigadier General Douglas H. Cooper, suffered more than six hundred.

HEADQUARTERS DISTRICT OF THE FRONTIER,
In the Field, Fort Blunt, C. N., July 26, 1863.

GENERAL: I have the honor to report that, on my arrival here on the 11th instant, I found the Arkansas River swollen, and at once commenced the construction of boats to cross my troops.

The rebels, under General Cooper (6,000), were posted on Elk Creek, 25 miles south of the Arkansas, on the Texas road, with strong outposts guarding every crossing of the river from behind rifle-pits. General Cabell, with 3,000 men, was expected to join him on the 17th, when they proposed attacking this place. I could not muster 3,000 effective men for a fight, but determined, if I could effect a crossing, to give them battle on the other side of the river.

At midnight of the 15th, . . . I immediately commenced crossing my forces at the mouth of Grand River in boats, and, by 10 p.m. of the 16th, commenced moving south, with less than 3,000 men, mostly Indians and negroes, and twelve pieces of artillery. At daylight I came upon the enemy's advance about 5 miles from Elk Creek, and with my cavalry drove them in rapidly upon their main force, which was formed on the south side of the timber of Elk Creek, their line extending 1 1/2 miles, the main road running through their center. . . .

As my men came up wearied and exhausted, I directed them halted . . . to rest and eat a lunch from their haversacks. After two hours' rest, and at about 10 a.m., I formed them in two columns, . . . The infantry was in column by companies, the cavalry by platoons and artillery by sections, and all closed in mass so as to deceive the enemy in regard to the strength of my force. In this order I moved up rapidly to within one-fourth of a mile of their line, when both columns were suddenly deployed to the right and left, and in less than five minutes my whole force was in line of battle, covering the enemy's entire front. Without halting, I moved them forward in line of battle, throwing out skirmishers in advance, and soon drew their fire, which revealed the location of their artillery. The cavalry, which was on the two flanks, was dismounted, and fought on foot with their carbines. In a few moments the entire force was engaged. My men steadily advanced into the edge of the timber, and the fighting was unremitting and terrific for two hours, when the center of the rebel lines, where they had massed their heaviest force, became broken, and they commenced a retreat. In their rout I pushed them vigorously, they making several determined stands, especially at the bridge over Elk Creek, but were each time repulsed. In their retreat they set fire to their commissary buildings, which were 2 miles south of where the battle commenced, destroying all their supplies. I pursued them about 3 miles to the prairie south of Elk Creek, where my artillery horses could draw the guns no farther, and the cavalry horses and infantry were completely exhausted from fatigue. The enemy's cavalry still hovered in my front, and about 4 p.m. General Cabell came in sight with 3,000 re-enforcements. My ammunition was nearly exhausted, yet I determined to bivouac on the field, and risk a battle in the morning if they desired it, but the morning revealed the fact that during the night they had retreated south of the Canadian River.

The enemy's loss was as follows: Killed upon the field and buried by my men, 150; wounded, 400; and 77 prisoners taken, 1 piece of artillery, 1 stand of colors, 200 stand of arms, and 15 wagons, which I burned. My loss is 17 killed, 60 wounded, most of them slightly.*

My forces engaged were the First, Second, and Third Indian, First Kansas (colored), detachments of the Second Colorado, Sixth Kansas, and Third Wisconsin Cavalry, Hopkins' battery of four guns, two sections of Second Kansas Battery, under Capt. E. A. Smith, and four howitzers attached to the cavalry.

Much credit is due to all of them for their gallantry. The First Kansas (colored) particularly distinguished itself; they fought like veterans, and preserved their line unbroken throughout the engagement. Their coolness and bravery I have never seen surpassed; they were in the hottest of the fight, and opposed to Texas troops twice their number, whom they completely routed. One Texas regiment (the Twentieth Cavalry) that fought against them went into the fight with 300 men and came out with only 60. It would be invidious to make particular mention of any one where all did their duty so well. . . .

Very respectfully, your obedient servant,

JAS. G. BLUNT,

Major-General.

Maj. Gen. JOHN M. SCHOFIELD,

Commanding Department of the Missouri. . . .

* But see revised statement, p. 449 [revises to 13 killed and 62 wounded].

The War of the Rebellion: A Compilation of the Official Records of the Union and Confederate Armies, ser. 1, vol. 22 (Washington, DC: Government Printing Office, 1888), 447–49.

"THE ONWARD MARCH OF ANTI-SLAVERY"

Many antislavery advocates believed the war would eliminate slavery, and so the editor of the Council Grove Press *urged readers to sell their slaves. This issue paid particular attention to Missouri, as two* Press *columns address its "gradual emancipationists." The first argues that their slow approach placed them on the road to perdition; the other argues that soon there would be no slaves in Missouri, as slaves who enlisted in the Union army received their freedom while their owners received $300.*

SLAVERY.

We yet have a few people in this country, and we fear in this county, who cannot give up their love for Slavery; they really hope to see the Union restored, but with it Slavery.

Gentleman, it is no use, we were among those always Anti-Slavery to the "manor born," but with others had hoped that the contest between Slavery and Freedom would end as a moral conflict, and that the pulpit and ballot-box would settle the contest, and civil war be avoided, but the evil was too great, it required "blood to purify and become the moral atmosphere."

Slavery had triumphed time after time.—Missouri, after a terrible conflict was admitted a Slave State; Texas was admitted a Slave State. The Missouri Compromise was repealed. Kansas and Nebraska thrown open to Slavery, which was sought to be established here by the bayonet. After all this we did not suppose the slave power would attempt to tear down our entire Government, because in this conflict of opinion, the Northern ideas should for once triumph. We stated years ago that we feared Slavery could only be wiped out in blood. We recollect saying, in this place, three years ago that, "the moment that the Slaveholders raise a hand against this Government, they strike the death blow to Slavery," and they have done it. We now tell our readers, if you have any interest in Negroes, you had better sell at once. Negroes are low to be sure, but the market will never be so good again.

The first shot at the Star of the West, shot the "sum of all villianies" to the very heart; ever since it has been writhing in its agonies. Conservative doctors have tried to nourish it up again, but all of no avail. Die it will; when this Rebellion is put down, and peace restored to the country, Slavery will be numbered with the past. There is no use in fighting "manifest destiny," you might just as well attempt to stop the current of the Mississippi with a cane, as to try to stop the onward march of Anti-Slavery in this country.

"His spirit is marching on,"

and the principles of Anti-Slavery will continue to "march on," until the cause of the war is removed; until

"A Slave cannot breathe *American* air."

Then, and not til the, will the war come to a close.

Council Grove Press, December 14, 1863.

WORRIED THAT AFRICAN AMERICANS WOULD GAIN THE VOTE IN KANSAS

Although Andrew Harris's regiment had been sent to fight in Georgia, he kept up with the news from home and, eighteen months after the Emancipation Proclamation, he was worried that Kansas would extend suffrage to African Americans.

Camp 3 mile from atlanta
July 22nd 1864

Dear Parents

I take this opportunity of letting you know that I am well at present and hope those few lines will find you enjoying the same blessing: We are on the front line here and are having a noisy time of it There is a continual roar of rifles on the skirmish line some of them is not more than 50 yards in front of the works The bullets is whistling over our heads mostly all the time and a shell occasionally we have been lucky so far there has only been 6 men wounded in the regiment. Some of them acadentaly and two gard disabled too night. We are getting close to atlanta but the rebs seems to have an objection to us going any further at present. They show fight [unclear] considerable we have had to build several breast works since we came to the brigade but every time the army moves it has to build and there is no grumbling at hand to work but it is every man pitch in and work for his life all most. This [?] Army has only built 5 or 6 hundred miles of breast works in this campain

The rebs says that we dont fight fair The prisoners wants to know why we dont come up in front of their works to drive them out. . . . I dont know as I will write any more about war Sherman will carry it on to suit himself we belong the the 1ˢᵗ Brigade 3ʳᵈ Division 4ᵗʰ Army Corps

I see by the papers that there has been a convention called in Kansas to allow Nigers to vote if they do I hope that every one that goes just one half of them will turn blacker than the blackest niger that ever come from afar if it comes to vote I want every one that for it to turn to a niger as soon as he casts his vote and then let the white man leave the State to the nigers but I have a better opinion of the people of Kansas than that I don't think that they like nigers quite so well as that I don't know of any thing more to write at present. I will bring my scribbling to close.

Give my love to all

I. Harris

Your son

A. W. Harris

Co. E. 8ᵗʰ Kansas. . . .

1ˢᵗ Brig 3ʳᵈ Div, 4ᵗʰ A. C.

(in, Marrietta GA

"THEY BEGIN TO THINK THAT THE COLLORD MEN CAN FIGHT"

A member of the Twelfth Regiment Kansas Volunteers, Willard Hubbell of Paola wrote his wife, Maria, during the Camden expedition. This campaign was part of the failed Union effort to gain control of Arkansas, Louisiana, and Texas in the spring of 1864. It was also when the battle of Poison Spring occurred, which proved so costly to the First Kansas Colored Volunteers.

Head Qtrs "C" Co. Thayers Division Steels Army

Camden Ark

April 25ᵗʰ 1864

Dear Maria

. . . We have mooved our camp up in the south west part of town near the fortifications the Rebles built. They are a nice thing for us to defend our selves. They (the Rebles) built fortifications all around the town to keep the *Yankee's*

Captain Willard O. Hubbell of Paola served in the Twelfth Regiment, Kansas Volunteer Infantry. *Reproduced by permission from the Kansas State Historical Society.*

out, but we took the town without fireing a gun they found out that if they undertook to hold the town we would open a sige & starve them out, for there communication was cut of & they had no way to get supplys only as they got it through the country. We have had several skirmishes with them since we have been here but they will not actact us in the fortifications they will try & take in our forage parties. Col Williams of the 1ˢᵗ Collord Reg & some of the 6ᵗʰ K & 2ⁿᵈ KS & 14ᵗʰ & 18ᵗʰ Iowa went out on a foragin trip some 10 miles west of camden, & on there return Rebles surounded them & tried to take them in, but Col Williams went in for fight he lost his train of one hundred ninty waggons mules & all—they ware over powerd by the Rebs & compleetly surounded but the niggers cut there way through & had it hand to hand fight but the niggers was badly cut up. Col Williams lost 100 men killed & wounded & missing The 18ᵗʰ Iowa lost some. We lost one section of Rabbs Battery & Two Howetsers. The niggers fought well. They begin to think that the collord men can fight.—Three of our boys out of the company ware teemsters in the train & they narowly escaped, lost there clothing & gun's came to camp sometime turing the night. There was great excitement in the camp for several days. One night after we had gone to bead there was an alarm given & the 2ⁿᵈ Brigade was called out. We sleeped on our arms all night our Reg was in the center & we suported the 1ˢᵗ Arkansas Battery at the Brow of the hill in front of our camp, near the road. . . .

Tuesday Apr 26ᵗʰ Dear Maria, . . . I forgot to tell you that young Colman (Yankee Colmans son) 1ˢᵗ Lt in the 1ˢᵗ Collord was killed. when Col Williams had his fight. the Rebles have a spite towards the officers of the nigger Regiments. Col Williams lost five officers in the fight The Collord troops have all the hard work to do & running around & escorting forage trains, & c . . .

Little Rock May 4ᵗʰ While writing this letter . . . we received orders to march for Little Rock—I Packed up & at dark we started & traveld all night until 10 o clock. The next morning—tired & hungry—we started again on force marches. the Boys got out of grub & had nothing to Eat only what we could pick up along the road & that was not much—after traveling night & day we got to Saline River . . . at 11 o clock we ware orderd to the field of action we started on quick time & got whare the cold lead came down like hail we had not got far in the timber before Col Hayes was mortely wounded & several men in the Reg was wounded & one man killed we ware left for a time without a commander finely I took my company & formed a line of battle fasing the Rebles & the rest of the Reg formed on & Evrything was all right Capt Chesnut took command & change position we had not been there long before the Rebles came back in force of about fifteen thousand with the intention to break our lines & drive us back we open fire on them with the Two Ill Reg one Wisconsin Reg & the 12ᵗʰ Kans & the

2nd Colord & such aroaring of musketry was never heard before we had not been fighting long before I was struck with a spent ball & liked to knocked me over I thought at first the ball had went through. but come to look it had not but it hurt me verry bad & I had to leave the field. I was awful sick the ball took struck me in the right side just graced the hip bone. . . .

We left Camden Apr 25th & arrived at this place Little Rock May 3rd tired out hungry & evrything that would make a soldier sware. . . .

We have traveled since we left Fort Smith 350. I think we have done well

From yours for Evr
W. O. Hubbell

Kiss the Babies & Except
Lots for yourself

Willard Ovis Hubbell Papers, Kansas State Historical Society.

THE LESSONS OF THE WAR

The Union Sentinel *began publishing in Hiawatha at the end of August 1864 and, in this editorial shortly before the end of the war, contemplated whether the war had imparted greater value on liberty. Located in the northeastern corner of Kansas, Hiawatha is the seat of Brown County, bordered by Nebraska to the north and one county removed from Missouri.*

WHY SO LONG?

Many a time, we—as a people—weary of the war, its blood shed, its tumults, its dread suspenses, its rumors and terrors, with its bereaving, taxing, conscripting hand—have cried out—Why so long? Where is the "coming man" to put an end to all this?

Ah, it is not in man to divine the reason of all the ways of Him whose thoughts are not as man's thoughts. And yet, we can see some thing—how slow, and dull, and stupid man is in comprehending his true relations and duties to his neighbors, to his country, the world, and to coming generations.

The war has revealed to us the fact that even in the North there was an immense amount of prejudice against the black, consequently a bitter feeling against "abolitionists," often so strong as to give a positive moral influence in favor of the slaveholder.

To educate this class past and above the fatal point on which their prejudices had fastened them, has cost—we can now have some idea, when we look at the wilderness of suffering through which we have already passed, and yet—who can tell what still lies before?

But what lesson did the South need! and how long has it been continued! Both sections needed to be made to feel the chastising hand of the God of justice and of the poor, so heavily and so long for the monstrous crime and the inhumanity of slavery, that they would forever cast it from them.

It was not meet that the war should end with the brief campaign which it is estimated might have crushed the rebellion in its incipiency, had the North sprung to arms at the first signs of an armed insurrection at the South, and when a kind of "order" might apparently have been restored at not one-thousandth part of the cost in life and treasure we have already suffered.

No. We can better appreciate the value of anything when we have labored and suffered to gain it.—Liberty will henceforth be worth more to us at the North. We know what was paid for it, and will watch, and guard, and protect it with its "price"—"eternal vigilance;" and we know the antagonism and deadly hostility of Slavery.

And the South promises to learn well this lesson of Providence, having reaped the bitter fruits of secession and rebellion to maintain her darling Slavery until she is glad to see all go out together once and forever!

Hiawatha Union Sentinel, March 10, 1865.

SEVEN

~

Politics and Prosperity

*A*s the foregoing letters demonstrate, Kansas's soldiers had little patience for, as Samuel Ayers put it, the "traitors in our midst." Ayers was able to find some honor in Southerners who had the courage to openly advocate and fight for their beliefs, but little admiration for those "northern sympathizers" who hid behind professions of loyalty. As he wrote in mid-1863, "of all the low mean and contemptible beings in the world such men are the most base and vile for they have not the manhood to come out as men should and publicly avough their real sentiments but secretly in the dark do all they can to supplant that government that for years has fostered them protected their rights and secured to them every advantage that a good and wholsom government could secure to any nation."[1] For many Northerners, but especially for those willing to sacrifice their lives to defend their country, opponents of the war trod a fine line between honest opposition and treason. Although soldiers like Samuel Ayers wrote of their disgust with the activities of copperheads, opponents of the war had a much quieter presence in the state than in other regions of the Union.

There was, however, persecution of Democrats, largely over issues of freedom of the press. In Leavenworth, for example, Daniel R. Anthony killed the editor of the *Leavenworth Herald* in June 1861 for "printing supposedly unpatriotic remarks." Eight months later, after another Democratic paper was started in town, a mob attacked the offices of the *Leavenworth Daily Inquirer* for criticizing the administration of President Lincoln. However, the editor of the *Leavenworth Daily Conservative,* whose press printed the opposition paper, persuaded the mob not to destroy its offices. In June 1862 the editor of the *Daily Inquirer* was arrested and released without incident. Other Democrats complained of another type of harassment—intimidation at the polls.[2]

Issues of loyalty were also tied to economic policies. Many Missourians, for instance, complained that jayhawkers stripped them of their property after accusing them of disloyalty. Similarly, if one suddenly appeared to be too prosperous, it might lead to suspicion that greed was a stronger motivator than the cause. And there was ample opportunity to prosper from the business of war. As the *Neosho Valley Register* noted, "Financially, the existence of the present war has proved a godsend to Kansas. Our farmers now find a ready market for all their surplus produce—money is plenty and business proportionately lifely."[3] And this difference was stark for Kansans. At the time of the 1860 census, Kansas residents had a per capita income of only $84, just slightly more than half that of free residents in the United States.[4] However, situated on the frontier, Kansas was an important military supply post both supporting the war effort and facilitating overland trade further west. Heavy government purchasing persuaded many Kansans to move from agriculture to raising stock due to the increased demand for cattle, mules, and horses.[5] Towns such as Leavenworth, Atchison, and Fort Scott boomed due to the war, and the war's effects were astounding. In 1860, Kansas had 1.8 million acres in farms; by 1865, it had 3.5 million acres. In 1860, its farms were valued at $12.3 million dollars; by 1865, their value had soared to $24.8 million. The value of all property in Kansas in 1860 was $31.3 million dollars; by 1865, that value had more than doubled to $72.2 million dollars.[6] Indeed, although fraught with fear and terror, wartime nonetheless provided a welcome economic contrast to the drought and hard times of the territorial period.

Prosperity was not the only marker of the transition from peace to war. In 1854, when Kansas was organized, the proslavery faction was dominant in the territory. However, with each passing year, the Democratic Party's fortunes waned as those of the newly formed Republican Party rose. Perhaps the best evidence of Kansas's ideological affiliation during the war resides in the fact that the two most notorious proslavery Democrats of the territorial period, Sheriff Samuel Jones and Judge Samuel Lecompte, joined the Republican Party.[7] As the migration of Jones and Lecompte to the opposition demonstrates, there was little incentive for being a Democrat in Kansas in the 1860s. In truth, the Democratic Party in Kansas simply could not recover from the inept prewar administrations of Presidents Pierce and Buchanan. Their Kansas policy had been interpreted by territorial residents as proslavery and unresponsive to popular opinion. Furthermore, the party alienated even more citizens with its economic policies. Buchanan's land policy, for instance, had shown scant sympathy for cash-poor territorial residents.[8] As a result, the Republican Party quickly came to dominate Kansas. And while there was a definite political struggle within the state, it was an intraparty squabble as conservative Republicans maneuvered for place, prestige, and patronage with the radical faction of the party.

By the midterm election of 1862, the Republican Party was divided. Senator James H. Lane cast such a large shadow over the state that there was little room for Kansas's other ambitious men. As Lane controlled the official Republican Party, anti-Lane Republicans united as the Union Party. Kansas Democrats opted not to put forward a slate of candidates in the election but were reluctant to fade away. To preserve their identity as Democrats, they merely put forward a simple slogan, "the Union as it was," and consequently garnered little support. With the

Democrats a nonfactor in 1862 and with the splinter Republicans having little influence, Thomas Carney, the candidate backed by the regular Republican Party, won the governor's seat by almost five thousand votes.[9]

In local politics, Lane's influence in the state was at its lowest ebb in 1864 due to a variety of factors. His interference with Governor Carney's efforts to organize a home guard, for instance, had backfired in the aftermath of the 1863 Lawrence massacre when the absence of adequate border security proved devastating for the town. Nonetheless, military events greatly aided Lane and his friends. In late September 1864, Confederate general Sterling Price moved into Missouri and the Kansas militia was called out to pursue him. Gubernatorial nominee Samuel J. Crawford volunteered for service as an aide-de-camp and participated in the pursuit. Although the anti-Lane candidates were optimistic about their chances beforehand, the resultant publicity from the pursuit of Price lifted Lane and his favored candidates to victory in the state elections.[10]

On a national level, with Abraham Lincoln under siege within his own party, Kansas catapulted into the spotlight with the circulation of the Pomeroy circular of early 1864. His own ambitions for the White House thwarted in 1860 with the nomination of the lesser-known Lincoln, Secretary of the Treasury Salmon P. Chase of Ohio put forth his own name for the presidency once more. Kansas senator Samuel Pomeroy chaired the national executive committee organized to support the Chase candidacy, and he suffered unwanted publicity when the version of the circular with his name attached to it was leaked to the press. As a senator, Pomeroy ought to have benefited from his position, but with Lincoln favoring Lane to such a degree, Pomeroy actually had little patronage at his disposal. As such, it is hardly surprising that Kansas's other senator yearned for a changing of the guard.

During the presidential contest of 1864, for most Kansans there was only one option. As Brigadier General Powell Clayton wrote shortly before the presidential election, "at this juncture, it is the duty of all Patriots, independent of past party predilections, to vote for Lincoln and Johnson."[11] As had happened during the election of 1862, Kansas did not have much copperhead activity, but it did have a divided Republican Party. In September 1864 the Republican state convention met in Topeka on the eighth while the Republican Union state convention, an anti-Lane organization, met in the same city on the thirteenth. Both claimed to represent the state's Republicans, but because the latter accepted Democratic support, many observers dismissed it as copperhead in orientation.[12] Ultimately, the Republican Union state convention supported the reelection of Abraham Lincoln. Angered by this decision, the convention splintered yet again and a faction met as the Radical Democrats later that day, urging Lincoln to reject the nomination so that "loyal men" could support the party. This group chose Pomeroy and Charles Robinson, another Lane rival, as delegates to the anti-Lincoln convention, held in Cincinnati.[13]

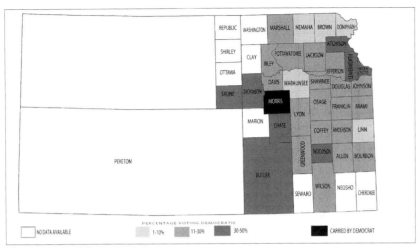

Electoral Map of Kansas, 1864

In 1864 the Democrats did not select candidates and endorsed the Union Republicans once more. By this time, the party had neither a real organization nor a significant newspaper, yet the state was home to an estimated eight thousand to ninety-five hundred Democrats.[14] Despite so many Democrats, a divided state Republican Party, and a cadre of anti-Lincoln Republicans, the people of Kansas knew their own minds. Supportive of Abraham Lincoln's administration and his goals, especially the elimination of slavery, they voted overwhelmingly for the president. In fact, in their first presidential election, Kansas's vote was the most decisive of all the Northern states, with 79.2 percent of voters choosing Lincoln over his Democratic opponent.

DECRYING THE "DEPART IN PEACE" DOCTRINE

Located in Junction City, just south of Fort Riley, the Union *was concerned about the lack of loyalty allegedly revealed by its rival newspaper, the* Kansas Frontier. *As this 1861 editorial demonstrates, other presses noticed the contretemps. Indeed, the* Wabaunsee Patriot *presaged the events of five months later, when loyalty concerns spilled more than just ink. On March 10, 1862, soldiers stationed at Fort Riley attacked the office of the* Kansas Frontier; *five days later, they destroyed it and forced its editor to enlist.*

NO HALF-WAY HOUSE.

The *Union* and *Frontier* newspapers, at Junction City, are having quite a warm time, by way of variety, the trouble, it seems, growing out of a charge by the Union that the Frontier editor was a traitor and in the habit of promulgating traitorous sentiments. We trust that some good may come of the discussion, notwithstanding it may have been called up more with a view of influencing the approaching election than any thing else. Both editors are candidates for office and respectively run on opposing tickets. We should be glad to see the Frontier change its course, somewhat. Its extreme sensitiveness on the Slavery question argues badly, and the solicitude it manifests for the "rights" of rebels in arms against the government is rather out of place, considering circumstances. Let rebels take care of themselves, neighbor. If an enemy stood with drawn blade, ready to sever your windpipe at a single thrust, we hardly think you would be over fastideous in the matter of hurting him and shedding his blood. No, the issue would be, fight or submit. If he has rights, let him look after them himself; it's quite clear, they have no claims upon you. Now, we would not be so uncharitable as to call you a traitor, but if we had no better patriots to stand by the flag, we would have long ere this been the crouching vassals of a proscriptive and lordly South. There can be no reserve; there is no middle ground. Your influence, directly or indirectly, must go to promote the interests one side or the other, for or against the government. Are you sure your position is not one to encourage the rebels, and to discourage men upon our own side? Do you not exert an influence which rebels understand to be favorable to granting their claims of independence—favorable to their being allowed to "depart in peace"—and while they have their bloody fingers upon the throttle of our government, favorable to their sinking the knife to the vital flow? Is not your position that of the soldier who goes out to battle for our flag, yet who stands back in the rear and clamors for the "rights" of the enemy? He regrets that the war against the enemy cannot be carried on with a better feeling—more in a spirit of love—he loads and fires blank cartridges, shouts that he is in favor of a "vigorous prosecution of the war," yet creates anything but unity of sentiment and concert of action by his counsels and influence, and by his actions, which speak louder than words, says to those in advance of him, "Boys, I think we had better lay down our arms, and let them depart in peace," which if logically translated, means, let them ride over us rough shod, let them transfer their government to Washington, and by the aid of the spiritless, lilliputian element at the North, garrison their soldiery in every city and town.—This is the legitimate tendency of the "depart in peace" doctrine, which many weak kneed brothers advocate indirectly, if not in so many words.

Wabaunsee Patriot, October 19, 1861

THE BOND SWINDLE

The Truth Teller *was published daily in Topeka under the slogan "Truth is Mighty and will Prevail." Editor Josiah C. Trask was a fervent antislavery advocate who*

came to Kansas Territory in 1857 from Massachusetts. He worked at the Herald
of Freedom, *taking over that paper and changing its name to the* Kansas State
Journal *in 1861, and was the printer of the state laws. These two editorials
concerned the political firestorm that broke out over bonds the state sold to raise
funds. Trask died in the Quantrill raid on Lawrence, in 1863.*

February 24, 1862.

READ AND REFLECT.

Word has gone forth to the people of Kansas, that the State has been swindled
in the sale of Bonds, and that a committee has been set to work to investigate the
fraud, this may be all right and proper. If the State has been or is thought to be
swindled, it is the duty of the Legislature to investigate the matter. But are the
people of Kansas aware of the disgraceful course pursued by the Investigating
Committee. We opine not. Let us give them a little insight into the business.

It is reasonable to suppose that men under oath would set about the work of
investigation with the utmost firmness, giving an impartial report of the evidence,
and above all, permitting the persons accused to vindicate their character, if they
could so do. But such was not their course. When the Committee are finely in operation, Gen. Lane, to the neglect of the interest of Kansas in the Senate, makes his
appearance in town, and straightway the committee are closetted with him, con-
cocting plans to blast the character of our State officers. A beaten path is soon visible
between the committee room and that of Lane, like unto a deer trail from the forest
to a salt lick, and the committee receive and obey orders and instructions from him,
as readily and implicitly, as if the one were Commander-in-Chief of an army and
the other that army itself. He is permitted to testify in the matter—or rather, to give
vent to a quantity of his pent up spleen, hatred and malice—and that evidence (God
save the word!) is published to the world as incontrovertible evidence that the State
officers should be impeached, and their characters ruined forever; while, at the same
time, testimony favorable to the officers is suppressed by the committee; and, owing
to the whirlwind of excitement which sways the Legislature, the committee cannot
be compelled to put forth the suppressed evidence.

This unfair testimony goes before the House, and that body is crowded to
a vote without time to reflect, even though reason and wholesome discussions
must be stifled in the operation. The members, one after another, vote unanimously for impeachment, although many of them feel in their hearts that they
are doing a terrible wrong, to at least, some of the accused. But they have not
the moral courage to say so; for the public mind has been prejudiced, and he
who votes contrary to public mind, will be assailed with the charge of complicity with robbers and swindlers.

The work being accomplished as far as the House is concerned, the Senate is now looked to. Two thirds of that body are necessary to complete the work, and it contains too many members who are not sufficiently pliable to answer the desired purpose. Lane again sends forth his fiat, and members are ejected from their seats and others substituted in their places, as coolly and deliberately as old household furniture is displaced to make room for new. And this is Constitution, law, right, justice, violated, because a demagogue, a debauchee, a murderer, says men are his enemies, and must be punished.

Is it not time for honest members of the Legislature to pause and reflect.—Will they continue to bow down to the tyrant, public opinion, which is for the time being swayed by an excitement, the work of misrepresentation and falsehood. Will they continue to obey the behests of such a man as Jim Lane, to gratify his private revenge, when their innermost conscience tell them they are perpetrating a great injustice? Let them not give themselves to regret, in the future, that they permitted themselves to be blinded and carried away in a brief moment of excitement, by men who are bent upon accomplishing their designs, though the best interests of the State are ruined.

February 25, 1862.

THE GREAT SWINDLE.

Some persons are very industrious, trying to make it appear that a great swindle has been perpetrated by Messrs. Hillyer, Robinson and Stevens. What are the facts? Judge Ewing, the Leavenworth and Lawrence Banks and others, were offering Kansas Bonds at 40 cents on the dollar. While such was the fact, these gentlemen, by some management, obtained 60 cents for the State, over and above all expenses; and Stevens proposes if that is not legal and satisfactory he will make it up to 70 cents. Where, then, is the swindle? The truth is, Mr. Stevens and the officers obtained more for the State than any other men could obtain, and should be entitled to praise rather than censure, if we understand the facts. Had they not effected a sale, the interests on the Bonds would not have been paid, no money would have been received for the incidental or other expenses of the Legislature, and State Bonds would have been worthless. Look at both sides and then condemn.

Truth Teller, February 24 and 25, 1862.

WAR AND PROSPERITY

Located only five miles from the Missouri border, Fort Scott had been abandoned and its buildings sold at government auction in the territorial period. When the war began, the army moved back and transformed Fort Scott into a busy hub. A military prison, an icehouse, a blacksmith shop, warehouses, and other necessities sprang up, as did more than forty miles of fortifications. Ultimately, the Quartermaster's Department would supply all troops within forty miles through Fort Scott, which housed regiments from Kansas, Wisconsin, Ohio, Iowa, Indiana, Colorado, and the Indian Home Guard.

PROSPERITY OF KANSAS.

While the war has produced a decline of business in nearly every other loyal State, its effect on Kansas has been to increase our prosperity fourfold. It is now more than a year since hostilities first broke out in Missouri, and during all the intervening time, there has been one constant stream of emigration into Kansas. Not only has the increase in population been great, but nearly every family has brought with it a quantity of stock—horses, mules, cattle, sheep and swine, from Missouri, now constitutes a large portion of the material wealth of our State.

Military operations have also aided us largely. At least a million dollars have been disbursed by the Paymasters, in this Department, of which a large proportion is still retained among us. Another million has been issued from the Quartermaster and Commissary departments, for cattle, horses, mules, grain, &c. Hundreds of men—mechanics and laborers—receive profitable employment from Government officers. As nearly all of this is additional to our usual business operations, its effect is plainly perceptible in increased energy and activity everywhere, but more especially in the eastern and south eastern portions of the State.

The town building "mania" which raged so extensively a few years ago, has entirely died out. Men of means prefer investing their money where they have a prospect of an immediate return, rather than trust to the chances of a visionary fortune, in the dim future. This concentration of capital, will soon lead to the establishment of large manufacturing interests, one of the surest roads to public and private prosperity. We can look forward with confidence, that the day is not far distant, when Kansas will take her place among the leading States of the Union.

Fort Scott Bulletin, June 21, 1862.

STUTELY STAFFORD NICHOLS AND THE OPPORTUNITIES OF WAR

Originally from Vermont, Stutely Stafford Nichols was reluctant to join a regiment when his personal prospects were on the rise, reflecting the feelings of many Kansans who had struggled financially in the territorial period.

Lea'th City, Kan. Aug. 27th/62

Dear Brother,

. . . I suppose you have often wondered why I did not join the Army. Well, I will tell you all about it. "Three years or during the War" seems like a long time for a man of my age and in my circumstances to be taken from his business, but I have felt all the while that I was not doing my duty to my country in remaining an idle spectator while the best blood of the Nation was being poured out in defense of the one great principle for which we are fighting. When the last call for Volunteers came out, I thought that I would enlist, although I was then making and am still making, more money than at any time previous to this War, but just at that time I had a slight bilious attack and when I had recovered an order was issued for the enrollement of the Militia. Of course I enrolled with the rest, but three or four of us commenced the organization of what is known here as an independent Militia Company, and have got the company organized. When every-thing is complete, we shall tender our services for the defense of the State. . . . As Kansas will have to call on other States for men, unless her own citizens nearly all turn out to defend the border, it is thought that a few Regs. formed in the same way of ours, would be of as much service to the Government as though we were in the regular service. . . .

Yours as ever,
S.S. Nichols

~

Leavenworth, March 29th 1863

Dear Brother:

. . . We have never been called into service here in Kansas, and I don't know that we ever will be. Everything is quiet on the border at this time, but how long it will remain so is hard to tell. It is rumored that Price has crossed the Mississippi and that his friends in some of the upper counties of Mo. have raised the Secession flag. Kansas, as you already know, is a great place for excitement and especially at such a time as this. The Copperheads here have a hard road to travel but if they were strong enough they would drive all the Union men out as they did in fifty six. I believe we have about as much to fear from the Copperheads in the loyal States as we have from the Rebels. . . . That wool speculation of yours was quite a nice thing. If you had a large am't of it your profits would be great if you had it now. Farmers who are in the wool business at this time will do very well in spite of heavy taxes. I hope father has a large lot of sheep on hand. I am in the fruit tree business still, and will give you an account of my business when I finish sales this spring. Business of all kinds is pretty good in Kansas. Hoping to hear from you again soon, I remain, your affectionate brother.

S. S. Nichols

~

Camp Jennison near Ft. Leavenworth, Nov. 9th, 1863

Dear Brother,

... New Orleans will furnish a wide field for speculation, and if you should strike a "lead" you will become a millionaire in a very short time. This War is making rich men poor and poor men rich. Well, what is your opinion in regard to the War now? The Telegraph yesterday brought us the glorious news that the old flag was flying over the walls of Sumter. If this be true it is cheering indeed. As you see by the heading of my letter, I am in the service at last. I recruited a part of a Co. for the 15th, and should have filled it if they had given a little more time, but they were in such a hurry to raise the Reg't that they made us recruiting officers consolidate our men. ... My address will be, Co. "I" 15th Ka's Vol' Cavalry Ft. Leavenworth, Ka's. Hoping to hear from you again soon, I remain as ever, your affectionate brother,

S. S. Nichols

Stutely Stafford Nichols Papers, Kansas State Historical Society.

KANSAS MEN "ARE STEALING THEMSELVES
RICH IN THE NAME OF LIBERTY"

Along the Kansas-Missouri border, some Kansans were determining the loyalty of Missourians and, if finding them lacking, taking their property. On June 26, 1863, General Thomas Ewing spoke against jayhawking, warning that his patience with that behavior had run out.

GEN. EWING'S POLICY.

On Friday last Gen. Ewing, in command of this Military District, made a speech in Olathe, Johnson County, which is reported in part in the Kansas City *Journal*.

I hope to soon have troops enough on the Missouri side not only to prevent raids into Kansas, but also to drive out or exterminate every band of guerrillas now haunting that region. I will keep a thousand men in saddle daily in pursuit of them; and will redden with their blood every road and bridle path of the border, until they infest it no more.

I mean, moreover, to stop with a rough hand all forays for plunder from Kansas into Missouri. The militia companies recently organized along the line, at the suggestion of the Governor and Gen. Blunt, and armed by the Government, will do good service in repelling invasion, and I shall be glad to have their aid. But they are authorized no more than other citizens to seize property of rebels or sympathizers on either side of the line. I will have property seized in the District only by order of officers in the service of the United States, who are responsible for abuse of discretion or violation of orders in making such seizures, and in disposing of property seized.

There are many men in Kansas who are stealing themselves rich in the name of Liberty. These men must find some other mode of giving effect to their patriotic zeal. As they want to kill rebels, let them join any old regiment, or either of the new ones about being raised. They can find in the service positions equal to their energy, daring and talent; and can adorn the service, and be honored in it. The Government will welcome them; it needs and has a right to the service of all men of enterprise who are at large, and it will not too closely discriminate against such men because of irregularities in the past.

But, whether they enter the service or not, I now notify them that they will be compelled to quit stealing, or get out of this District, or get me out of it. I mention this by way of an amicable understanding in the outset.

* * * * * *

Some men in the State, who are influential by reason of boldness, position or talent, have been long engaged in distorting the honest sentiment of the State, and giving respectability to robbery when committed against any whom *they* declare disloyal. They arrogate to themselves and their sympathisers, all the radical antislaveryism and genuine loyalty in Kansas. Under their aegis many of the worst men that ever vexed a civilized community have flocked and been protected. If a farmer came to Kansas originally from a slave State, and especially if he has good stock, he is in danger of being suspected, and if suspected by even the most suspicious of this sect, his stock is taken and sold, and put in the pockets of the vigilant patriots. Any citizen who denounces this mode of conducting the war, is regarded as a sympathiser, and politically unsound. They have refused to enter the service—the Administration is not radical enough—but they claim to be doing more service than the soldiers who abandon their homes and business, and, obedient to the orders of their Government, peril their lives in the front of battle.

Now, I propose, if these men do not enter the service of the United States and subject themselves to the discipline of the army, to get along without their help; and I fully expect to be able to punish rebels, their aiders and abetters on both sides of the line with as much severity as they have heretofore been punished by these men, and with the advantage in my favor of not harrassing harmless men, and turning over to the Government all property seized.

* * * * *

I am neither in favor of slavery, nor indifferent to it; but hate it and wish it utterly destroyed. Before the war, I felt bound by the Constitution and laws of the country to tolerate the institution I abhorred. I now rejoice from my heart of hearts that we shall be compensated for all the precious blood shed in this rebellion, by sweeping from the land this atrocious and intolerent despotism. I will go to the verge of my authority to give effect to the emancipation policy of the Government and the Department; and shall never remain in command of the District an hour to execute any policy at war with the spirit of liberty I revere.

Leavenworth Daily Conservative, July 2, 1863.

GOVERNMENT CORRUPTION IN KANSAS

With the war machine gearing up, funds flowed into Kansas as regiments moved through the state's many forts. With this increase of government business came concerns about men enriching themselves to the detriment of the war effort. An early abolitionist who came to Oskaloosa in 1862, John Wesley Roberts addresses this issue in these two editorials. Located in Jefferson Country, about twenty miles northeast of Topeka, between Fort Leavenworth and Fort Riley, Oskaloosa was founded in 1855.

July 25, 1863.

HOW IS IT?

Sam. Wood, in the Councel Grove Press, tells of a recent visit made by himself to Fort Scott to attend the sale of confiscated stock. After stating the sale of cattle was stopped by order of Gen. Schofield, and that the horses on hand were nearly worthless—all the good ones minus the ranche—and that there were but 530 head of cattle, one-fourth of which were bulls and the balance old cows and young calves, with "scarcely a saleable creature in the whole lot," he adds:

"Now it would not do to suppose that all the good, saleable cattle had been taken out and sold. It won't do to suppose that an officer, when he confiscates 100 head, more or less, of cattle, quietly sells all that will sell, and drives in a few bulls and old colds [cows]. We must suppose that the stock at Fort Scott is just the stock confiscated; no more, no less; but to our mind, the rebels are overdoing the bull business a little. Can it be that the only cattle that rebels raise are bulls and old cows that no one else will have?"

What constitutes a rebel at Fort Scott? The evidence of loyalty is *poverty.* A man that has nothing, his honesty is unquestioned; but if he lives in Missouri, and owns a good horse, or some cattle, there is no evidence in the world by which he can prove himself loyal, and save his property. Men are now at Fort Scott, working by the day for a living as loyal as Gen. Blunt himself, who have had every hoof confiscated, or jayhawked, which is about the same thing, for all the benefit it is to Government. Good men at Fort Scott, admit that wholesale swindling is going on, but deny that Gen. Blunt is privy to it. Our opinion is that Gen. Blunt cannot be ignorant of it, and if he cannot stop it at once and forever, he is unfit for his position. What a pity it is that Gen. Ewing's District does not extend thirty miles further south, so as to take all Kansas, that is settled.—There is no danger of any officer in the District of the Frontier getting into limbo, on account of cattle speculation, if we wait for "one without sin to cast the first stone."

It is our deliberate opinion, and has been for months past, that when the day of reckoning comes, and "righteous revelations" are made, it will be found that some asses have been covered with lion's skins, and that when the covering is removed the beast will appear in all its deformity.

That there have been enormous swindlings, base corruption and gigantic frauds committed in this region of Uncle Sam's dominions since the war broke out, no man of even half discernment can fail to see; and that those who ought to have put a stop to the villainy have not done so, is quite as plain. Something is wrong and somebody is to blame. Who is it? Time will reveal these matters. Then look out!

October 1, 1864.

WHERE THE MONEY GOES.

We have repeatedly spoken of the shameful waste of the funds of the government in this hour of the nation's greatest need. We see by the Topeka *Record* that our remarks have hit the nail on the head. That paper speaks of the matter as "twaddle." Why? Because the editor is one of the very men we hit, who is robbing the treasury by receiving a salary for which he makes no just return. He says it is necessary for the military population of Kansas to be enrolled, whether there is any draft in the State or not, in order that it may be known how few or how many men we are justly responsible for. Very well. But what is the use of paying *three* sets of hands for doing what *one* set could *easily* accomplish? Why don't you answer that, Mr. Record?

You say in large congressional districts the law provides for more than one set of officers. Certainly, where there is a *necessity* for more. But is that the case in Kansas? Every man of ordinary intelligence *knows* it is not. Take your own case. You get $1,300 a year and perquisites, and you have not performed $50 worth of work per annum. A clerk, we have no doubt, will do all you have done for that sum, and glad of the chance. Are you not taking something from the government then without returning a just equivalent? And have you not enough intelligence to know that the government *needs* every cent of that $1,250 and perquisites you take from it annually for nothing? And do you not know that this is no better than downright robbery in the essence of the thing? Can you be a *true* friend of the government while you are thus robbing it, in its hour of utmost peril, of the very life-blood of its existence? Answer these questions fairly and honestly. Meet them as a patriot and a man—*if you can.*

All your loud professions of loyalty and radicalism amount to nothing with thinking and honest men while you thus belie your words by your acts. It is easy enough to *talk* patriotism. "Words are but wind," But it is quite another thing to *act* patriotism by giving up a hold upon an office, the pay of which is a shameless robbery of the treasury; *Do* something if you wish *any* honest man to believe in the genuineness of your loud-mouthed loyalty.

And what we say of you, we say of the whole class of which you are one. All the men who are holding *needless* offices in Kansas and getting pay for doing next to nothing, are no better than thieves and robbers. They are getting rich off the blood and tears of the nation. They are *bushwhackers upon the national treasury,* and they will yet become a stench in the nostrils of the people.

You officers get your pay—for nothing—and who foots the bill? The people, your neighbors and fellow-citizens. You are robbing them, Morally, you had just as well go into their houses and take the money from them. Of every dollar they invest in stamps, in high prices for living, one half goes to pay the *bushwhackers upon the treasury.*

Think of this, citizens of Kansas,—One-half of all the expenses of the war goes to the useless officeholders and plunderers. Remember that when you pay one dollar to the government, fifty cents of that sum goes into the pocket of a plunderer. You are patriotic, you are noble and generous. You give freely because you believe that what you gave goes to sustain the government and carry on the war. But it is not so in full. Only half of what you give goes for that purpose; the other half is swallowed up by the miserable wretches who are growing rich out of the war, and the troubles of their country, and are trying to *prolong the conflict that they may grow richer.*

And who is responsible for this state of things in Kansas? *James H. Lane.* You have all heard him speak, and in his speeches *boast* that *he got the offices for his friends.* You know this is one of the *burdens* of his speeches, and we need not repeat the fact. Then, so far as you are concerned you are paying fifty cents on the dollar on the *extra* price of your living, and on all the revenue tax you pay, to support the office-holders of Lane in Kansas, Lane himself declaring the fact that *he* has "got the offices."

Now, we ask, do you intend to do this any longer? Are you so foolish as to tax yourselves so heavily to keep up a brood of blood-suckers around you, who get rich at your expense, and then snub you because you are poor? Do you intend to let these monsters fatten off of your toil, that they may become aristocratic, and sneer at you as "poor dogs?"

No, you will not do it! You are made of different stuff. You have not braved the perils incident to the settlement of this State; you have not killed of[f] one aristocracy, that built upon Slavery and human blood, to build up another aristocracy founded upon robbery of the government—of yourselves—and the blood and tears of your friends! No, you will not do it; and we ask you not to be deceived by any one. Believe no demagogue, but take the *facts* and make your own conclusions. Stop the stealing and robbery, and you will stop the war—it will speedily be ended by the crushing of the rebellion. You believe this; you feel, you know it to be true. Then strike for your country, when you can, and let your ballots tell to the confusion of the plunderers.

Oskaloosa Independent, July 25, 1863; October 1, 1864.

QUARTERMASTER'S REPORT, FORT LEAVENWORTH, 1863

Named for Colonel Henry Leavenworth, a veteran of the War of 1812, Fort Leavenworth was established in 1827 and is the oldest continuously active army post west of the Mississippi River. The fort was an important staging area for moving needed supplies through the western theater of war, and Camp Lincoln was established there to train Kansas volunteers. On July 17, 1862, President Lincoln signed legislation authorizing the purchase of land to create national cemeteries for soldiers who died serving their country. That year, twelve national cemeteries were established, two of which were in Kansas, at Fort Leavenworth and Fort Scott.

QUARTERMASTER'S OFFICE,
Fort Leavenworth, September 21, 1863.

General M. C. MEIGS,
Quartermaster-General, U. S. Army, Washington, D.C.:

GENERAL: . . . I have the honor to report that during the year ending 30th of June, 1863, I was stationed at this place, attending to the various duties pertaining to the quartermaster's department at this depot. . . .

During the year I have promptly furnished the necessary transportation for all the troops, subsistence, quartermaster's, ordnance, and medical stores required for all the troops serving in Utah, New Mexico, Colorado, Nebraska, Kansas, the Indian country west of the State of Arkansas as far south as the Arkansas River, the two western tiers of counties of the State of Missouri north of the thirty-eighth parallel and south of the Missouri River, and the western tier of counties of the States of Missouri and Arkansas south of the thirty-eighth parallel and to the Arkansas River. I have provided all the quartermaster's supplies, clothing, &c., for all this vast extent of country, except Utah and New Mexico, and for the latter Territory I supplied 600 cavalry horses and 100 wagons and teams complete. With railroads and water communications the supply of the section of country referred to would be but a small undertaking, but the magnitude and labor of the duties I have performed can be better understood when you recollect that the troops scattered over this vast extent of country have been supplied by the common road wagon over unimproved roads, obstructed by high water in summer and by ice in winter, and the most of them passing through a perfect wilderness, where there is no forage or other supplies except grass. I say this is no small undertaking when you take the above circumstances into consideration, together with the distances of the points to be supplied from this depot. That you may understand this, I will give you some of the principal points to which I have had to send large quantities of supplies and their distances from this depot, with the weight of stores sent to each, viz:

Post or station.	Number of miles from Fort Leavenworth	Stores transported (pounds)
Salt Lake City, Utah Terr	1,837	662,720
Fort Union, N. Mex	735	6,364,263
Fort Laramie, Nebr	600	832,134
Fort Lyon, Colo	500	440,900
Fort Larned, Kans	266	811,956
Fort Kearny, Nebr	275	592,206
Fort Scott, Kans	125 ⎫	
Fort Gibson, Cherokee Nation	300 ⎭	8,106,501
To other posts and stations		1,801,664

A much larger business has been done by other officers at other points, but the facilities for doing business and the number of officers to perform the labor and divide the responsibility have been in the same proportion to the magnitude of the business. I do not say it with any spirit of fault-finding or complaint, but all the duties of this depot, comprising every description of business transacted by the quartermaster's department, have been performed by myself, with no officer to share the labor and responsibility except one military store-keeper in charge of clothing. There was shod at this depot during the year 11,101 mules and 5,058 horses; 2,500 wagons and ambulances have been repaired in the shops under my charge. In addition to my other duties I have conducted two very large Government farms, on which was cultivated and secured for the use of your department 2,200,000 pounds of timothy hay, 749 bushels of corn, 650 bushels of oats, besides furnishing pasturage for a large number of public animals. The repair of tents, wagon covers, harness, tent poles, &c., I have no account of, but

they have been large. Transportation has been furnished for the supplies and
equipage of a large number of troops moving from one point to another. Means
furnished was Government wagons, which returned to this depot, and I have no
account of the number of troops so transported. The troops in the section of
country I have had control over have all been promptly supplied, and no troops
have ever been better supplied, so far as the quantity and quality of the supplies
are concerned. Their means of transportation, clothing, equipage, &c., have
been excellent and the character of their artillery and cavalry horses superior.
I have worked hard, have accomplished a great deal under the circumstances,
every branch of my business, to its minutest particular, having been conducted
under my own immediate personal superintendence, and I hope at least to
obtain credit for industry, attention to duty, and at all times having the best
interest of the service in view and laboring constantly to that end.

Very respectfully, your obedient servant,

L. C. EASTON

Major and Quartermaster, U. S. Army.

The War of the Rebellion: A Compilation of the Official Records of the Union and Confederate Armies, ser. 1, vol. 53
(Washington, DC: Government Printing Office, 1902), 570–71.

"WHO IS LOYAL?"

*The following is less an editorial than a personal disagreement publicly aired, but
it does raise the question of how to demonstrate loyalty in wartime, revealing the
tensions between those who served in the military and those who did not. Although
editor S. N. Wood charged rival editor R. B. Lockwood with disloyalty, Lockwood
became mayor of Council Grove in 1870. On the Neosho River, the city is in central
Kansas, about 170 miles west of the Missouri River and about 40 miles south of
Fort Riley.*

WHO IS LOYAL?

Examine the Council Grove *Press* of the last nine months, and see if the pen-
dency of its editorials and extracts do not tend to disparage and weaken the government in the eyes of the people.

We find the above the above in the Smoky Hill circular, from the pen of R. B.
Lockwood of this place. And who is it who thus questions our loyalty to the government? A man too cowardly by nature and education to raise a hand in defence of
his country. While we were for two years in the army battling for our government,
Lockwood was in Council Grove, afraid to call his soul his own. He listened to treason every day upon our streets, without the courage or manhood to once rebuke it.

After we came home he allowed an avowed rebel to shout his foul treason in his face. and strike, and spit upon him as a "damned union man," and did not resent it. He would not consent to even prosecute the traitor for a breach of the peace. About the same time he cautioned us against talking so plainly and avowing our union sentiments so strongly, as our life was in danger, or our office would at least be destroyed. Our reply was "Morris county must be a union county."

When we came home from the army it was a notorious fact that union men dared not speak their sentiments here, The reputation of our place was that of a "sink-hole of treason." To-day we are as loyal a county as there is in the state. No thanks, however, to Lockwood for it. No one could be more humbly non-committal than he was when the emissaries of treason were splurging about here, and giving the impression abroad that our county was a nest of traitors.

In a locality where treason is the popular sentiment, no one would be a bigger traitor than he, but he would be one of the very last to go into the army on either side.

Council Grove Press, July 2, 1864.

THE DEATH OF PRESIDENT LINCOLN

This moving eulogy of Abraham Lincoln comes from an agricultural journal and praises him as a man from a background similar to its readership's. The editorial also reflects early convictions that John Wilkes Booth must have been directed to assassinate the president by officials of high rank in the Confederate States of America.

THE DEATH OF PRESIDENT LINCOLN.

Since the last issue of the FARMER our country has been called to mourn as few nation's have ever mourned before. On the night of April 14th, President Lincoln was shot in his private box at Ford's Theatre, and Secretary Seward was stabbed at his own residence. The President died the next morning at 7:20. Mr. Seward still lives, and will probably recover. The murderer of the President was Booth, the tragedian. The assassin of Secretary Seward is not positively known. Neither have as yet been taken. The inspiration of the deed, no doubt, came from Richmond. The plot was a complicated one, and included other high officials.

The grief of the nation is deep and sincere. It is not "official" mourning, but a real personal sorrow. No President since Washington, has ever endeared himself to the people as President Lincoln had. We had passed through the fires together, and felt bound to him by that peculiar tie which common trials create. No defeat of the war has spread such universal gloom. Each man feels it as a personal bereavement, for we had learned to look to our President as a personal friend—party lines were well nigh obliterated, and all truly loyal men began to place implicit confidence in his judgment and integrity. Added to our personal grief, is our anxiety for the nation which has lost its head and guide. Will the storms drift us into dangerous places now the pilot is gone? And our grief and anxiety are deepened by the method of the President's death. We had supposed the knife of the assassin was laid aside in this land of the free. We seem to be rolled suddenly back several centuries, to the days when despotism and anarchy struggled for the supremacy. But it is only other exhibition of the hate and lawlesness which the slave power has developed. These are the last and greatest of a long list of martyrs who have fallen for freedom in our nation. The course of the country will not be hindered. The nation that has borne the shock of armies will not quail before the assassin's knife. The slave power has simply shown its venom. True to the instincts of the viper, it has stung the hand that had crushed out its life. But the national cause will not be affected. "The viper bites the file—let him bite on."

President Lincoln rose from the people. It is fitting that the people should mourn his loss. From a laborer he rose to the highest position in the world. But from first to last, he retained that unaffected simplicity of manners and purity of life which always characterize the truly great.

Kansas Farmer, May 1865, 73.

EIGHT

The Continuing Mission

*T*HE OFFICIAL OPENING of Kansas to white settlement, in 1854, put pressure on Indian commissioner George W. Manypenny to settle Indian claims in the territory. From 1854 to 1855, Manypenny signed a number of treaties with tribes in eastern Kansas, including the Delawares, Shawnees, Kickapoos, Miamis, Wyandots, and Sauks and Foxes. With the lands given up by the Otoe-Missouris, Omahas, and Iowas in northern Kansas, over the course of two years the United States reduced Indian claims to Kansas land from 15 million acres to just over 1 million acres.[1] Although this was a significant clearing of claims in the territory, it would still not be enough for Kansans. By early 1863, officials were trying to remove even more Indians from the state, often to make room for railroad construction.[2] During the war, however, claims could command only minimal attention, because a different threat was on the horizon.

In the aftermath of the firing on Fort Sumter, Kansans feared a Confederate-Indian invasion, but the first American Indians who crossed the border were seeking succor, not conquest. With war imminent between the North and the South, American Indians caught in the middle had a choice to make: would they support the federal government, an often untrustworthy ally, or wager on a better outcome with the unknown Confederate States of America? When war broke out, the Union and the Confederacy responded distinctly to the challenge posed by Indian Territory. While the Union stopped disbursing tribal annuities and withdrew from its forts, the Confederacy sent officials to negotiate new treaties and recruit military forces.[3] In return for offers of protection and representation, Indians of the Five Civilized Tribes organized three regiments for the defense of Indian Territory: a Choctaw-Chickasaw regiment, a Creek-Seminole regiment, and a Cherokee regiment composed largely of Cherokee chief John Ross's supporters. In addition, Confederate colonel Stand Watie, a Cherokee, organized a second regiment of Cherokees opposed to Ross. Altogether, these regiments numbered five thousand men. By the end of the war, some ten thousand Indian troops had fought for the Confederacy.[4]

Although the Confederacy successfully courted these tribes and signed a July 1861 treaty, not all of them wanted to participate in the Americans' war. Most significantly, Opothleoholo, an important Creek leader, chose to remain loyal and led his followers north. He was pursued by Confederate Indian forces and Texas cavalry commanded by Colonel Douglas Cooper and, on November 19, they fought at Round Mountain, the first engagement of the Civil War in Indian Territory. Two more engagements at Chusto-Talasah and Chustenahlah followed. This last battle on December 26 resulted in devastating losses, forcing these loyal Indians to continue their exodus with scant supplies in the middle of a particularly severe winter. They would begin the new year in Kansas in desperate need of food, clothing, and medicine. By April, more than seven thousand Indians had sought refuge in the state.[5]

In June 1862, the Union sent an expedition of six thousand men—American Indians as well as Kansas and Wisconsin regiments—under Colonel William Weer of the Tenth Kansas Infantry, into Indian Territory in order to drive out Confederate forces and restore these refugee Indians to their homes. Initially, this expedition was successful: they captured Tahlequah, capital of the Cherokee nation, and were moving toward Fort Gibson, the most important fort in Indian Territory. However, led by Colonel Frederick Salomon of the Ninth Wisconsin Regiment, Weer's troops mutinied, and the white soldiers returned to Fort Scott, leaving the Indian regiments behind. Only the timely arrival of Brigadier General James Blunt resulted in the reinforcement of the abandoned Indian troops. Nonetheless, the Indian expedition was successful and resulted in the permanent occupation of the upper portion of Indian Territory.[6]

Once the Confederates had been driven out of the area of Indian Territory north of the Arkansas River, the Union organized the loyal Indians of the Cherokee, Creek, and Seminole nations into three regiments, each with one thousand men, for defense of their country. The Indian Home Guards were officered by white men. William A. Phillips of Kansas was active in organizing the regiments and was in command throughout the war. These regiments saw action at Locust Grove, Honey Springs, and Perryville in the Cherokee nation; Newtonia in Missouri; and Maysville and Prairie Grove in Arkansas. Among the most notable engagements in Indian Territory itself was that at Baxter Springs.

After the Lawrence massacre of August 21, 1863, William Quantrill headed south to spend the winter in Texas. On October 6, Union and Confederate forces met in Indian Territory at Baxter Springs. Quantrill led his men south along the Texas Road, killing two Union teamsters who had been posted there. One of Quantrill's columns led by David Poole encountered Union troops, largely African American soldiers, and killed many before they could reach the fort. At the fort, the Confederates attacked but were held off. Led by Quantrill, the second column approached from another direction, coming across a Union detachment escorting

Major General James Blunt to his new headquarters at Fort Smith. Quantrill's men killed seventy of the one hundred men in Blunt's detachment—shooting, stripping, robbing, and mutilating them—but Blunt and a few mounted men made it back to Fort Scott. Blunt was removed from command for his failure to protect his column (he, in turn, blamed the men for cowardice) but was reinstated with a sharply curtailed domain.[7] This Confederate victory has often been called the Baxter Springs massacre.

For American Indians, ultimately the war had a negative impact on their fate in America. Although as many members of the Five Civilized Tribes served in the Union army as served in the Confederate army, the federal government declared its treaties with the tribes to be void, forcing the tribes to negotiate new treaties that ceded the western part of Indian Territory to the United States.[8] For Kansas's Indians, the repercussions were equally grim. Without solid control in the region, by July 1864 full-scale war had broken out as Kiowas, Arapahos, and Comanches moved along the Santa Fe Trail, robbing people and killing eighteen of them. By September 1864, Major General Samuel Curtis, at Fort Leavenworth with the Army of the Border, was quite blunt in stating that he required "the bad Indians delivered up" and "wanted no peace till the Indians suffer more."[9]

And suffer they would, because the forays continued in 1865, with attacks largely along the overland line. These attacks proved to be deadly and represented a significant change in the character of the conflict between Kansans and Indian tribes. During the first four years of Kansas's statehood, 74 whites were killed by Indians; during the second four years, from 1865 to 1869, more than 250 were killed and hundreds more wounded. In 1867 alone, 128 people were killed. As a result of these deaths, Kansas governor Samuel Crawford pushed the federal government to act and when it did, he resigned to take command of the Nineteenth Kansas, a regiment raised specifically to combat the region's Indians.[10] By 1875 fewer than one thousand Indians remained in the state of Kansas.[11]

"THE CHEROKEES ARE ARMING AND ARE PREPARING TO INVADE KANSAS"

On July 12, 1861, Confederate colonel Stand Watie organized the First Cherokee Mounted Rifles. In August, Cherokee chief John Ross called a general assembly to meet at Tahlequah, where the Cherokees voted to join the Confederacy and submitted the treaty they signed to the national council for ratification. Indian agent George Cutler urged Commissioner of Indian Affairs William Dole to act swiftly, but his warning came only one week before the Cherokee national council declared war on the United States.

Topeka Oct 21st 1861

Dear Sir,

I have just returned from a visit to the borders of the Cherokee country, and find affairs there in a most deplorable condition. The Cherokees are arming and are preparing to invade Kansas. A body of 1,000 who were to have joined some 3,00 whites and in conjunction with them lay waste the Neosho valley failed to get to the place appointed in time; the whites burned the town of Humbolt and then retreated to Missouri. The next day the Cherokees came in, but found their alies had fled, they then sent a body of 5,00 under the command of a white man to the westward, it is supposed to avoid the settlements, and come in some distance up the Neosho, and then sweep everything before them on their way back.

The people of southern Kansas are leaving as rapidly as possible; many of them will loose all they have in the world,

The secessionists are arming all the Indians they can get arms for.

If, there is not something done, and that immediately, there will be terrible work in the southwest. Let me beg of you that you will lay the matter before the President, and see if possible that some measures are taken to rescue the southern Indians from the Rebels. We have what we believe to be reliable information that the Cherokees have seceeded, we *know* they have done so virtualy, yet there are large numbers in the nation whose sympathies are with the government, but who are compeled by their surroundings to take up arms against us.

I was visited a few days ago by a delegation of Creek Indians who assured me, that, although a large number of their warriors were in the rebel army, yet the entire portion of the full bloods were with the government in heart; and they begged me to ask their "White Father" to send some of his children down there to protect them." They also assured me that the moment a body of Union troops occupied the country a majority of the nation would join them, But that now they were being *pressed* into the Rebel Army. We hold a council at Humboldt the 16th of next month; I would be very mutch pleased if I could then assure them, that they should have assistance. I think the Administration would do well to authorise the formation of a Brigade of *friendly Indians* Three thousand Indians would be sufficient to restore confidence to those who are disposed to be friendly to the Government, and would insure peace and quiet to southern tribes. It would be necessary perhaps that a Regiment of Whites should accompany them, This plan meets the approbation of all the Indian Agents; and Gen'l Lane is also heartily in favor of it.

I have taken pains to find out the sentiment of some of the Kansas tribes and am satisfied they would enter heartily into the matter—should it be sanctioned by the Government. The secessionists are now tampering with the Osages. Unless some steps are taken they will secede next.

This matter cannot be pressed too earnestly, nor can it be consumated too soon. Hoping it may receive your early and earnest attention

I am your's truly

G. A. Cutler

Agent of the Indians of the Creek Nation

George A. Cutler to William P. Dole, October 21, 1861, Abraham Lincoln Papers at the Library of Congress, Manuscript Division (Washington, DC: American Memory Project, 2000–2002), http://memory.loc.gov/ammem/alhtml/malhome.html.

LOSSES SUSTAINED DURING AN 1861 CHEROKEE RAID

This claim filed by Elizabeth Kimerlin (variously recorded as Kimberlin) testified to losses sustained during a July 1861 raid by Cherokees. It is possible that the raid Kimerlin remembered actually occurred a month later. In August 1861, a Confederate group under John Matthews invaded the Cherokee neutral lands and forced out sixty families. Matthews was killed when the Sixth Kansas drove the Confederates from the field in September. Kimerlin's deposition also reveals the value of agricultural products at the start of the Civil War.

In the matter of the claim of Mrs. Elizabeth Kimerlin for losses sustained by Indian depredations in the year 1861.

State of Kansas
Labette County

Mrs. Elizabeth Kimerlin being duly sworn according to law deposed and says; that she is a resident of Bourbon County State of Kansas, and has been ever since 1858. That her husband now deceased (William Kimberlin was the owner of a claim on Lightening Creek in what is now Crawford County Kansas. That on Sunday July the 20th 1861 a band of about one hundred Cherokee Indians under command of a certain Col. Liaudwayty [?] and one Matthews came into that portion of Crawford County Kansas. Killed several of the inhabitants, drove off stock and killed the same and forced the people of that region to abandon their homes and property; that this deponent and her now deceased husband were forced to abandon their property for fear of the Indians This deposed further states that there was abandoned on her husbands place in said Crawford County state of Kansas, the following property because her late husband was unable and could not for fear of his life take any part of it away.

Eight thousand rails at 6 cents pr piece	480.00
Deponent says these rails were all in a fence	
and were burned and destroyed	
Thirty five acres of corn in the field which it was	
estimated would yield 50 bushels pr acre 17^{50} bush at 75^{c} pr bushel.	1312.50
Deponent further states that corn was worth	
$1.$^{25}_{100}$ pr bush, in the Spring following being 1862.	
Two and a half acres hungarian growing	50 00
Six acres of wheat cut and in the shock, and estimated to	
yield 20 bushels pr acre. Deponent also says that wheat was	
then selling in that County for $2 pr bushel	240.00
Fifty head of hogs which deponent swears were worth	
$10 pr head, the same averaging near 200 lbs each.	500.00
Total amount of claim	$2582.50

Deponent further swears that she has not recovered reclaimed nor recaptured any portion of said property, nor recovered any compensation therefor. Deponent further swears that she never sold or in any other manner disposed of this claim and that her husband, now deceased, never sold or in any other manner disposed of this claim, and that she is the heir and representative of this claim.

David Kelio [?]   } Witnesses   Elizabeth Kimerlin
Henry Brandley   }

Sworn to and subscribed before me this 20 day of March 1872

F. P. Baker
Chairman of Board of Commissions
State of Kansas
Labette Country

Aaron Decker of Bourbon County and Levi Price of Crawford County State of Kansas being each first duly sworn deposed and each for himself says that he is personally acquainted with Mrs Elizabeth Kimerlin the claimant herein named, and have carefully read the foregoing affidavit and know the contents thereof, that they were neighbors of Mrs. Kimberlin at the time the Cherokee Indians made the raid referred to in the affidavit and know that the facts set forth are true; that while they can not state positively to the number [bushels?] destroyed, they believe the number stated to be correct and further more deponents each for himself say that he believes the charges for the other items in the afidavit are just; and that from his personal knowledge the loss was sustained as stated.   Aaron Decker

David Kelio   } Witnesses   Levi Price
H. Brandley   }

Sworn to and subscribed before me this 20 day of March 1872

F. P. Baker
Chairman of Board of Commissions

On back:

Cherokee Depredation Claim

Claim of Mrs. Elizabeth Kimerlin

For losses sustained on account of depredations 1861

Amount claimed $2582.50

20 July 1861

This claim shows on its face that at the time the depredation was committed claimnant was resident of the Cherokee Neutral Lands.

The Commission find that the claimant sustained the losses as set forth and report in accordance there with, and recommend that this claim be referred to the Congressional Delegation representing Kansas in Congress of the U. S., to be by them laid before the proper authorities for such action as may be deemed just in the premises[?].

F. P. Baker
Chairman Commission

H. Brandley
Clerk of Commission
Elizabeth Kimerlin
Care of I. M. Keener
Fort Scott Kans.

Elizabeth Kimerlin Miscellaneous Collection, Kansas State Historical Society.

"THE MOST EXPERIENCED MEN ARE UNABLE TO CONTROL THESE SAVAGES"

With Indian Territory directly to the south, Kansans were interested in the controversial plan to recruit American Indian troops. Ultimately, the policy Marcus Parrott derided was pursued. Two regiments of American Indian troops were raised in Kansas: the First Regiment, Indian Home Guard, in May 1862 and the Second Regiment, Indian Home Guard, in June and July 1862. A third regiment was raised in Indian Territory.

Born in South Carolina, Parrott grew up in Ohio and moved to Kansas in 1855; in 1857 he was elected territorial delegate. Once Kansas became a state, he ran for the Senate, but came in third. His congressional campaigns of 1862 and 1874 were also unsuccessful.

Leavenworth Kansas Apl 21. 62

Dear Father

. . . Our troops are distributed or at least the distribution is ordered—part
to New Mexico & part to the Indian Territory. The government has recently
authorized the raising of two Indian regiments for service in their own country
but to be commanded by white officers and associated with regiments composed
of white men. The policy of this proceeding is in my opinion fatally erroneous.
It is a fact, that at the battle of Pea Ridge the bloodiest fighting took place
between the Indians and an *Arkansas* regiments of white men. This is doubtless
to be attributed to the fact that when their savage nature is aroused they are
incapable of distinguishing friend from foe. I mention this circumstance as it has
entered largely into my determination not to accept service in the Expedition,
though on general grounds it is a very undesirable field because it promises little
or no active service unless the inhumanity of the savages shall lead to it. . . .

Afftly Yr son

Marc

~

Leavenworth Apl 28th 1862

Dear Mother,

. . . I introduced Mr Corwin to Genl Sturgis yesterday & the Genl advised him
that *no Indian* regiments would be raised—that he thought the policy a mistaken
one on the part of the government and calculated to make a disgraceful record
in history. He has besides given out a general order, in which he declares his
purpose to arrest any one who shall attempt to form or enlist the Indians for
military service. So our youthful Lt. Col. is stopped on the threshhold of his
career. More than likely you will have him return to you without the sight of a
red-skin. His cousin a young man named Wright of Urbana is here with him,
also holding a majors Commission in the Indian service. What such boys as
these could Expect to do with mild Indians Excited by the prospect of blood or
plunder is more than I can tell. The most Experienced men are unable to control
these savages, boys would no doubt be despised by them. But I sincerely hope
that we shall hear no more of Indians as soldiers in this war, however much I
may sympathise with my young friends who will lose their commissions. . . .

. . . Give my love to all & believe me your affectionate

Son

Marc

Marcus Junius Parrott Collection, Kansas Collection, RH MS 554, Kenneth Spencer Research Library, University
of Kansas Libraries.

"THEIR COUNTRY SHOULD BE REDEEMED"

In mid-1861, some six thousand Creeks and Seminoles left Indian Territory for Kansas. Pursued by Confederates, many died before reaching Kansas; losses were especially heavy in a December 1861 engagement. After raising the First and Second regiments of Indian Home Guard, in Kansas, the Union returned these Indians to their homes, defeating the Confederates at Cowskin Prairie and Locust Grove the following summer. Some Confederate Indian regiments defected to the Union and, after the withdrawal back into Kansas, the Cherokee nation fell into disarray. The next major engagement occurred when the Union defeated the Confederates at Fort Wayne on October 22, 1862. Reporting to Secretary of the Interior Caleb Smith a few weeks later, James Blunt argued that poor leadership had stranded Indian refugees and led to disaffected troops.

Headquarters First Division Army of the Frontier
On Boundary Line Between Arkansas & the "Indian Nation"
14 miles south of Maysville, November 21st 1862

Sir,

. . . As early as last winter . . . it was agreed, that two Regiments should be raised of loyal Indians, to act as Home Guards, who, with a military force of white men to accompany them, would move into the Indian Territory, to expel the Rebel Forces and hold the country; and that the Refugee families should then be taken home.

On the arrival of the officers appointed by the President, to organize those Indian Regiments, Genl. Sturgis was in command of Fort Leavenworth, the Headquarters of the District of Kansas, who not only refused to co-operate with them, but issued an order prohibiting the execution of the instruction of the Interior Department upon the subject. On my taking command of the Department of Kansas, about the first of May 1862, I immediately countermanded the order of Genl. Sturgis and directed the organization of the Indians, to proceed with as little delay as possible.

As soon as they were mustered, armed and equipped, I sent them, accompanied by a sufficient force of white men, all under command of Colonel Wm Weer, who had specific instructions from me, to expel the Rebels, possess and hold the Indian country and, to relieve and restore the loyal Indians.

The expedition had proceeded as far South as Fort Gibson and was proving eminently successful in accomplishing the object of its mission, and but for the insubordination and mutinous conduct of Col. (now Genl) Salomon and the forcible arrest by him, of Col. Weer and the assumption of command himself, followed by his utterly unjustifiable and disgraceful retreat and the abandonment of the Indian country, the 3.000 refugee women and children, who followed the retreating Army and are now suffering for the want of suitable clothing and shelter, in the vicinity of Fort Scott, would to-day be comfortably settled in their homes and this country, would have been saved from the desolation, that has since been visited upon it.

On learning the condition and movements of the command, I sent a despatch to Col. Salomon, ordering him to advance and support the Indian Regiments, under Col. W. A. Phillips, who had determined to remain and hold the country as long as it was possible to do so, and left Fort Leavenworth, to take command myself in the Field.

On arriving at Fort Scott, I found, much to my surprise, that Salomon with his command was there. I found that my orders had been received by him, when yet seventy miles South of Fort Scott, on his retreat, but had been purposely disobeyed. The Indian Regiments, after holding out as long as they were able, for want of support and supplies, became discouraged and distrustful of either the ability or willingness of the government to protect them; and, before I took command in the Field, for the purpose of recovering with as little delay as possible, what had been lost by Col. Salomon's retreat, many of them,—particularly the First Regiment, composed chiefly of Creeks—went to their families at Le Roy, Kansas. I had some difficulty in inducing the Indians to return to their commands. They claimed, that the government had failed in its promises made to them; and it was only by assuring them, that their country should be redeemed and their families, taken home and protected, that I could persuade them to enter Missouri and Arkansas, on the present campaign, which has already resulted so favorably, in defeating the Rebels and redeeming the Indian country.

A large number of women and children had followed the Army out of the Indian territory and, I learned that thousands more were coming. I immediately sent persons to prevent their leaving their homes and to induce them, to remain until succor should reach them. This, to a certain extent, I accomplished. Those that had already arrived in the vicinity of Fort Scott, I ordered to be fed. As to clothing and shelter, I had none for them. Convinced that the Refugees at Le Roy, were all desirous of returning home and knowing that it was the interest of the government, as well as that of the Indian country,—to say naught of the question of humanity involved—that they should be restored, without unnecessary delay, I determined to make good my own promises, as well as those of the agents of the government, previously made.

The Superintendent [of Indian affairs], Mr Coffin, was absent and the condition of the Refugees, with the non-fulfilment of the promises made them, called for some prompt action in the matter. While I did not desire to interfere with the business of any Department, with which I was not legitimately connected, the interests of these Refugee Indians, were so intimately blended with the military affairs of the Indian Territory, that I deemed it my duty to act in the premises, as indicated in my letter of Sept to the Indian Agents at Le Roy—and I have yet to be convinced, that I committed any error. As the military commander, having jurisdiction over the Indian Territory, I regarded it as my duty, to make every effort in my power, to restore and protect its loyal people and, to save the country from rebel devastation. The Indians mustered into the Federal service, were not willing to make a second expedition south, unless assurances were given them, that their families should be taken to their homes, as soon as we obtained occupation of the country. With that assurance, they were willing to encounter any danger and to make any sacrifice.

Another reason for my interfering with the Refugees—one indicated by humanity, as well as to subserve the interests of the government—was the fact, that their welfare was disregarded, by those whom the government had appointed as their guardians. The fact had been patent, that these Refugees were the victims of a clique of mercenary and unscrupulous speculators, who were resolved upon robbing the Indians and the government of every dollar they could; and the longer the former could be kept in Kansas, the greater their profits. Hence they have not only endeavored to prevent those who were originally in their charge, from being returned, to their homes, but have made every effort in their power, to get the others, who had followed the U. S. Army for protection to place themselves under their care and guardianship; which the Indians, thus far, have had the good sense to protest against. The latter well know that they have not only been unnecessarily kept from their homes, but also, that they are the victims of a corrupt swindle. . . .

The advantages of taking the Indians home this fall, are briefly these: the Indian country is in our possession. The Indian Regiments in the U. S. Service are able to hold and occupy it. They would be much more willing and contented to do hard service, could their families be restored to their homes; and their families are equally anxious to return. There is no good reason why they should not have been taken back. There is plenty of beef and pork in the Indian Country; and salt can be manufactured in abundance there. The deficiency in grain, can be supplied from Arkansas and, but few supplies would have to be furnished by government. They could occupy their own houses with comfort, instead of passing the winter in a much colder climate, without roof or shelter and, compelled, half-clad, to wear away the tedious days and nights, shivering by a log fire, in the open air.

Another reason why they should be returned this fall is, that they might be there early in the spring, to cultivate the soil. The season is early, commencing in March, and by putting in early vegetables, they would soon be able to furnish their own subsistence; whereas, they cannot be taken home in the spring as early as March, or in time to prepare and make a crop next season. Consequently the government must feed them and thus, corrupt officials and swindling contractors, may be enabled to prey upon them another year.

But, I am entirely content, to leave this matter to an impartial investigation, to decide whether Mr Coffin or myself, has labored most faithfully, to protect the welfare of the Indians and the interests and honor of the government.

In connection with the foregoing history of affairs, pertaining to the Indian Territory generally, I desire for the information of the War Department, to state further, the following facts in regard to such of the Indians, as have been mustered into the service of the United States.

Under instructions from the War Department, in organizing the *first* and *second* Indian Regiments, white men only were made Field and Staff Officers; but no white man was mustered in as a Company Officer, though I had recommended to the Department, that at least one officer in each company, should be a white man, for the purpose of keeping the company books and taking care of the government property.

The third Regiment, under Col. W. A. Phillips,—formerly a Major in the first Regiment—was organized during Col. Weer's occupancy of the Indian Territory in July last. A portion of the men had previously belonged to the Rebel Regiment of Col. Drew and took part against us, in the battle of Pea Ridge; but, having been forced into the rebel ranks, they availed themselves of the first opportunity, to give evidence of their loyalty to the government.

This regiment, (the third), was organized, with twelve full companies. The officers were chosen by election and, experience in the first and second regiments, having proven the necessity, for at least, one white officer for each company, they were accordingly so organized, the first Lieutenants being selected from among the meritorious non-commissioned officers of the white volunteers, whom I discharged, to enable them to accept their promotion. This Regiment is composed entirely of Cherokees and, it is but justice to say of them, that their discipline and deportment are as good as those of other troops and, their services of as much, nay more value to the government, in this section of country, than those of any other Regiment in the Service.

The first Regiment, (Creeks), now numbers but eight companies, two others having failed to report themselves at Fort Scott, on my order to that effect, after they had left their command and gone to Le Roy as before stated. The reason of their failing to comply with my order was, probably, the influence exercised over them by their old chief, Opothleoholo; Whether they return or not, there will be no difficulty in filling that regiment with Loyal Creeks, so soon as this command reaches a point in somewhat closer proximity to their Nation. Said Regiment also saw the advantage of having one white officer in each company and accordingly, one of the Lieutenants in each of them resigned and their places were filled—as in the case of the third Regiment—with non-commissioned officers, selected from the white troops.

The Second Regiment was originally composed of Indians of various tribes—Cherokees, Osages, Delawares, Shawnees and Qua-paws. They were thus organized, against my advice upon the subject and all, except the Cherokees, proved worthless as Soldiers. Of six companies, all but about twenty, deserted after the return of Genl. Salomon from the Indian Territory, in July last. Had there been an officer over them, fit to command, it might have resulted differently; but their commander, Colonel Ritchey, was entirely incompentent as an officer. He is now under arrest and, should be discharged from the service by order of the President. When this Regiment was last paid, about the middle of October—payment for the 31st of August—I ordered the fragment of the six companies, before mentioned (about 20 in all) to be paid and mustered out. The remainder were treated as deserters. The effect of this course has been salutary upon the other Indians. Since then six new companies of loyal Cherokees, have been organized and mustered into this regiment.

These Indian Regiments are all mustered as Infantry, but nearly one half of them are mounted on their own ponies and, do excellent service as mounted men, especially as scouts. They do [not] receive, or ask any pay, for the services of their horses; but in consideration of the valuable services they render, as mounted men, I have ordered their horses to be shod. As the forage is taken principally from the enemy, there is but little expense to the government on that account. Some irregularities have been permitted by me, in the cases of these Indian Regiments, viz: the employment of citizen teamsters for the Regimental transportation, as the Indians could not be made to fill the places to advantage; but recently, negroes—slaves of rebels—who have come within our lines, have been employed as teamsters, under the provisions of a late Act of Congress. Another irregularity, has been the detailing of white soldiers from other regiments to act as clerks and keep the company books, in the Indian Regiments and allowing them extra-duty pay, 25 cents per day therefor. Also—in some cases—the employment of interpreters. These were contingencies, that could not be avoided and, which the interests of the service, required to be met.

In conclusion, I may add, that the whole Indian Country is now, substantially, in our possession. The Confederate or Rebel power in it is destroyed. The great majority of its people always have been loyal at heart. Many, who for a long time sided, ostensibly, with the Rebels, did so because of their inability—in the absence of any aid afforded them, by the Federal Government and, surrounded

as they were constantly, by Confederate Agents, who made them the victims of
grossly false representations—to protect and take care of themselves.

All the circumstances, by which they were encompassed, being considered, it
is by no means surprising, that they acted as they did. They availed themselves of
the first opportunity they could embrace, to prove their allegiance, by tendering
to the government their services. In this, they have been earnest and devoted;
and, no men in the service are more patient and untiring, in their efforts to serve
the government, than the Cherokee soldiers.

The rebel portion of the Indians, have become disheartened and have
abandoned the hope of controling the country. With other troops occupying
north-western Arkansas, the Three Indian Regiments, are amply sufficient to
hold and take care of the whole Indian Territory. They are in high spirits at the
prospect of returning very soon to their own country, and are only desirous
of having their families restored to their homes at an early day, which it is
manifestly, the interest of the Government, as well as of the Indians, to have
done with as little delay as possible.

Very respectfully
Your Obedient Servant '
Jas. G. Blunt.
Brigadier General.
Commdg 1st Division Army of the Frontier

Official.
    Thos. Moonlight (signed)
    Lieut. Col. & Ch'f of Staff

James G. Blunt to Caleb Smith, November 21, 1862, Abraham Lincoln Papers at the Library of Congress,
Manuscript Division (Washington, DC: American Memory Project, 2000–2002), http://memory.loc.gov/
ammem/alhtml/malhome.html.

A MEMBER OF THE INDIAN HOME GUARD WRITES OF NEOSHO

*The Third Regiment, Indian Home Guard, was organized in September 1862 and
mustered out in May 1865. This correspondent, likely one of the regiment's white
officers, shares his opinion of the regiment and of the society found in Neosho,
Missouri, near the headquarters of the Indian Home Guards, at Fort Scott.*

From our own correspondent:

NEOSHO, Feb. 11, 1863.

EDITOR BULLETIN:

It is so long since you heard anything from "your own," that you must think us
dead or lost but We are happy to inform you that we not only still live and have our

being, but relish our victuals anxiously. Now when you talk of gay places, "that's" Neosho. The population consists of Whites, Indians, Negroes, and Codfish Aristocracy, the latter class may be unknown to your readers, so I will try to explain. They are what Sam Slick terms the ragged bottoms, have not got a dollar, very little sense, and think themselves too good to associate with their superiors in intellect, etiquette, and wealth; But we are happy to state they form but a small portion of our population.—Last week our commander of the post, Maj. Foreman, was relieved by Capt. Spillman. Major during his short stay among us endeared himself to all loyal citizens, and was the terror of traitors and all evil-doers. But possessing such excellent qualities as a commander, a wider sphere was given him, he is now in command of the 3d regt. of Indian Home Guards. Before leaving he gave a supper, and it was such a one as any one might think it an honor to attend.—Speeches were made, songs sung, toasts drank, and sad havoc made among the edibles.

Our new commander, Capt. Spillman, has already shown that he is every way worthy to be the successor of Major Foreman young and energetic, he is just the man for the place. . . .

The Indians make excellent soldiers, never grumble at any duty, no matter how laborious, always ready for a scout, and woe be to any unfortunate individual who is caught in the brush. The officers are untiring in their efforts to discipline and encourage the men.—Capt. Henning organized a company of State Militia, such a ragged, filthy looking set you never seen I know. As he was enrolling them, he had them drawn up in line, I noticed an Indian officer watching them very intently, and steped up to him and asked what he thought of the "outfit."—Oh no he says very mysteriously, shaking his head "Bushwhack, me watch," laying his hand on his revolver.

. . . Give my kindest regards to all the folks at the Fort and tell them "we are coming soon."

S. Big Injun,
Lieut. 3d Indian.

Fort Scott Bulletin, February 27, 1863.

"THE INDIANS SEEM TO WANT TO MAKE PEACE"

Writing to his sister, Margaret Price, Henry A. Dutton seemed optimistic about his mission to the west. He believed the Sioux were ready for peace, but on July 22, 1865, the Sioux attacked his regiment. Dutton was a member of the Eleventh Regiment Kansas Volunteer Cavalry, which marched from Fort Riley to Fort Kearney, Nebraska, in February 1865. They halted at Sioux Agency, thirty miles to the south, before continuing to Fort Laramie and then through to Platte Bridge,

where they protected the telegraph line over the Oregon Trail. Colonel Preston Plumb
was assigned to protect the Overland Stage Line from Camp Collins, Colorado, to
Green River, a distance of some four hundred miles.

April 12th 1865

In camp on the North Platte, Mountains

Dear Sister Daffie,

. . . we are now about forty miles west from "Fort Laramie" on our way west, we are now about eight hundred miles west of Fort Leavenworth, Since I wrote last the Indians seem to want to make peace a good many of the Sioux Indians have already come to "Military Posts" and ask protection and draw government grub I believe the Indians expedition has already played out, and our Regt is agoing to be stationed along on the wire road from Laramie to Salt Lake all the way from here to the "South Pass" some of our Regt is agoing into Idaho Territory to protect the miners there. I understand that Col Plumb is agoing to make his "H^d Q^{rs}" at the bridge on the North Platte about one hundred and thirty miles from here and I suppose probably we shall stay there with him when you write again direct to the Band *via* Fort Laramie, I would like to go as far west as any of the Regt, We left the "South Platte" at Julesburgh and crossed over to high ridge about sixty miles to where we struck the North Platte and we followed the North Platte about fifty miles at which point we found Laramie situated on the south bank near the mouth of the Laramie River. We have had a cold march all the way, not a day that our over coats were uncomfortable only with the cold, as snow storm nearly every day We are north & west of Denver City now and the wildest country your ever saw, it is fit only for the Indians we saw Laramie Peak about one hundred miles before we reach it and we have crossed a rougher country than I ever saw before. . . . . If Richmond has been surrendered as is reported with a good part of Gen Lee's Army I think we shall soon have Peace but I must close as it is late, we march again tomorrow. . . .

Your aft Brother Henry A. Dutton.

Margaret Price Collection, Kansas State Historical Society.

THE ELEVENTH KANSAS IN THE WEST

Organized in 1862, the Eleventh Kansas was one of three regiments Kansas furnished
in response to Abraham Lincoln's call for three hundred thousand soldiers to serve
for three years or until the end of the war. Isaac B. Pennock kept a diary and this
excerpt covers the regiment's final months as they headed west. They had a hard
winter and spring campaign beset by severe cold and inadequate supplies. Leaving

Four members of Company G, Eleventh Regiment, Kansas Volunteers. *Reproduced by permission from the Kansas State Historical Society.*

Fort Laramie on April 9, the Eleventh Kansas was sent to Platte Bridge, 130 miles west, with orders to protect the telegraph line, gather intelligence on the American Indians, and prevent their crossing the Platte River. From there, Company I went to Deer Creek and then Sweet Water station, fifty miles farther west, where they discovered twenty days' ration of corn to last the whole summer and no ammunition for their carbines. They were to support the Eleventh Ohio Cavalry, who, dispatched to guard the three hundred miles of telegraph lines from Laramie to South Pass, had been dismounted by skirmishes with the Indians. As Pennock details, this was difficult country with a determined enemy.

DIARY OF ISAAC B. PENNOCK, FIRST SERGEANT COMPANY "I," ELEVENTH KANSAS CAVALRY

May 10 [1865]. Reveille at 2 o'clock in the morning. Started on march as soon as we could saddle up, without any breakfast. Extremely cold. Our boots so frozen almost impossible to get them on—had to thaw them out. No wood at this camp; had to cook our coffee with sage and grease brush. After starting froze our whiskers until arrived at stopping place to get breakfast. Sage and grease brush

for cooking. No wood. Seen three human skulls on the roadside. Traveled about
18 or 20 miles. Rolled out after dinner, 1/2 past 2 p.m.; traveled until 15 minutes
of 11 o'clock at night. Camped on trail between Powder and Wind river, among
sand hills. Traveled about 30 miles—50 miles in all today. Fed our last corn to
night. Horses commence giving out this evening. All very tired. Man and beast
went to bed. This day crossed two or three of branches Powder river.

May 26. . . . Hear that Indians tried to stampede stock at Sweetwater yesterday
afternoon—30 to 40 of them. They did not succeed.

May 27. . . . Platte bridge is composed or built entirely of pine hewn. The piers
are 28 in number built up in the river of hewn pine logs, filled in with stone. The
piers are about 30 feet from center to center. It is a very substantial structure for
this wooden country. Price of crossing 6 mule team from one to five dollars each,
according to stage of river. We have news that the Indians attacked Rocky Ridge
station today in strong force. The fight is still going on; don't know what the
result will be. The operator says there is an immense number of the enemy. . . .

June 1. . . . Hear that Rocky Ridge station was burned by the Indians; don't
know whether the garrison escaped or not. Some anxiety on their account. Two
companies of galvanized troops started for there escorted by a detail from our
regiment, last night at 7 o'clock p.m.

June 2. . . . After noon hear that Indians attacked the bridge today; 100 men sent
to its relief; no particulars yet. . . .

June 3. Fine day. At 3 o'clock p.m. received despatch from Col. Plumb that Indians
have attacked station at upper bridge; ordered to cross lower bridge with 20 men and
attack them in rear. Captain Greer and 20 men started but the Indians were gone
when we got there but plenty of fresh tracks. Col. Plumb is in close pursuit and was
in firing distance at 2 hours before sundown. We have heard from the fight; two
or [of] our men killed and one Indian, and several ponies. One of our men had 10
arrows shot into him, scalped and finger cut off and terribly mangled. Barnwell of
Co. "F" got some distance in advance and Indians in superior numbers turned on him
and two others. His horse being shot, he was dismounted and unable to get away.

June 20. Mosquitoes very troublesome. Indians committing depredations at
various points on the road. This camp not so healthy as heretofore; nine men of
our company sick.

June 24. Fine day. Our boys back from Sweetwater. The Indians in the fight there
were Arapahoes, about 40 of them, and 9 of our troops. Three Indians were

supposed to have been killed; one of our men killed and one wounded. The man killed, they scalped all the hair off his head, cut off his hands at the wrist, took the sinews out of his arms; took out his heart and liver, ran a lance into him and stuck him up on a pole. Several Indians wounded. Col. Moonlight is relieved of command of this district. . . .

July 2. Fine pleasant morning. Call for inspection sounded at 9 a.m. Just as we were falling in three shots were heard in quick succession which was the signal in case Indians were seen. All except a small party to keep camp, started to save the horses which were grazing some 3/4 of a mile from camp. When horses were started safely to camp, we pressed on a little beyond to the brow of the bluffs on the west and down in the valley 1/2 a mile distant were the Indians. We fired a few shots and returned to camp. Sent out a few mounted men to ascertain their strength. Horsemen soon returned. Indians came nearer, within range of camp, shooting from ravines. Sent out 5 or 6 men to engage them; fought them awhile from one ravine to another. Didn't pay. Sent 12 or 14 men under Captain Greer and charged them; drove them; shooting one; capturing a great many of their trinkets, bows, shields, &c. Indians then drew off on the hills to the east. Captain Greer and 9 or 10 mounted men pursued, endeavoring to cut off some of their stragglers. Proceeded 1/2 a mile when the Indians were discovered to be in force just beyond a hill we were about to ascend. After some hesitation we fell back slowly, which we had no sooner began than they charged on us in greatly superior numbers endeavoring to cut us off from camp. We put in what shots we could to the best of our ability but in spite of our efforts to repel them, they drove us a few hundred yards. Sergeant Holding was wounded in this engagement; ball entered back part of the neck and passed out through the lower part of the left ear. The man who shot him was supposed to be a white man; was shot himself through the breast by one of our boys, Hammond, just after he had shot Holding. Could not ascertain anything about how many Indians were killed, only by the blood which marked the field and which proves that quite a large number of men or ponies were killed or wounded. This fight on Reshaw creek 4 miles from lower Bridge.

July 3. Lieut. Drew with 20 men ordered on a scout to Deer Creek, 28 miles east, started at noon. Captain Greer ordered to send 10 men to Sweetwater to escort operator and repair the line. Boys refused to go in so small a party. Ten more were detailed; still they refused to go. Ten more volunteered to go with them; 2 teamsters, operator and one citizen, in all 34 men. Just at sunset they started out, Sergt. Pennock in command.

July 23. Pleasant morning. Five of our horses stolen from near camp on last night by a party of Indians. Captain Greer with detachment of 26 men pursued Indians but unable to overhaul them. Indians crossed mountains about 14 miles southeast of our old camp, about 10 of them, one white man with them. Captain Greer's party found where the war party that fought us three weeks ago today first stopped after the fight; found where they had dressed the wounds of their party received in the fight. A great many bloody rags were discovered. One of their warriors was found hidden under a rock, supposed to be a great warrior or chief from the trapping found with him, silver ornaments, &c. Supposed a number of killed buried there from appearances, and a number wounded. Detachment that went the other way found another fresh grave of warrior.

July 24. . . . Indians around camp during night. Sentinel Stewksbury saw two but did not get a shot at them. Later at night, just before daybreak, Corporal May fired on one but without hitting him. Dark night, no moon. Suppose we will have mail today. Mail detained at Horse Shoe on account of a body of Indians in that vicinity. . . .

July 25. . . . Considerable noise among the horses on last night. The guard thinks Indians were prowling around; too dark to see very well. Immediately after dinner, the cry of "Here come the Indians" rang through the camp. I ran out of the tent when sure enough, they were coming up the opposite side of the river. The boys commenced shooting and made some very good shots. Fifteen of them rode along the bank, yelling and hooting like madmen. We crossed the bridge, 10 mounted, following them a couple of miles. We killed two if not three of them. They were gradually reinforced until we found we would be taken. We fell back to camp. They commenced crossing the river two miles below and ran into the cattle herd. Twelve or fourteen of the boys went after them and had a severe fight, killing one, a head chief who was scalped, also two or three others mortally wounded. We finally drove them across the river. They killed one steer but we stuck it and hauled it into camp. We fought them across the river until dark. When we returned to camp, they did not disturb us during the night. About 50 to 100 in sight.

July 26. Terrible day for our command and no knowing how it will end. At daybreak a few Indians were seen in the hills north of the river. Lieut. Britney and 10 men arrived from Sweetwater before daybreak. Detachment of companies "H" and "D" to be here by 12 or 1 o'clock. They camped three miles this side of Willow Springs. Captain Greer received an order to send a detachment to meet "H" and "D" companies. I took charge of it by request of the captain. On reporting to Major Anderson, found that Lieut. Collins of

"G" company, 11th Ohio was going along, but the captain, thinking it would
be best, I went along, 20 or 25 in all. We crossed the bridge and got about one
mile from camp when from the N.,E.,S.,W., and every point of the compass,
the savages came. It appeared as thought they sprang up out of the ground.
They completely surrounded us. There was no other alternative. Death was
approaching on every side in its most horrible form, that of the tomahawk and
scalping knife of the Indian. We turned and charged into the thickest of them,
drawing our pistols and doing the best we could. It was a terrible ordeal to go
through; it was really running the gauntlet for dear life. After a terrible break-
neck race of 3/4 of a mile, we arrived at the bridge where the boys had run
out to our support. In the charge we lost 5 killed and about 12 wounded. Lieut.
Collins was killed. Everything was in full view of the station. Over 1500 Indians
were around our little party. The Indians suffered dreadfully as our pistols were
pushed right against their bodies and fired doing great execution. We were
forced to come back. Every horse nearly was wounded in one or more places,
4 were killed. They now cut the wire both east and west. Twenty men under
Lieut. Walker went two miles east to repair it. The enemy attacked him killing
one and wounding two of our company. He had to retreat, not getting the wire
fixed. At one-half past 11 o'clock, "H" and "D" companies detachment came in
sight west of us. The savages surrounded them. Five of the boys crossed the
river 3 miles above; two were killed, three came into camp afoot, their horses
being killed. One, on horseback, was the mountains, but several Indians were in
close pursuit. All this we could see plainly from the station but could do nothing
for them. "H" and "D" detachments corralled or tried to corrall their wagons
but did not succeed very well. We could see the Indians in swarms charge down
upon our boys, when they would roll volley after volley into them. It seemed to
us as though the boys were in a strong position, 20 in all being the number. At
about 4 o'clock p.m., the firing ceased and a smoke, that of the burning wagons,
commenced ascending. The enemy commenced going off north by twos and
threes till at sundown not a living being was to be seen. We are certain that all
the boys were killed but from the length of time they held out the immense
numbers of the Indians charging in solid masses upon them, they must have
suffered terribly in killed and wounded. Two Snake scouts started at 1/2 past 9
o'clock p.m. with despatches to Deer Creek. Would get there before day.

July 27. Up at daybreak. Went on top of the post with the glass. Soon the Indians
commenced appearing on the ridge just opposite on the north side of the river,
first one and then two, until by sunrise hundreds were in sight on all the hills.
Some of them halloed across it in the Cheyenne language, telling the women
to leave as they were going to burn us out and kill all the soldiers and men here.

They are now going southwest on the high ground towards Red Buttes, but few in sight at 8 a.m. The Indians are very mad. They told the Indians (Snakes friendly) that they had killed all the men of "H" and "D" yesterday and were going to kill more white men today, and that our men had killed and wounded heaps of Indians. Copy of papers found on battle ground of yesterday, viz: "Blackfeet, Cheyenne, Arapahoes, Sioux and few Comanches are here now. They want to fight four days more. I was taken prisoner down on the Platte river. You killed a chief yesterday evening. They say they do not want to have peace. There is over one thousand (1000.) They want your stock and want to fight. They are moving to battle on the place." A party of us crossed this afternoon to try and bring in some of the dead. We found Lieut. Collins and McDonald and one other man in a dreadfully mangled and cut up condition. Our scouts at the west discovered the Indians in force about 2 miles off, dancing, encircled by their horses. Think this body is 600 strong. Another body of men from the east came in sight when we were recalled. They proved to be a reinforcement of 50 men from Deer Creek. Our Indian scouts got there after daybreak. Lieutenants Hubbard and Grim started immediately. Another party is just starting to try and bring in the dead bodies nearest the river. The boys are all in safe (sundown) and brought in the three dead bodies left nearest; 58 arrows were found in one body; 24 in the body of Lieut. Collins and several in McDonald's body. Two Indians showed themselves in the west on the hills. The three boys that escaped from the train on yesterday fought their way for 7 miles. Sixty Indians crossed the river and followed them, killing all their horses and two out of the original five that were cut off from the train at the first charge of the Indians. Four of the Indians were killed and several wounded. The fighting was distinctly seen by all at the station. The three boys got into the bed of a brushy creek when the band of Indians pursuing nearly all left them, only 14 Indians continuing the pursuit of these. They disabled two or three when they also gave over pursuit. The boys were "D" company boys of our regiment: Henry Smith, Byron Swain and Corporal James Shrader. "H" 13 killed; "D" 8; "I" 3; "K" 2 in battle at Platte Bridge; "I" 11 wounded; "K" 2. . . .

July 28. Sentinel on guard fired a shot at two o'clock in the morning. Three Indians came near the post and ran as soon as fired upon. They were mounted. We all ran into the breastworks immediately, but a daybreak no one was in sight on the surrounding hills. No Indians appeared up to 2 o'clock p.m. A detachment started to find our boys above. About 5 miles out west from the station, 20 of the dead bodies were found, the wagons burned. The Indians had a great many killed and wounded. They had to cut up a great many telegraph poles and split them to drag off their killed and wounded. The Indian scouts (Snake) say there were 3000 Indians at least went north from the trail. The telegraph line is destroyed as far west as the party went, about 6 to 8 miles.

July 29. Move back this morning from station to camp. A strong party went out to bury the dead. Twenty-one bodies were buried on the battle ground, a horrible sight; all scalped but one who was nearly burned up. The savages set the wagons on fire and heated the irons and bolts and burned the men with them, and turned their feet into the fire, torturing them, if alive, in every possible manner. They were buried in two graves, 7 in one and 13 in another. One body was buried on the other side of the river from where the train was taken. Wire cut east.

July 30. Company "K" left this morning for Deer Creek. No signs of 6th Michigan said to have passed La Bonte on yesterday. A detachment of Ohio 11th came in from Sweetwater this morning. They tried to fix up the wire but too much of it down. A detachment went out to guard operator, to telegraph west for repair train to return, about 300 yards of wire down. Nine o'clock at night, no news from the east, wire still cut. Great anxiety on account of 6th Michigan not being heard from. Fears for "K" company. Strong guard.

July 31. . . . Sixth Michigan not up yet and no intelligence from them, some alarm on their account. Our rations of provisions out today. The messes have had no meat for 3 days and are out of flour this morning; things begin to look serious. If nothing turns up today, we will have to commence butchering and jerking beef for our subsistence. Draw one day's rations of bacon and flour of Ganard, a ranchman here, owner of the Bridge. Picket on herd. Saw two Indians below camp a couple of miles. The herd was brought in immediately. It is now sundown, nothing further has been seen. On account of nothing being heard from below, we all moved into the trenches and station. The scouts did not attempt to go to Deer Creek as they thought the danger too imminent to attempt going through. Succor must come soon; this suspense is terrible..

August 1. . . . No news whatever from below. We cannot imagine what can be the matter. Gen. Connor telegraphed when the line was up that 6th Michigan would reach here by last Saturday night. It is now Tuesday and not a word of any kind from below and Indians between here and Deer Creek. Surely today we can hear something. A party went this morning as far up the line west as where the wire had not been disturbed, but it could get no communication west. Wire cut west somewhere. We have strong working parties throwing up additional dirt works for fortification as we don't know at what moment the enemy will attack. Our ammunition is very short, but a few rounds. Our fortifications are now nearly perfected and we can hold the fort for two hours if assaulted by the enemy in force by firing 10 shots each from our carbines, but our pistol ammunition is plenty for close quarters. At four o'clock in the afternoon, we were working in the trenches. The joyful cry came, "The line is working." Spades and shovels were instantly thrown down, a general rush was made for the telegraph office. The joyful tick, tick, tick put a glad smile on every countenance. Soon we heard that the 6th Michigan would be here on tomorrow; Sergeant Todd and rations for 15 days with them. All is gladness and joy.

August 10. Reveille at 3 a.m. Roll out at 4. Travel about 14 miles to Horse Creek; good stream of running water. At 10 o'clock a.m. got breakfast. This is the spot where Captain Foulks and his men who were escorting some Indians to Fort Kearney were attacked, and he and several of his man killed by the Indians. They were friendly Sioux, armed and clothed by government to kill soldiers. No wood nearer than the river, over one mile; good grass for stock. Start again at 3 p.m. Camp five miles west of Fort Mitchell on Platte river; excellent grass. Rained this afternoon. Not much wood to be had. Scott's Bluff in view all day. Several dead bodies of Indians found at Horse Creek by our men.

August 26. Reveille at 3 1/2 o'clock a.m. Marched 1/2 an hour before sunrise about 10 miles. Pass Midway Station, camp three miles east of it; plenty of good grass all over the river bottom. Start for afternoon march at 3 o'clock. A large train with Mormon emigrants camped alongside of us at noon, Swedes, Norwegians, Danes. Third Massachusetts Cavalry camped near us on their way west just before we started from our noon camp. Marched 10 or 11 miles to good camp on river.

August 30. Reveille at 3 o'clock a.m. Marched at a little before sunrise, arrive at the Fort in about 3 hours. Universal indignation at Connor's course in dismounting and taking our horses from us; it is nothing but petty spite doing it. Turned all our horses over, also tents and equipments. March at 5 o'clock p.m., passing through Kearney with repeated groans for Connor, the miserable commander of this district. Camp about 3 miles east of Kearney; grass good.

September 22. . . . At 1/2 past 5 p.m., Company "I" was mustered out of the service of the United States by Brevette Brigadier General Lowe, mustering officer for the state of Kansas.

September 25. . . . Paymaster has paid off Company "I" and scattered it to the four winds of the earth.

Thus concludes the history of Company "I," 11th K.V.C. Its organization is no longer known, its members are flying hither and thither to mothers, sisters, wives and the loving arms of friends at home.

Pennock Diary [transcript], Kansas State Historical Society.

MAJOR HANCOCK ON INDIAN AFFAIRS IN KANSAS

In 1867 the commander of the Department of Missouri, Winfield S. Hancock, requested his report on Indian affairs be circulated lest an injustice be done to soldiers serving on the frontier. Hancock was angered by Louis Bogy, the commissioner of Indian affairs, who had argued in a separate report that the current troubles with the Indians could be traced, in part, to orders that arms and ammunition not be traded. But Hancock insisted that "officers and troops, who have so recently engaged in a long and bloody war have no inclination to commence fresh campaigns unless duty requires it." Part of the disagreement between Bogy and Hancock stemmed from unclear jurisdiction: if difficulties with American Indian tribes arose, was the Indian Department or federal troops responsible? Hancock's report is also of interest because it provides a window, albeit imperfect, into the concerns of the various chiefs in Kansas.

REPORT.
REPLY TO THE REPORT OF COMMISSIONER BOGY, OF FEBRUARY 5, 1867, ENCLOSED UNDER THE FRANK OF THE INTERIOR DEPARTMENT.

Major General W. S. Hancock, U. S. Army, to Brevet Major General W. A. Nichols, Assistant Adjutant General.

HEADQUARTERS DEPARTMENT OF THE MISSOURI,
FORT LEAVENWORTH, KANSAS, *March 6, 1867.*

Brevet Brigadier General W. A. Nichols, *Assistant Adjutant General, Military Division of the Missouri, Saint Louis, Mo.*

GENERAL: . . . The fact is, that there are other and graver reasons existing for our present troubles with the Indians, than those given by Commissioner Bogy. One of our most important appears to be, that the extension of our great lines of travel across the plains is driving the buffalo away, and thus interfering with the hunting-grounds of the Indians, and with their only means of support. The Government makes no sufficient arrangement to subsist them, when the game has disappeared, and they are obliged to roam over the country after the buffalo, to support themselves. The extension of railroads and other thoroughfares, the military authorities cannot prevent, nor can the Indian department control such circumstances. The only feasible plan, in view of these facts, would seem to be, to remove the Indians entirely from the main lines of travel across the plains, to place them on reservations, . . . and, if necessary, feed them. They should then be required to remain on their reservations, and not be permitted to roam at large;

and to this end (as the Indian department has not the force necessary to control them) they should be placed under the charge of the military authorities.

Indians have no regard for Indian agents, save so far as they may be useful to them. They only fear and respect force. . . .

WINF'D S. HANCOCK,
Major General U. S. A., Commanding.

~

HEADQUARTERS DEPARTMENT OF THE MISSOURI,
FORT LEAVENWORTH, KANSAS, *March* 11, 1867.

Colonel J. H. Leavenworth,
     U. S. *Indian Agent for Arrapahoe, Apache, and [blank]*
Colonel: . . . I am at present preparing an expedition to the plains, which will soon be ready to move. My object in doing so at this time is, to convince the Indians within the limits of this department, that we are able to punish any of them who may molest travellers across the plains, or who may commit other hostilities against the whites. We desire to avoid, if possible, any troubles with the Indians, and to treat them with justice and according to the requirements of our treaties with them, and I wish especially, in my dealings with them, to act through the agents of the Indian department, as far as it is possible so to do. Concerning the Kiowas of your agency, we have grave reasons for complaint. Among others, it is officially reported to these headquarters, that that tribe has been making hostile incursions into Texas, and that a war party has very recently returned to Fort Dodge from that State, bringing with them the scalps of seventeen (17) colored soldiers, and one (1) white man. I am also informed that the Kiowas have been threatening our posts on the Arkansas, that they are about entering into a compact with the Sioux for hostilities against us, and that they have robbed and insulted officers of the United States Army who have visited them, supposing that they were friends. . . . I desire you to particularly explain to them, that one reason why the Government does not at once send troops against them to redress these outrages against our people is that their "Great Father" is averse to commencing a war upon them (which would certainly end in destroying them,) until all other means of redress fail. . . .

(Signed,) W. S. HANCOCK,
Major General Commanding.

     Official copy.
         W. G. MITCHELL,
            Captain and A. D. C.

~

TALK WITH "TALL BULL," CHIEF OF THE CHEYENNES.

[Tall Bull was responding to Hancock's assertion that American troops, while not eager for war, were prepared for it and that those guilty of depredations should be cautious.]

. . . "Tall Bull" replied as follows:

You sent for us; we came here. We have made the treaty with our agent, Colonel Wynkoop. We never did the white man any harm; we don't intend to. Our agent told us to meet you here. Whenever you want to go on the Smoky Hill you can go; you can go on any road. When we come on the road, your young men must not shoot us. We are willing to be friends with the white man.

. . . The buffalo are diminishing fast. The antelope, that were plenty a few years ago, they are now thin. When they shall all die we shall be hungry; we shall want something to eat, and we will be compelled to come into the fort. Your young men must not fire at us; whenever they see us they fire, and we fire on them. . . . .

~

HEADQUARTERS DEPARTMENT OF THE MISSOURI,
IN THE FIELD, CAMP No. 17,
NEAR FORT DODGE, KANSAS, *April* 23, 1867.

TALK HELD WITH KIOWA CHIEFS KICKING BIRD, STUMBLING BEAR, "THE MAN THAT MOVES," HALF-BROTHER OF THE LATE CHIEF TO-HAW-SON, AND SEVERAL OTHER WARRIORS PRESENT.

[In this meeting, Hancock stated that he wished to confirm the good feelings of those Indians friendly to the U. S., to fight those who wished to wage war and to find those responsible for depredations.]

. . . "Kicking Bird" then said:

. . . We want peace in it and not war. We have seen you, (General Hancock,) and our hearts are glad. We will report the talk you have had with us to all of the nations, so that they will know what you have said. When there is no war south of the Arkansas our women and children can sleep without fear of being molested, and our men can hunt buffalo there without fear of enemies. My heart is big and glad that you have told us you will not make war on Indians whose consciences are good. We have often wished for the Sioux and northern Cheyennes not to come down here; they steal our horses when they come here, and we do not want them to come. I have heard that our goods are coming early this spring. When they arrive, that will be the time to pick out young men for guides and scouts. After I get back to my people, I will tell the words you have said to our chiefs, and when it has been told our young men, they will report what they will do. You can see for yourself that we are peaceably encamped on the other side of the river, and no matter what kind of a storm came, we have stayed to have a talk with you. Whatever you have to tell we will listen to, and we know that it is the truth. Now and then we have robes to trade for sugar and coffee for our women and children. On the prairie we eat buffalo meat. We are encamped close by here. . . .

∼

FORT DODGE, KANSAS, *April* 28, 1867.

TALK HELD WITH "LITTLE RAVEN," HEAD CHIEF OF THE ARRAPAHOES; YELLOW BEAR, CUT NOSE, BEARDY, AND SEVERAL WARRIORS PRESENT.

"Little Raven" said as follows:

We have heard from the Sioux above here; about their going away and leaving their lodges; but for all that we have come in as fast as our horses would carry us. This route and the Smoky Hill route are now free. We don't stop the roads. We love the whites. We make peace with the commissioners from Washington at the mouth of the Little Arkansas, and that peace we have kept for two years. We have a great many brothers and friends in the southern country, and we have sent runners to tell them to listen to what you (General Hancock) have to say. The Sioux in the north do not listen to me, nor the Arrapahoes who have lived in the north for years. They do not belong to the nation. They are the same as the Sioux. The commissioners in Washington look to me as the head chief of the Arrapahoes. I have told all the Indians of all the nations the same as I tell you now. You send for me to come and see you, and I came as fast as I could. My heart is glad to see you. We wish you to inform your soldiers on the roads that we are not with the Sioux and Cheyennes. We will report what you say to us to all the nations. Whatever you have to say, let it be said in plain language, so that we can understand it. We do not belong north at all—with the Sioux or any other tribe. We belong south. Until the Sioux and Cheyennes go north of the North Platte, we will remain south of the Arkansas. It is a good thing for the soldiers to camp along the different streams, for we can then come in and trade with them. We don't want to stop the railroads at all. Our hearts are glad when we come here without wives and children, and meet all your chiefs with friendship. What you say we will listen to, and when our people come in for their treaty goods, we will have a good chance to report to them what you have told us. It is likely that you have heard of the Arrapahoes committing depredations. That is false. Other Indians have done so, and have laid it to Arrapahoes. All the other villages of our people, save mine, are a great ways off, and that is the reason we came in first. They will all be in; their lodges are further off south. The Arrapahoes, Comanches, Kiowas, Apaches, and Osages, are almost all camped at Salt Plains. We hope that you will give us provisions to take home with us. We hope that when you to go Washington you will report that "Little Raven" has a good heart towards the whites. The Great Spirit listens, and knows that this is true. I am getting old; these young men are my children. I am working hard myself for peace. We are glad to meet all of your chiefs here, and glad to take you by the hands. We want to know if you have heard of forty animals being taken by us from the whites up the road. Three Cheyennes and three Arrapahoes took them. The Arrapahoes got twenty-five head, and the Cheyennes the remainder. . . .

~

PROCEEDINGS IN COUNCIL HELD BY MAJOR GENERAL HANCOCK, COMMANDING DEPARTMENT OF THE MISSOURI, WITH THE HEAD CHIEF "SATANTA," OF THE KIOWA TRIBE OF INDIANS IN KANSAS, AT FORT LARNED, KANSAS, MAY 1, 1867.

. . . Satanta said:
. . . The Cheyennes, Kiowas, and Comanches are poor. They are of all the same color. They are all red men. This country here is old, and it all belongs to them. But you are cutting off the timber, and now the country is of no account at all. I don't mean anything bad by what I say. I have nothing bad hidden in my breast at all; everything is all right there. I have heard that there are many troops coming out in this country to whip the Cheyennes, and that is the reason we were afraid, and went away. The Cheyennes, Arrapahoes, and Kiowas heard that there were troops coming out in this country; so also the Comanches and Apaches, but do not know whether they were coming for peace or for war. They were on the lookout, and listening, and hearing from down out of the ground all the time. They were afraid to come in. I don't think the Cheyennes wanted to fight, but I understand you burned their village. I don't think that was good at all. . . .

Satanta continued: . . . I want peace, and will try to make them keep peaceful. The Kiowa braves have grown up from childhood, obtaining their medicine from the earth. Many have grown old, and continue growing old, and dying from time to time, but there are some remaining yet. I do not want war at all, but want to make friends, and am doing the best I can for that purpose. There are four different bands of Comanches camped at different points in the south, along on the streams, and there are five different bands of Kiowas, those of Lone Wolf, Heap of Bears, Timber Mountain, Black Bird, and Stumbling Bear, and they profess to be chiefs, although they have but two or three lodges each. They are waiting, however, to hear what they can learn before taking the war path. The Kiowas do not say anything, and whatever the white man says is all right for them. The Kiowas and the white men are in council to-day, but I hope no mistake will be made about what the Indians say here, and that nothing will be added to it, because I know that everything is sent right to Washington. . . .

Satanta continued: As for this Arkansas wagon road, I have no objection to it; but I don't want any railroad here, but upon the Smoky Hill route a railroad can run there, and it is all right. On the Arkansas and all those northern streams, there is no timber; it has all been cut off; but, nevertheless, if anybody knows of anything bad being done, I do not like it. There are no longer any buffaloes around here, nor anything else we can kill to live on; but I am striving for peace now, and don't want anything construed to be bad from what I say, because I am simply speaking the plain truth. The Kiowas are poor. Other tribes are very foolish. They make war and are unfortunate, and then call upon the Kiowas to aid them, and I don't know what to think about it. I wan't peace, and all these officers around this country know it. I have talked with them until now I am tired. I came down here, and brought my women with me, but came for peace. If any white men steal our stock, I will report it openly. I continue to come often and am not tired. Now I am doing the best I can, and the white man is looking for me. If there were no troops in this country, and the citizens only lived around here, that would be better. But there are so many troops coming in here that I fear they will do something bad to me. . . .

I heard that the railroad was to come up through this country, and my men and other tribes objected to it; but I advised them to keep silent. I thought that by the railroad being built up through here, we would get our goods sure, but they do not come. I would like to get some agent who is a good and responsible man—one who would give us all our annuities. I do not want an agent who will steal half of our goods and hide them, but an agent who will get all my goods and bring them out here, and give them to me. I am not talking any thing badly or angrily, but simply the truth. I don't think the great men at Washington know any thing about this, but I am now telling your officers to find it out. Now I am done, and whatever you (General Hancock) have to say to me I will listen to, and those who are with me will listen, so that when we return to camp we can tell others the same as you tell us. . . .

～

HEADQ'RS FORT DODGE, KANSAS, *February 24, 1867.*

Brevet Brigadier General CHAUNCEY MCKEEVER,

A. A. General, Headquarters Department of the Mo.,

Fort Leavenworth, Kansas.

SIR: I have the honor to report, that yesterday I had a council with "Satanta," "Stumbling Bear," and other chiefs of the Kiowas. Satanta stated he had heard no bad news yet; that he did not wish to go to war; that he had not yet accepted the tobacco and blankets of peace from the Sioux; that he was friendly to the whites, and expected to remain so; that he might tell me something pretty rough, and I might kill him if I wanted to; he had not much to tell me, but he would conceal nothing; the grass, wood, and water at this post belonged to him; he did not ask the white man to come here, and they must leave; no more wood must be cut on Pawnee Ford; they must stop putting up houses to live in, and white men must not come here to run off the buffalo, and eat up the grass, and drink all the water. He said he told me this now because he would never see me again; he was going to move away from this country; he could get no buffalo, (his party killed four on the way in here,) and he was going away south to hunt; what he was telling me was the truth and no lie. . . .

During this incoherent speech, Satanta was frequently interrupted by the other chiefs, particularly when he gave expression to anything like war-talk, when he would abruptly change his tone, and ask for something to eat.

I replied to his speech as follows:

Satanta has talked half peace and half war to me, and I do not understand what he means; he says his heart is good, and he don't want war; and then he says the white man must move out of this country; that the wood, water, and grass belong to him.

I do not understand such talk; if he wants peace, I advise him to have nothing to do with the Sioux; that they had behaved badly, and the white people were very angry, and it will ruin him and his tribe if they get mixed up with them; I was friendly, or I would not tell him this; if he wanted peace, I did not understand what he meant about the roads and railroads stopping west of Council Grove; neither the roads nor the railroads would be stopped; if they disturbed them, there would be war, and the country would swarm with white men; they would come on him from all sides, and destroy him and his people; . . .

(Signed,) H. DOUGLASS,

Major 3d U. S. Infantry, commanding Post.

Winfield S. Hancock, *Reports of Major General W. S. Hancock upon Indian Affairs, with Accompanying Exhibits* (Washington, DC: GPO, 1867[?]), 3, 8, 11, 43–47, 57–62, 68–72, 126–28.1.

NINE

~

The Promise of Kansas

WHEN WAR BROKE out in 1861, Kansas was still young: after nearly seven years as a territory, it had become a state only weeks prior to Fort Sumter. The war hastened its development and with the return of peace, the state boomed. Many of the changes Kansas saw during Reconstruction were demographic. As Americans were drawn to the state by opportunity and cheap land, Kansas's population grew by a factor of fourteen in the first two decades of statehood. Part of that growth was due to internal changes, such as the negotiation of new treaties with Kansas's American Indian tribes, which officially opened fertile lands in the southern part of the state to settlement. In addition, railroad construction throughout the state increasingly made Kansas an attractive proposition for both investors and those seeking work. Finally, external factors led to an exodus of African Americans out of the South and into Kansas during Reconstruction.

When its first federal census was administered in 1860, Kansas Territory had 107,206 people living within its borders. Although its antislavery reputation might lead one to believe that the state had been settled largely by Massachusetts abolitionists, the settlement pattern was much more diverse. Of its residents in 1860, 12,691 individuals had been born outside the United States. Of the remaining 94,515 individuals, children born in the territory since organization accounted for almost 11,000 residents. Aside from the foreign born, settlers to Kansas came most often from Ohio (11,617), Missouri (11,356), Indiana (9,945), and Illinois (9,367). Kentucky, Pennsylvania, and New York each furnished approximately 6,500 settlers to the territory. Despite common assumptions fed by Bleeding Kansas propaganda, Massachusetts was, in fact, far down the list of settlers' home states, sending only 1,282 emigrants to Kansas—nearly the same number as the Southern state of North Carolina had sent.[1]

By the last year of the war, Kansas had grown to 142,456 residents. Although the 1860 census revealed 13,846 residents born in the states of the future Confederacy, by 1865, Kansas would have only 1,901 residents who had been born in the Deep South.[2] But by far the most significant demographic change Kansas experienced during the Civil War came in the numbers of fugitive slaves who sought refuge in the state. The influx of so-called contrabands began almost immediately as James

H. Lane and his cohorts crossed the border to liberate Missouri slaves. In September 1861, H. D. Fisher claimed to have formally freed the first slaves in wartime. Not all slaves awaited assistance from federal military forces; some crossed into Kansas on their own initiative. When they arrived, many found work as soldiers and farmers, but others needed assistance. In early 1862 the Kansas Emancipation League was formed to alert eastern philanthropists to the need for aid. In addition, the league planned to meet refugees' future needs, pledging not only to "assist all efforts to destroy slavery" but to "encourage industry, education and morality among these people, to find them a benefit and not a burden to the state which shelters them" as well.[3]

As a territory, Kansas had only 625 free black residents and 2 slaves in 1860; yet five years later, African Americans formed 8.9 percent of the Kansas population—the highest ratio the state would ever have—with 12,691 residents. This trend would continue during Reconstruction as black migration came in two waves: from Tennessee in 1875 and from Texas, Louisiana, and Mississippi during 1879 and 1880.[4] Sadly, many fled the South only to discover that Kansas was not the promised land they expected. Instead, these black migrants found "climatic extremes, early crop failures, and other reverses" in "what a St. Louis paper described as a 'bleak and arduous land.'" One group who decided to return to Texas appended a sign to their wagon that captured their experiences in the state: "Farewell to Kansas, / Farewell forever, / I may go to hell, / But back to Kansas, never."[5] Others managed to adjust to the weather and agricultural differences and settled in Kansas. However, a number of the "Exodusters" who fled the racism of the South were disappointed to discover the hardening of racial attitudes in Kansas in the 1880s and 1890s. Some of these individuals left the state, heading for Nebraska and Colorado, while others followed E. P. McCabe, a leader of the Nicodemus colony, the last remaining town in Kansas settled by former slaves, into modern-day Oklahoma.[6] Ultimately, more stayed than left and this influx of black residents significantly affected the state. After three decades of statehood, Kansas's black population would soar from the initial 627 to almost 50,000 residents.

The Civil War brought another major change to Kansas: increased attention to railroad construction in the state. Before the war, there were only five miles of completed track between Elwood and Wathena, in the northernmost part of the state near the Missouri border. In order to support the construction of telegraph lines and railroad tracks from Missouri to the Pacific Ocean, Congress passed the Pacific Railway Act of July 1862. The Union Pacific, Eastern Division (later the Kansas Pacific), and the Atchison and Pikes Peak (later the Union Pacific, Central Branch) both received a federal land grant and a loan of United States bonds to support their construction efforts. These two companies received more than 4 million acres of land in Kansas to build their railroads. In addition, the federal government gave the state another 4 million acres of land to transfer to railroads; a third company, the Atchison, Topeka and Santa Fe, would receive the largest share, a land grant of 2.9 million acres when it reached the western border of Kansas.[7] By 1867 the state had more than 300 miles of track, while in another year that count would reach more than 500 miles.[8]

The railroad also changed Kansans' focus; they moved from the eastern half of the state, where settlement in the territorial period had clustered, to the west, where many Indian tribes still resided. As a result of this shift, the federal government would have to negotiate with the various tribes, and the increased American military presence in this area is not coincidental. In 1859, Fort Larned was constructed, followed by Forts Harker and Zarah in 1864. But 1865, the last year of the American Civil War, saw four forts rise in western Kansas: Dodge, Hays, Kirwin, and Wallace.[9] This is also the year the federal government moved more seriously to negotiate with tribes. The Little Arkansas Treaty of 1865 and the Medicine Lodge Treaty of 1867 with the Cheyennes, Arapahos, Kiowas, and Comanches pushed Kansas's Plains Indians toward Indian Territory and those regions of Kansas that remained unsettled.[10]

These negotiations combined with the frontier war against the tribes demonstrate that the promise Kansas represented for white Americans and for black Americans fleeing the South came at a great cost, especially for the original inhabitants of the state. However uneasily white Kansans welcomed African Americans settling into their state in the aftermath of the war, they were less sanguine about the continued presence of American Indians. As Kiowa Satank stated during the 1867 negotiations, "The white man once came to trade; he now comes as a soldier. He once put his trust in our friendship and wanted no shield but our fidelity. But now he builds forts and plants big guns on their walls. . . . He now covers his face with the cloud of jealousy and anger and tells us to be gone, as an offended master speaks to his dog."[11] And gone they would be, for the promise of Kansas was not all-encompassing.

These documents on postwar Kansas reflect the ambiguity of what Kansas represented. For African Americans, it represented the brightest part of the spectrum: hope that a better life could be forged away from the entrenched racism of the South. For American Indians, it represented the darkest aspects: they were unwanted and standing in the way of white advancement. For white Kansans, the end of the war would bring new challenges: not just contending with other Americans, but wrestling with nature, from drought to grasshoppers, and with "progress" in its many forms, from the unrelenting path of the iron horse to the extension of suffrage to new groups to the election of the nation's first female mayor.

"TRAVERSED BY THE IRON HORSE"

As anticipated by James Humphrey, editor of the Manhattan Express, *President Lincoln signed the Pacific Railway Bill on July 1, 1862.*

THE PACIFIC RAILROAD BILL

Congress and the country are thoroughly awake to the importance of a speedy construction of Railroad to the Pacific shores. The prompt passage of the bill for this purpose by the house on the 6th inst., and the fact that the same bill is reported by the Senate Committee without amendment and its passage urged, is sufficient indication that the great leading interests of the country are now in safe hands. The bill which will undoubtedly become a law, if it has not already passed, creates a body corporate and politic, by the name and style of the Union Pacific Railroad Company. They are empowered to lay out, locate, construct, furnish and maintain a continuous Railroad, with the appurtenances, from points on the one hundred and second meridian of west longitude to the western boundary of Nevada Territory. The capital stock is to consist of 100,000 shares of $1,000 each. Whenever 40 consecutive miles of road shall be completed the Government will issue bonds of $1,000 each to the amount of 16 of said bonds per mile, payable in thirty years after date, bearing six per centum per annum interest.

The line of Railroad and telegraph shall commence on the one hundred and second meridian of west longitude, at the termination of the Leavenworth, Pawnee and western Railroad and Telegraph line, to connect therewith, thence running westerly upon the most direct central and practicable route through the Territories of the United States to the western boundary of Nevada Territory.

The question of the speedy construction of a Railroad to the Pacific coast is now practically settled. Its general location however, is yet a matter of doubt. It is this which now chiefly concerns us as a State. The bill provides for the construction of a line commencing at Leavenworth, with two branches starting from the western boundary of Missouri, and the western line of Iowa. We can hardly concieve how the Leavenworth Pawnee and western Railroad can miss the Kansas valley, through at least a large portion of its length. Indeed, the charter of this latter company provides that they shall construct a line of Railroad as far as the Fort Riley reserve, or to Pawnee. It may then be run in a northernly direction, until it reaches the one hundred and second meridian of longitude west from Greenwich. It would be almost impracticable, were it not at the same time a violation of the terms of their charter, for the company charged with the construction of the road from Leavenworth to the western boundary of Kansas, or the 102 meridian of west longitude, to deviate from the Kansas valley before reaching Fort

Riley.—Every impartial observer will admit that the valley of the Kansas presents the most direct and practicable route for a Railroad, but whether local interests may not rob us of a portion of the road remains to be seen. In any event we doubt not that but a comparatively short time will elapse until the whole length of this beautiful and fertile valley will be traversed by the Iron horse.

Manhattan Express, May 17, 1862.

FARMING CONTINUES AMID THE DISTRACTIONS

As this letter from a member of the executive committee of a newly formed farmers' club attests, the war affected agriculture in Kansas. The state had so few men that the absence of those serving was keenly felt. Close to the Missouri border, Gardner had a reputation as a free-state town in the territorial period. It was invaded by bushwhackers on October 22, 1861, and then twice more in the first three years of the war. The journal to which the writer directed his letter began publishing monthly on May 1, 1863.

LETTER FROM GARDNER.

Gardner, Jan 20th, 1864.

Editor of the Kansas Farmer:

Notwithstanding the distracted state of things here on the border, and the necessity of persons and property which has existed for the last two years, we have succeeded in organizing quite a respectable Farmers' Club. We believe in the sentiment advanced by the Father of his country: That Agricultural Societies contribute greatly to the increase of improvement by stimulating to enterprise and experiment, and by drawing together the results and developments of individual experience, everywhere, thus giving each individual the benefit of the experience of all.

The object of our society being, as declared by our Constitution, to improve the mechanical and agricultural interests of our country. . . .

But very little improvement has been made on the farms in this vicinity for the past two years. Our farming interest are now beginning to revive a little. The energy which our excellent Governor has manifested during the past year in protecting the border, has had to some extent restored confidence in the ability of the State authorities to protect the persons and property of its citizens, and we now occasionally see a *farm building* and field fence in process of erection. Should nothing occur to mar the confidence already gained, we will very soon become an interesting and prosperous agricultural community.

There is at present a great scarcity of common laborers among us. Very many of our able bodied men are in the service of their country; our itinerant population all driven back in the interior for safety; the consequence of this is it is impossible to obtain a day's labor at any price. To obviate this difficulty in some measure our Legislature should immediately adopt some measure to induce emigration to our State. In any part of our State improved land lies idle from scarcity of labor. Now if some measure could be adopted to induce the emigrant to Kansas this land may be made to add to the wealth of the State. Kansas for enterprise is not often behind her sister States, and it is ardently hoped that she will not in this matter prove recreant to her most vital interests. . . .

W. M. Shean.

Kansas Farmer 1, no. 11 (March 1, 1864): 220.

"WE DONT WANT ANY MORE CRY OF FAMINE"

The grasshoppers that periodically invaded Kansas affected the availability of food. This letter addresses the probability of famine and reflects a sensitivity about the state's ability to stand on its own.

Ft Scott, Kansas
May 20, 64

To the Board of County Commissioners
Crawford Co.
Gentlemen,

Reports come to us of distress among the people of the new Counties for want of breadstuffs. I have apprised the Governor that it *may* become necessary to take measures for the relief of some in a *quiet way*. He is anxious to know the exact condition of things and concurs with me in the propriety of working quietly. We dont want any more cry of famine to go up from Kansas. Our state must support her own poor if it takes our last cent—although it is true that if any are to suffer it will be those who have recently come in from other States.

Inasmuch as the law makes you the guardians of the poor I have thought it best that you make quiet inquiry and inform the Governor of the exact present and prospective condition of the people. After much inquiry and some observation I had made up my mind that the people can get through without help *unless* the grasshoppers shall take the garden stuff and the corn crop. If this should occur I think some will have to be helped or be moved to where they can get employment. I wish you would learn all about it and inform the Governor.

If it shall be found necessary to do something towards their relief I would suggest the following. The suffering Counties to issue "Aid Bonds" to be put in the hands of the Governor and traded for corn and bacon. The County Commissioners of each County to receive and distribute the provisions bought by their county bonds and take receipts of the parties. The next Legislature to legalize the Bonds and make the receipts of the destitute a lien on their real and personal property (when recorded) on behalf of the County.

In this way the Counties would be re-imbursed.—If you shall need to do anything and can think of a better plan please do so.

—If you think it best to solicit *donations* we will do so rather than let anybody suffer—but we could scarcely keep our distress out of eastern papers.—Besides it is best—and many would prefer—to feel that they had merely *borrowed* of the County.

—Please keep the Governor informed on the subject.

Respectfully
George A. Crawford

George A. Crawford Papers, Special Collections and University Archives, Wichita State University Libraries.

KANSAS SUFFRAGE SONG

After women failed to gain suffrage in the Wyandotte Constitution, the campaign for women's rights continued. The Impartial Suffrage Association, founded in Topeka in 1867, supported two constitutional amendments (to extend the vote to women and to African Americans), but both were defeated. This suffrage song, with lyrics by P. P. Fowler and John W. Hutchinson, was sung during the 1867 campaign.

THE HUTCHINSONS' KANSAS SUFFRAGE SONG
WORDS BY P. P. FOWLER AND J. W. H.

O, say what thrilling songs of fairies,
Wafted o'er the Kansas prairies,
Charm the ear while zephyrs speed 'em!
Woman's pleading for her freedom.
    CHORUS—Clear the way, the songs are floating;
    Clear the way, the world is noting;
    Prepare the way, the right promoting,
    And ballots, too, for woman's voting.

We frankly say to fathers, brothers,
Husbands, too, and several others,
We're bound to win our right of voting,
Don't you hear the music floating?

We come to take with you our station,
Brave defenders of the nation,
And aim by noble, just endeavor
To elevate our sex forever.

By this vote we'll rid our nation
Of its vile intoxication.
Can't get rum? Oh, what a pity!
Dram-shops closed in every city.

Fear not, we'll darn each worthy stocking,
Duly keep the cradle rocking,
And beg you heed the words we utter,
The ballot wins our bread and butter.

All hail, brave Kansas! first in duty.
Yours, the meed of praise and beauty,
You'll nobly crown your deeds of daring,
Freedom to our sex declaring.

Elizabeth Cady Stanton, Susan B. Anthony, and Matilda Joslyn Gage, eds., *History of Woman Suffrage*, 2nd ed., 6 vols. (Rochester, NY: Charles Mann, 1889), 2:934.

"LANDS FOR THE LANDLESS"

Located in the southeastern corner of Kansas, the Cherokee neutral lands were created by an 1825 treaty with the Osages and contained all of Cherokee and Crawford Counties and part of Bourbon County. It created a barrier between the Indians and white settlers in which neither group was to settle, but white settlers moved in. In 1867 when James F. Joy bought land for the Missouri River, Fort Scott and Gulf Railroad, settlers demanded the right to purchase their land and questioned the legality of his title. Surveys were to begin in 1869, but after the settlers threatened violence, troops arrived in June to keep order and remained through 1873. The dispute was litigated and Joy's 1872 victory was upheld by the U.S. Supreme Court. Ultimately, the settlers bought the land through Joy.

Fort Scott, Kan., May 11, 1869

James F. Joy Esq
Dear Sir,
    Last week I made a trip to the neutral Lands and spent 5 days among the people. . . .

I found a very excited state of feeling in some localities. It is personal against yourself, Mr. Cox, Mr. Grinnel, Mr [Wms?], and the Editors of Baxter & Ft Scott.

The [Land] Leagues are strong about Arcadia and Monmouth, in Crawford Co. and Wirtonia and Columbus in Cherokee. My opinion is that the men who favor violence are in a minority in Crawford Co. In Cherokee they at least have control. I think that if an immediate attempt to *force* the R.R. through the lands is made the Leagues would control the two Counties for the time being—compelling everybody to be with them or leave. The Baxter Springs people and those of Girard are firm and outspoken for the Railroad. In fact the Leagues have become so embittered against Baxter that they are ceasing to trade there. I staid all night at Wirtonia the night the ties were burned. The next I staid at Baxter. Mr. Chaunte was there. All sorts of rumors came to town. It was reported that the town was to be attacked—that Mr. Chauntre was to be interrupted on his return &c &c.

—There are many men opposed to you on the question of title who do not favor violence against the building of the Railroad. I find, however, that there is a very settled determination to resist by force of arms the progress of the R.R. through the Netural Lands. They will do violence to anybody who comes to help locate or build the Road. They can control the country from the Dry Wood to Baxter on that question.—I tried to convince them that in resisting the R.R. they were taking the weakest ground—in opposition not only to the Treaty Making power but to the Act of Congress granting the right of way—also to the act of the Legislature granting the right of way &c &c.—They comprehend fully the responsibility they assume, but claim that they are justified by the circumstances of the case.—I urged an appeal to the Courts and offered to bear a share of the expense in order to avoid violence. They said they would take the case to the Courts but in the meantime no R.R. could be built. The question was now, they said, beyond the control of the leaders and in the hands of the people.

—I think their idea is to have the sympathy of the country. They claim to have been soldiers—entitled to lands—poor and unable to pay even the interest which you ask. There is a Working Men's League started in the east by Gen Casey and others which they claim numbers hundreds of thousands. They expect to arouse the country and Congress in case a collision occurs, by the popular cry of "lands for the landless". They are starting a paper at Columbus on that issue. They claim to have the sympathy of the Governor.–and there may be some ground for this as it is understood that he and Hon Sidney Clarke work together politically and personally.

My impression was that they (the leaders) wish to drive you to a compromise—so I tried to learn what terms would be acceptable. As matters now stand they would demand

1st To go into Court in an agreed case.

2^{d} To have every present occupant secured in his title at $1.25 per acre in case they are beaten

3^{d} to have a contract to this effect in each case so as to bind the land.

4th For this consideration they will allow the R.R. to go through.

—Others in the lands—not Leaguers—have suggested that $1.50 per acre for the occupied lands might be satisfactory.—I suggested that the Government price for R.R. lands is $2.50 per acre usually.

This, briefly, is the result of my observations.—I scarcely know what to suggest. The appeal to arms on either side should be the last resort. You would find Leavenworth & Lawrence and every other rival interest against you in case of conflict.

—I am in hopes that as the R. R. progresses its friends will multiply in advance of it so as to give it protection.—It will pay you to offer the very easiest terms you can afford. The money saved to them in the price will go into improvements and add to the value of your unoccupied lands.—I find, in my experience with towns, that we make as much money in the long run by giving away alternate lots and getting the value in improvements as by selling them.–You can best judge what is best.–If I can be of any service in aiding the R.R. and avoiding blood-shed, I shall be very glad indeed.

Respectfully &c
Geo. A. Crawford

George A. Crawford Papers, Special Collections and University Archives, Wichita State University Libraries.

THE RAILROAD'S ROUTE

The railroad was critical to the development of many small towns in Kansas. Located on the Delaware River in the eastern part of the state, Grasshopper Falls grew slowly until the railroad arrived. Eventually the town would be at the junction of the Atchinson, Topeka and Santa Fe and the Kansas Central railroads. Trains for the former began running in 1872, while the latter was extended from Leavenworth that fall.

G. H. Falls, Kan.
June 10th 1869.

S. D. Cabaniss Esq.
Huntsville, Ala.

Dear Sir:— . . . I thought to give you the news from G. H. F. would not be amiss. . . . I have written Mr Lakin to know if he would secure me a situation

with him; or to assist the Surveyors of the A. T. & S. F. R. R. with their surveys.
I have not yet received an answer from him. I hope to be able to engage at
something by which I can make an honest living. . . .

The general opinion of the knowing people is, that the R. R. will certainly
pass through G. H. F. this year. It is reported that these Surveyors will commence
to survey a permanent route, so even as they complete and perfect their
agreements on the Road south from Topeka, which will consume some three
weeks yet, Mr Lakin seems confident that the Road will be built, and his opinion
is worth speaking [?] after, with regards railroad matters. It is thought now that
the permanent survey will run in the eastern portions of the towns, near Dr.
Northrup. . . . The Cobb place remains uncultivated and unimproved, so also
the Bowles place, I understand the present prospect for good crops on the other
above mentioned places is very favorable. However, the grasshopper have made
their appearance through the country in myriads, and in some localities have
already ruined fall wheat, and Oats.

Immigrants continue to come nearly every day to whom lands have been sold
from $10. to $20. per acre, owing to the locality and improvements on the lands.
I will now close. . . .

R. M. Spring
P. O. Box 76

Kansas Territory Papers, Special Collections and University Archives, Wichita State University Libraries.

ROCKY MOUNTAIN GRASSHOPPERS COME TO KANSAS

*Grasshoppers were a periodic problem in Kansas; under normal conditions,
grasshoppers swarmed in sufficient numbers to "threaten injury or do some damage,"
and when larger populations of grasshoppers invaded the state, the damage was
considerable, especially when drought left no margin for crop losses. For Kansans,
the outbreak of Rocky Mountain grasshoppers from 1874 to 1876 was particularly
noteworthy, coming in such waves that settlers reported they "hid the sun."*[12]

"THEY LOOK BEAUTIFUL BUT THEIR WORK IS FEARFUL"

Topeka Kansas Aug 30 74

Dear Daughter
. . . This is a beutiful country through here generally but now it has been all
eaten over by grass hoppers for hundreds of miles in every direction They come
in immense numbers and alight and eat up everything green and then rise in the
air and move on. They are now flying south having been up in Nebraska—When

I left Junction City 71 miles west of here they were flying south there and the air has been full of them all the way here and passengers in the cars say it is the same a hundred miles west of there and they have been passing that way for several days. You can only see them plainly in the direction of the sun and they then look like snowflakes it looks as if the sky was full of snow—their wings showing white in the sun light They look beautiful but their work is fearful. Thousands of families are moving east to escape starvation—You can see their white top waggons moving along the prairies as far as the eye can reach all returning home—East discouraged
Kiss Dora for me—Love to all

Affectionately yours,
James Hanford

Miscellaneous Hanford Collection, Kansas State Historical Society.

GRASSHOPPERS "LIKE A TRAIN OF CARS IN THE AIR"

Osage Mission Kansas
March the 26th, 1875

Dear Cousin Rob and Family,
. . . you wanted to know how close the grass hoppers came If you had got as many bumps on the nose & face as I did last fall you would thought you had been among them it no use for me to try to describe grass hopper senes I could not do it justice some days when they wase shifting you would hear a noise over your head like a train of cars in the air on looking up you would see the whole Elements darken with grass hoppers when they came down at night they would cover the ground complete Thoes that lit down on a corn field no difference how long it was would devour it in one days time neither leave blade husk corn on cob. We had to cut our hay in august on account of them and then they would jam the sickle so we could hardly cut they took every thing we had except our wheat last year was the only grass hoppers I have seen since I came here may be several years before they visit this part again they came from colerado and are called the colerado grass hoppers they hatch out on the dessert
   Well, Rob, there has been so much said about kansas destitution that I fear you have got out of the notion of coming its true we are hard up just now, but I aint the least discouraged I have done well since I came here I have sold two farms since I came and now living on the third one I think I have the best situation in the county I live on the crossing of two main traveled roads one mile and a half from the R Road, large running stream in 20 Rods of the house timber

the same distance the country is one of the grandest I ever saw all likes it that come here yet the climate is so mild the day you rote your letter the farmers was sowin oats all day frost had been out long before and it was warm i went to Fort Scott that day and about every one was sowing oats

. . . Well Robert, I think the best thing . . . is come to Kansas land is cheep yet and now is a good time to buy while the grass hopper fever is up as soon as we get a crop time will bee good again the spring has set in deliteful oats are all soed and plowing for corn. there will be grate [d]eal of corn planted in this month if weather remains warm we can rais anything here that canbe raised anywhere peaches ranges from 10 cts 25 to 50 cts per bushel I have four thousand young trees to give away

I want you to think on the subject of coming west and, if you want any further Information write to me and I will do all I can to assist you. I would like to see all of you out here. . . .

Old Osage Mission

Kansas   A. W. Johnson

A. W. Johnson to Robert S. Wickizer, Miscellaneous Asa M. Wickizer Collection, Kansas State Historical Society.

"HO FOR KANSAS!"

In 1878, "Ho for Kansas!" circulars could be found throughout the South calling for "Brethren, Friends, & Fellow Citizens" to leave for Kansas under the leadership of Benjamin Singleton, who became known as the father of the exodus. Born into slavery in 1809 in Tennessee, Singleton escaped to Canada and eventually settled in Michigan. He returned to his home state after the Civil War ended, hoping to help African Americans purchase land in the South, but hardening racial attitudes led him to abandon his hopes. Instead, he led an exodus to Kansas, where he established a colony in Morris County. By 1879 some fifty thousand African Americans had left the South, many heading to Kansas as well as Missouri, Indiana, and Illinois. In 1880, Singleton testified before the Senate about the hostile environment that led to the exodus. Singleton's motivations are further illustrated in an interview that same year.

TESTIMONY OF BENJAMIN SINGLETON

Washington, D. C., April 17, 1880.

Benjamin SINGLETON (colored) sworn and examined.

By Mr. WINDOM:

Question. Where were you born, Mr. Singleton?—Answer. I was born in the State of Tennessee, sir.

Q. Where do you now live?—A. In Kansas.

Q. What part of Kansas?—A. I have a colony sixty miles from Topeka, sir.

Q. Which way from Topeka—west?—A. Yes, sir; sixty miles from Topeka west.

Q. What is your colony called?—A. Singleton colony is the name of it, sir.

Q. How long has it been since you have formed that colony?—A. I have two colonies in Kansas—one in Cherokee County, and one in Lyon, Morris County.

Q. When did you commence the formation of that colony—the first one?—A. It was in 1875, perhaps. . . .

Q. When did you change your home from Tennessee to Kansas?—A. I have been going there for the last six or seven years, sir.

Q. Going between Tennessee and Kansas, at different times?—A. Yes, sir; several times.

Q. Well, tell us about it?—A. I have been fetching out people; I believe I fetched out 7,432 people.

Q. You have brought out 7,432 people from the South to Kansas?—A. Yes, sir; brought and sent.

Q. That is, they came out to Kansas under your influence?—A. Yes, sir; I was the cause of it. . . .

Q. How did you happen to send them out?—A. The first cause, do you mean, of them going?

Q. Yes; What was the cause of your going out, and in the first place how did you happen to go there, or to send these people there?—A. Well, my people, for the want of land—we needed land for our children—and their disadvantages—that caused my heart to grieve and sorrow; pity for my race, sir, that was coming down, instead of going up—that caused me to go to work for them. I sent out there perhaps in '66—perhaps so; or in '65, any way—my memory don't recollect which; and they brought back tolerable favorable reports; then I jacked up three or four hundred, and went into Southern Kansas, and found it was a good country, and I thought Southern Kansas was congenial to our nature, sir; and I formed a colony there, and bought about a thousand acres of ground—the colony did—my people.

Q. And they went upon it and settled there?—A. Yes, sir; they went and settled there.

Q. Were they men with some means or without means?—A. I never carried none there without means. . . .

Q. Tell us how these people are getting on in Kansas?—A. I am glad to tell you, sir.

Q. Have they any property now?—A. Yes; I have carried some people in there that when they got there they didn't have fifty cents left, and now they have got in my colony—Singleton colony—a house, nice cabins, their milch cows, and pigs, and sheep, perhaps a span of horses, and trees before their yards, and some three or four or ten acres broken up, and all of them has got little houses that I carried there. They didn't go under no relief assistance; they went on their own resources; and when they went in there first the country was not overrun with them; you see they could get good wages; the country was not overstocked with people; they went to work, and I never helped them as soon as I put them on the land.

Q. Well, they have been coming continually, and adding from time to time to your colony these few years past, have they?—A. Yes, sir; I have spent, perhaps, nearly six hundred dollars flooding the country with circulars.

Q. You have sent the circulars yourself, have you?—A. Yes, sir; all over these United States.

Q. Did you send them into other Southern States besides Tennessee?—A. O, yes, sir.

Q. Did you do that at the instance of Governor St. John and others in Kansas?— A. O, no, sir; no white men. This was gotten up by colored men in purity and confidence; not a political negro was in it; they would want to pilfer and rob at the cents before they got the dollars. O, no, it was the muscle of the arm, the men that worked that we wanted.

Q. Well, tell us all about it.—A. These men would tell all their grievances to me in Tennessee—the sorrows of their heart. You know I was an undertaker there in Nashville, and worked in the shop. Well, actually, I would have to go and bury their fathers and mothers. You see we have the same heart and feelings as any other race and nation. (The land is free, and it is nobody's business, if there is land enough, where the people go. *I* put that in my people's heads.) Well, that man would die, and I would bury him; and the next morning maybe a woman would go to that man (meaning the landlord), and she would have six or seven children, and he would say to her, "Well, your husband owed me before he died;" and they would say that to every last one of them, "You owe me." Suppose he would? Then he would say, "You must go to some other place; I cannot take care of you." Now, you see, that is something I would take notice of. That woman had to go out, and these little children was left running through the streets, and the next place you would find them in a disorderly house, and their children in the State's prison.

Well, now, sir, you will find that I have a charter here. You will find that I called on the white people in Tennessee about that time. I called conventions about it, and they sot with me in my conventions, and "Old man," they said, "you are right." The white people said, "You are right; take your people away." And let me tell you, it was the white people—the ex-governor of the State, felt like I did. And they said to me, "You have tooken a great deal on to yourself, but if these negroes, instead of deceiving one an other and running for office, would take the same idea that you have in your head, you will be a people."

I then went out to Kansas, and advised them all to go to Kansas; and, sir, they are going to leave the Southern country. The Southern country is out of joint. The blood of a white man runs through my veins. That is congenial, you know, to my nature. That is my choice. Right emphatically, I tell you today, I woke up the millions right through me! The great God of glory has worked in me. I have had open air interviews with the living spirit of God for my people; and we are going to leave the South. We are going to leave it if there ain't an alteration and signs of a change. I am going to advise the people who left that country (Kansas) to go back.

Q. What do you mean by a change?—A. Well, I am not going to stand bulldozing and half pay and all those things. Gentlemen, allow me to tell you the truth; it seems to me that they have picked out the negroes from the Southern country to come here and testify who are in good circumstances and own their homes, and not the poor ones who don't study their own interests. Let them go and pick up the men that has to walk when they goes, and not those who have money.

There is good white men in the Southern country, but it ain't the minority (majority); they can't do nothing; the bulldozers has got possession of the country, and they have got to go in there and stop them; if they don't the last colored man will leave them. I see colored men testifying to a positive lie, for they told me out there all their interests were in Louisiana and Mississippi. Said I, "You are right to protect you own country;" and they would tell me, "I am obliged to do what I am doing." Of course I have done the same, but I am clear footed.

Q. Now you say that during these years you have been getting up this colony you have spent, yourself, some six hundred dollars in circulars, and in sending them out; where did you send them, Mr. Singleton?—A. Into Mississippi, Alabama, South Carolina, Georgia, Kentucky, Virginia, North Carolina, Texas, Tennessee, and all those countries.

Q. To whom did you send them; how were they circulated?—A. Every man that would come into my country, and I could get a chance, I would put one in his hand, and the boys that started from my country on the boats, and the porters on the cars. That is the way I circulated them.

Q. Did you send any out by mail?—A. I think I sent some perhaps to North Carolina by mail—I think I did. I sent them out by people, you see.

Q. Yes; by colored people, generally?—A. Some white people, too. There was Mrs. Governor Brown, the first Governor Brown of Tennessee—Mrs. Sanders, she was a widow, and she married the governor. He had thirty on his place. I went to him, and he has given me advice. And Ex-Governor Brown, he is there too.

Q. You say your circulars were sent all over these States?—A. Yes, sir; to all of 'em.

Q. Did you ever hear from them; did anybody ever write to you about them?—A. O, yes.

Q. And you attribute this movement to the information you gave in your circulars?—A. Yes, sir; *I am the whole cause of the Kansas immigration!*

Q. You take all that responsibility on yourself?—A. I do, and I can prove it; and I think I have done a good deal of good, and I feel relieved!

Q. You are proud of your work?—A. Yes, sir; I am! (Uttered emphatically.)

Q. Well, now, some of those people that go there suffer a great deal; what have you to say about that?—A. I tell you how it is. I speak plainly. It is "root hog, or die." I tell the truth. Kansas is not a warm climate.

Q. Do you think that your people suffer more from the climate there than they do at home?—A. No, sir.

Q. Have you talked with the people that have gone there lately as to the reason for their going?—A. Yes.

Q. What reasons did they give?—A. They say they have been badly treated in their countries. . . .

Q. Is there any way to stop it?—A. No way, sir, on God's earth to stop it. . . .

U.S. Congress, Senate Report 693, 46th Cong., 2nd sess., 1880, 379–84.

INTERVIEW WITH BENJAMIN "PAP" SINGLETON

Mr. Singleton said—in substance I am 71 years old I am here for a special purpose—to tell the cause of the exodus. I have been in the cause thirteen years. I have been talking to my people, and they have seen the light and are seeking homes

In the South the colored men have been murdered, lacerated and whipped, and have cried for mercy in vain.

They have determined they would they would arise and seek a land in the West—a land unknown to us

I have been called the father of the exodus and am seeking homes for my People

Two hundred thousand are coming out of the South between now and the 1st of April unless the conduct of the Southern people is changed

I have been a slave fled to Canada when my children were small and nineteen years after when I returned they were grown

The treatment of the colored man is as bad now as in the time of slavery

When this act did not suit some scoundrel down there—the man offending would hear the fatal rap at his door, and the next morning his wife would have to cut his body down from the tree with a knife Many of the colored people have been beaten at their door many have been lacerated, many murdered—. . . their daughters debauched. . . .

When Senator from Indiana said the exodus was a scheme of the Rail-Roads was the machinations of politicians, he called many men before his committee to Washington, many who were interested in keeping the colored people South, & some who told the truth in regard to the conduct of the Southern people towards the colored men. He called me—I told him of the conduct of these people towards the colored men, how they were treated—and suffered—thus they had determined to come out of there—that I should find homes for 12,000 or 15,000 in Indiana Some 600—near Pontiac, Some near Springfield and other places—I was the last man examined.

I cant see what we will do if this man Garfield is not elected.

I am a Republican, a thorough Republican—

Why would men who have fought and bled for their country see this

I don't see how this man Hancock who has been in the army could run on the democratic ticket Democrats that say they are not like these Southern Democrats—they are as bad or worse—they are helping them, who boast of a solid South to carry out their purpose—the Ku Klux Klan originated in Indiana and New York.

The South want to make the colored people raise their cotton and Rice and be the hewer of wood and drawers of water—They want the colored men to work for small wages, and live on a little bread and water—and then be liable to be lacerated and murdered—The Southern people refuse to sell their land They ask Sixty-dollars for acre for land not worth more than one dollar and a quarter per acre.

Republicans at first persuaded us to stay and improve the country—while I told them to come out

I say I do not know what the colored People can do there unless this man Garfield is elected. He must buckle on his armor and run like a race horse

If there is not a change in the South between now and April next the remedy to relieve the colored people will be this exodus—It will grind the South to Powder—The South will suffer too cotton will go up to 25 to 40 cents a pound Sugar and Rice accordingly

These people will come out and make homes in the West, We would like the South—it suits us, is congenial to us if we could live there

In Kansas in Cherokee county and adjoining those who have gone before are making good homes fine farms, fine orchards, and are raising good crops, are building churches and school houses and soon will have fine society of their own

At the close the colored people present by a unanimous vote, promised their [help] and when they should hear of the exodus had commenced.

B. Singleton MSS, Kansas State Historical Society.

THE EXODUS "WILL TEST THE BOASTED
LOVE OF LIBERTY IN THE NORTH"

The eighth governor of Kansas, John Pierce St. John, was inaugurated in 1878, the year the exodus of freed people out of the South and into Kansas began. St. John headed the Kansas Freedman's Relief Association and, in this letter, he updated Horatio N. Rust, secretary of the Southern Refugee Relief Association, about how the influx of refugees was affecting his state.

State of Kansas, Executive Department
Topeka, January 16, 1880

Horatio N. Rust,
Chicago, Ill.,
My Dear Sir:

In answer to your letter of the 12th instant I have the honor to state, that I am of the opinion that, since last April, from 15,000 to 20,000 colored refugees have arrived in Kansas. Of this number perhaps not less than 12,000 were destitute of food and the means to buy it. Their clothing was wholly unsuited to this climate.

The Freedmen's Relief Association, organized here last spring, has, through its efforts, secured employment for at least 10,000 of this number. This has been accomplished through auxiliary societies organized in various portions of the State, some counties taking 20 families, some 50 and some as high as 100, and extending to them the opportunity of earning their own living. One or two carloads have been forwarded to Nebraska, where they were kindly received and cared for until homes could be secured for them. The Association has established a small colony in Wabaunsee County, about 50 miles west of here. This colony, taking everything into consideration, is getting along well, and I think, after say, July next, will be entirely self-supporting.

Barracks have been built near the city of Topeka that furnish reasonably comfortable quarters for about 200 persons, but during the past 6 weeks, the number crowded into these barracks would average perhaps 400 persons, while some have lived in tents, with very scanty bed-clothing and but little fuel. The result has been that the feet of quite a large number were frozen, during the cold weather about the time of the holidays. The weather however is milder now, and we hope that such exposure can be avoided in the future. These poor unfortunate creatures never murmur. They come to us, as friends, fleeing from their enemies. All unite in substantially the same story of cruelty, outrage and wrong heaped upon them by their oppressors in the South, the details of which I shall not undertake to relate to you now. Suffice it to say that, during the past few years, they have been subjected to a worse condition of things than ever existed in the South before;—the treatment extended to them being a disgrace to the civilization of the day and age in which we live.

The Relief Assn. is now needing lumber to build additional barracks and to finish houses that are already partly constructed by the freedmen. The average number being fed by the Assn. now is perhaps 300. This, as you are aware, costs money. In order to secure homes and an opportunity for these people to earn their own living, they are distributed in almost every direction, the greater portion of them in different localities through Kansas, wherever locations can be secured for them, while a few are sent to Iowa and Nebraska. In making this distribution it becomes necessary to pay railroad fares, which of course costs a great deal of money, hence you will see that money is necessarily required to carry on this work.

I have no means, right at hand, of stating to you the *exact* amount that has been expended by the Relief Assn. I incline to the opinion, however, that it will not vary far from $20,000 during the last 8 or 9 months. At times, the Assn. has been almost entirely destitute of funds; in fact I believe at one time, about 10 days ago, there was only ten cents left in the treasury; but we were not discouraged, for we had practically been in that condition before, yet we had full faith that God would open the way and replenish the treasury, and we were not disappointed. Just now, owing to the large numbers that are coming in every week and the correspondingly large expenditures, there is but little money in the treasury, yet we have faith that it will come as it is needed.

Having in view solely that which is for the best interest of these poor people, you will pardon me if I suggest to you, and through you to the philanthropic friends in your city, that, in my opinion, the great State of Illinois, that furnished to this country Abraham Lincoln who issued the proclamation that set these people free, and Grant at the head of the grand army that enforced it, could do no greater honor to herself and her martyred heroes than to open wide her doors to the unfortunate refugees, and furnish homes for 50,000 of them, where they could earn their own living, instead of sending supplies to them to a State that is already overcrowded with them to such an extent as to render it almost impossible to secure labor for them, so that they may be self-supporting.

I beg of you not to understand me as intimating that Kansas, in any sense, is complaining. Our people know what it is to struggle for freedom. They know its cost, and we shall never turn our backs upon any law-abiding human being who is willing to put forth an earnest effort to make an honest living. I only make these suggestions to the people of your State for the benefit of the colored people, as you are of course aware that Kansas, being yet in her infancy, can absorb only a limited number of this unfortunate race who depend upon their labor for support. Whenever the labor market is overstocked, of course means for their support is cut short, and they are thrown back upon the charities of the people. We have here to-day as many as can secure employment, yet they continue to come to Kansas at the rate of at least 250 a week. They seem to think that this is the promised land. Of course it is difficult to tell what will be the result; but of one thing you may rest assured, that, God helping us, we shall ever work earnestly and faithfully to do our whole duty. The refugees from the South would gladly go to Illinois, if they could only be made to feel that your people were not opposed to their coming.

Oh, for a Lincoln or a Lovejoy to step to the front in your grand State and speak out boldly upon these questions, and arouse your people to a realization of the magnitude and importance of this movement on the part of the blacks. I make the prediction that the present year will bring at least 100,000 of them northward. They must find a lodging place somewhere. This movement will test the boasted love of liberty in the north. It will try the spinal column of politicians; it will separate the doubting Thomases from the brave Joshuas; it will test the question whether any class of human beings are to have their liberties crushed out, in any portion of this country.

Kansas has never done anything to encourage the colored people to leave the South. We have simply, in dealing with this question, done as we believed God would have us do. It is not a political question; it rises above all politics. It is a question in which is involved human liberty, and the people of the North, through whose bravery and devotion to liberty the colored people were set free, should not forget that these same colored people have always been true and loyal to our government, that they were the friends of our soldiers in the darkest days of the rebellion, and now, in their hour of distress, we should stand by them in every laudable effort that they shall make to accomplish a second, and I hope their final, emancipation. They do not come North because they prefer the Northern to the Southern States, but they are compelled to come, for the reason that they no longer feel secure in either life or property, or enjoy any reasonable degree of liberty. The white people of the South could put a stop to this exodus at once, by simply extending to the blacks the same protection to life and property and equal rights before the law that the whites enjoy. But, until these rights and privileges are guaranteed to, and enjoyed by, the blacks, the exodus will continue, the refugees alleging that they would rather perish in their efforts to secure a lodgement in the North than to longer remain and suffer as they have heretofore in the South.

When the people of your State desire to know just what these poor people are in need of, they will find no difficulty in arriving at an answer, by thinking for a moment just what white people would require who are destitute of food, thinly clad, in a cold climate and without money, and among strangers. . . .

I am very glad to be able to state that the refugees who have come to Kansas are sober, industrious and well-behaved, and gladly embrace the opportunity of making their own living when it is offered.

Very truly your friend,
John P. St. John

STRUGGLING TO PROVIDE FOR THE REFUGEES

The Kansas Freedman's Relief Association was incorporated on May 8, 1879, to help refugees deal with their new circumstances. This circular letter details the difficulties Kansas's climate presented to those leaving the South.

A CIRCULAR LETTER

Topeka, Kansas, April 7th, 1880.

Although the rigor of winter's chilling blasts are in the wane, yet pneumonia continues the leading disease, and is taking many of these people who have fled from the "sunny South," where flowers that blossom all the year round lose their charms while bereft of "God-given rights to life, liberty and the pursuit of happiness."

In this city alone, during last month (March) there were thirty-two refugees buried by this Relief Association. Said a bereaved widow, "It 'pears hard to lose my man, but 'taint so hard as to see him shot dead, like the bull dozers shot Fairfax, las' fall a year ago. Now de Laud takes 'im."

I never saw so much suffering, with so little murmuring, as I have found among these people. No earnest worker for this people can escape a sip of the cup of persecution they have so long been compelled to drink in overflowing draughts, of the bitter waters of Morah. We are confident the friends of this oppressed people will not become weary in well-doing.

From present indications we do not see a prospect of decrease in this emigration. Money for food, shelter and medicine is needed.

LAURA S. HAVILAND,

Sec'y Kansas Freedman's Relief Ass'n.

"THEY STILL COME"

Kansas was not alone in providing for these refugees. The Southern Refugee Relief Association, headquartered in Chicago, also provided philanthropic aid. In this appeal, the association reprinted reports from agents in Kansas to illustrate the extent of need.

SOUTHERN REFUGEE RELIEF ASSOCIATION,
ORGANIZED FEB. 9, 1880,
FOR THE PURPOSE OF RELIEVING THE GREAT WANT
GROWING OUT OF THE NEGRO EXODUS, . . .

Chicago, January 22d, 1881.

AN APPEAL FOR HELP IN BEHALF OF THE COLORED REFUGEES IN KANSAS.

One year ago this month we published a statement from Mrs. Elizabeth L. Comstock, of Topeka, setting forth the destitution of the Refugees in Kansas, asking for your contribution of money, clothing and bedding. The response was generous. We received several carloads of goods, and forwarded them to Topeka, met the demand, and saved much suffering. Then we reported 20,000 arrivals in the new State. To-day comes a very similar appeal from Mrs. Comstock, saying the number has increased to over 60,000, and still they come. Our supplies are very short, extreme cold weather and exposure have induced much sickness, multitudes are suffering for fuel and shelter and the necessaries of life, and again we ask your contribution.

Below we give extracts from letters received from our agents in Kansas, whom the Association depends upon to distribute supplies, thinking this may be the best form of appeal we can use:

"Our people (refugees) here number from 700 to 800, principally Texans, poor, simple, field hands, the poorest of the exodites, those who came overland with Texas teams, trusting hearts, no money, large families, and devout Christians, about nine-tenths of them requiring aid. Fifty sick. During cold weather many were frost-bitten, some disabled. Coughs, pneumonia, ague, are the common sickness. This cold weather the people suffer much. I am out of funds, and twenty-five dollars behind. Two poor creatures from Texas just called on me for a bed-quilt to cover them to-night, and a dress each, *mothers;* I had none to give them. What we need most is medicine for the sick and help for the aged widows, then warm bedding and clothing.

"Oswego, Dec. 23, '80."   "W. S. NEWLON.

"It has been a very cold winter so far, and severe on our poor folks. Quite a number have just come from Texas. I wish I had some funds to relieve them. Great need of lumber for shelter.

"Parsons, Kas." "MILTON W. REYNOLDS, Pres't Labette Co. F. R. A.

Lucretia Fulton, one of our ablest workers in North Topeka, reports, under date of Dec. 30th, 38 widows with families of children in great destitution. Five of them with crippled sons; three with idiotic daughters, the result of southern cruelty and oppression.

Daniel Votaw, Independence, Kas., Dec. 25, 1880: "2,500 refugees in our part of the work, 1,500 of whom need assistance, so many came too late to make crops this year. Many of them are sick. They sleep so cold at night it is killing them. Fifty of them are not able to leave their rooms or tents."

L. M. Pickering, of Columbus, tells us, Dec. 29, 1880, that 500 in Chotopa and Oswego will perish, if not largely and speedily helped.

J. W. Wilson writes from Atchison, Kas., Dec. 18, 1880: "There are eight families here greatly needing help. They require clothing, bedding, fuel and provisions. I shall be very glad if the Relief Society will do something for them."

Dec. 31: In Oswego there are 900 refugees, 700 of them requiring aid. $200 per month required to give them the needful care, medicines, shelter and fuel. Much sickness, many little children and aged people.

Baxter Springs, 1000 refugees; 300 the age for going to school. Not much sickness. No color prejudice. School needed. Population of whites, 1,500. Too poor to sustain a school. Bedding, warm clothing, bed ticks, shoes, greatly needed.

Chetopa, 1,000 refugees; much sickness. Pneumonia, colds, &c., result of exposure. School greatly needed. Children's clothing, nourishing food for sick and aged. This village is the most direct point they reach in Kansas by railroad from Texas.

Dr. Newlon, Oswego, Kas., writes Dec. 30: "Relieving 200 a week. Our clothing all gone. Weather terribly cold. They still come. Send some bedding and clothing as soon as possible."

Daniel Votaw: "150 came last week, in great destitution. Many barefoot except rags wrapped and tied around their feet. We saw many new arrivals in Coffeyville whose condition beggars description. There was not a whole garment among them. Some had their tattered pants, coats, and shoes tied on with strings and strips of muslin. D. Votaw's field includes Independence, Coffeywille, Sedan and Cherryvale. Great distress and destitution in all these places."

A. B. Whiting, Topeka, Kas., says, Dec. 31: "The very old and physically helpless, the widows with large families of young children, 'the lame, halt and blind' among our exodites, can be counted by the hundreds. These are, and such as these always will be, objects of charity, and many children are needing clothing to fit them for school."

Wilmer Walten, our agent at Parsons, Kas., writes under date 12, 22, 80: "I was very thankful to hear that we are soon to receive supplies, for indeed we greatly need them. Bed ticks, bedding, shawls or scarfs for women, underwear for both sexes. Young and old in great need of shoes and socks or stockings. Weather extremely cold; much suffering for want of fuel and shelter."

A Letter from Mrs. Elizabeth L. Comstock.—We hope that our kind friends who have so liberally aided us during the past year will feel satisfied that their money and time has been well spent, as they hear the results of their kindness. Not a single colored tramp was seen last winter in Kansas, not one refugee has been arrested for stealing. Very little profanity has been heard among them, Of those for whom occupation and homes have been found in other States, we hear very good reports. They are spoken of as honest, sober, industrious and Christian people. We can bear testimony to their being more Christlike in disposition than any other race we have had anything to do with. Meek, patient, gentle, long-suffering and forgiving, our race owes a heavy debt to theirs. By their long years of unrequited toil, we and our fathers have been enriched, as we purchased the products of their labor at less price than we could have done had they been freemen. Our comforts, our luxuries, our wealth, have been drained from their life-blood; our pleasant houses, our well-supplied tables, our wardrobes, all plead for those who have contributed so largely to our national prosperity. Shall we treat these feeble, helpless children of God as they have been treated in the South, or shall we receive them as brethren and sisters created by our Father's hand, for whom our Savior has died? Send us warm bedding, send us clothing, send us shoes, bed ticks; provide shelter for the homeless wanderers, food for the hungry, help for the helpless to help themselves, and, in a coming day may we every one hear the blessed words: "I was hungry and ye fed me, naked and ye clothed me, a stranger and ye took me in!"

Elizabeth L. Comstock. . . .

The principal Railroads coming into Chicago have generously brought relief goods free, and will continue so to do. The Express Companies also bring *small parcels* free, which courtesy is duly appreciated by their patrons along the different routes, and by all friends of the cause.

Respectfully yours,
HORATIO N. RUST,
Secretary Southern Refugee Association.

Timeline

1854

January	Illinois senator Stephen Douglas introduces the Kansas-Nebraska Bill.
April	In Massachusetts, Eli Thayer begins organizing emigrants to Kansas.
May	President Franklin Pierce signs the Kansas-Nebraska Act organizing Kansas and Nebraska under popular sovereignty.
June	Residents of Missouri cross into Kansas, announce that slavery is instituted, and return to Missouri.
July	Settlers from the Massachusetts Emigrant Aid Company arrive in Kansas and establish the town of Lawrence.
	The Platte Country (Missouri) Self-Defense Association pledges to remove emigrants who go to Kansas under emigrant aid societies.
October	Territorial governor Andrew Reeder arrives in Kansas.
November	Territorial residents select John Whitfield as territorial delegate to the U.S. House of Representatives in their first election, one marked by fraud and voter intimidation.

1855

March	In their second territorial election, again marked by fraud and voter intimidation, Kansas residents select members for the territorial legislature.
May	A special election is held to fill seats vacated by the governor in April due to fraud.
July	The first territorial legislature convenes in Pawnee, then adjourns to Shawnee Mission, near the Missouri border.
August	Kansas's territorial legislature passes a harsh law protecting slavery.
September	Wilson Shannon replaces Andrew Reeder as territorial governor.
	The Free-State Party meets at Big Springs and resolves that African Americans, whether slave or free, should be excluded from Kansas.

The Free-State Party meets in Topeka and issues a People's Proclamation outlining the troubles in Kansas.

October   John Whitfield is elected territorial delegate once more, but in a separate election the Free-State Party elects Andrew Reeder.

In Topeka the Free-State Party holds a constitutional convention and creates the Topeka Constitution.

November   The proslavery Law and Order Party convenes.

Responding to Missouri's pleas for settlers, Jefferson Buford of Alabama issues a call in Southern newspapers for men to go to Kansas, funding his expedition, in part, by auctioning his slaves.

Proslavery advocate Franklin Coleman kills free-state advocate Charles Dow, sparking the two-week Wakarusa War.

December   Shannon ends the Wakarusa War by signing an agreement absolving Lawrence residents of complicity in rescuing Dow's roommate, Jacob Branson, from federal custody.

1856

January   Pierce informs Congress of the conflict in Kansas and requests funds to ensure order.

Charles Robinson is elected governor and Mark Delahay is elected representative under the Topeka Constitution.

February   Pierce issues a public proclamation against outside interference in Kansas, asking residents to obey the law and authorizing the territorial governor to call on federal troops at Fort Leavenworth.

March   The Topeka government selects Andrew Reeder and James Lane as senators-elect and sends a memorial to Congress asking for admission to the Union.

The House of Representatives forms a select committee to investigate the troubles in Kansas that is known as the Howard Committee, after its chair.

April   The Howard Committee opens hearings in Lawrence.

May   The Buford expedition arrives in Lawrence.

A grand jury in Douglas County indicts the leaders of the Topeka movement for usurpation of office and orders Lawrence's Free State Hotel, the *Herald of Freedom,* and the *Kansas Free State* be abated as nuisances.

U.S. Marshal Israel Donelson calls for a posse to help deliver subpoenas after determining that Lawrence residents are resisting arrest.

Douglas County sheriff Samuel Jones calls Donelson's disbanded posse back into service and leads a sack of Lawrence.

Massachusetts senator Charles Sumner is caned by South Carolina representative Preston Brooks in retaliation for his Crime against Kansas speech.

In retaliation for the sack of Lawrence, John Brown leads a small party to Pottawatomie Creek, where they execute five proslavery men.

Charles Robinson is arrested in Missouri and extradited to Kansas, where he and other leaders of the Topeka government are imprisoned near Fort Leavenworth for the summer.

June   Pierce places General Persifor Smith, commander of the Army of the West, in command of territorial forces.

Fighting commences in Kansas, especially in the southeastern counties of the territory where the battles of Black Jack, Franklin, Fort Titus, Osawatomie, and Hickory Point are fought over the next four months.

July   The House of Representatives accepts the Topeka Constitution by a vote of 99 to 97.

Federal troops disperse a meeting of the Topeka legislature.

August   Wilson Shannon resigns as governor.

The House of Representatives unseats John Whitfield as territorial delegate and orders a new election.

September Governor John Geary arrives in Kansas.

November Democrat James Buchanan of Pennsylvania is elected president of the United States.

1857

March   Governor John Geary resigns.

             The Supreme Court issues the *Dred Scott* decision.

May   Governor Robert Walker delivers his inaugural address.

October   The Free-State Party wins control of the territorial legislature.

             The Lecompton convention writes the proslavery
             Lecompton Constitution.

December   In a territorial referendum, 6,626 Kansans residents approve the
             Lecompton Constitution with slavery.

             Governor Robert Walker resigns.

1858

January   In a separate referendum, organized by the Free-State Party, 10,226
             Kansans reject the Lecompton Constitution.

February   With the Lecompton Constitution still before Congress, Kansas
             nonetheless plans for another constitutional convention, which will
             write the Leavenworth Constitution.

             James Denver is appointed governor of Kansas.

April   The Leavenworth Constitution stalls in committee in Congress.

May   Proslavery men kill five free-state men in the Marais des
             Cygnes massacre.

June   James Lane kills Gaius Jenkins in a land dispute.

August   Congress sends the Lecompton Constitution back to Kansas,
             where voters overwhelmingly reject it by a vote of 11,300 to 1,788.

1859

January   John and Charles Doy are arrested in Missouri with thirteen
             fugitive slaves.

March   John Doy is convicted and sentenced to five years in prison.

July   The Wyandotte constitutional convention convenes.

September   John Doy is rescued from prison in Missouri.

October Kansas voters ratify the Wyandotte Constitution.

John Brown leads a raid on Harpers Ferry, Virginia.

December Republican Abraham Lincoln visits Kansas Territory.

Under the Wyandotte Constitution, Charles Robinson is elected governor and Republicans gain control of the legislature.

1860

February Pennsylvania representative Galusha Grow introduces House Bill 23 and New York senator William Seward introduces Senate Bill 194 asking for Kansas's admission to the Union.

April The House of Representatives admits Kansas to the Union under the Wyandotte Constitution by a vote of 134 to 73.

June The Senate postpones action on Kansas's admission by a vote of 32 to 27.

November Abraham Lincoln is elected president of the United States.

December Led by William Quantrill, abolitionists raid the Morgan Walker farm in Missouri.

South Carolina secedes from the Union.

1861

January General Winfield Scott places Fort Leavenworth's soldiers on notice to go to Baltimore if necessary.

The Senate passes the Kansas bill 36 to 16, with an amendment making Kansas a judicial district of the United States. The House concurs to the amendment and the Kansas Bill passes 117 to 42.

President James Buchanan signs the Kansas admission bill and Kansas joins the Union as the thirty-fourth state.

February The Confederate States of America is formed by the seven states of the Deep South: South Carolina, Mississippi, Florida, Alabama, Georgia, Louisiana, and Texas.

Charles Robinson takes the oath of office as the first governor of Kansas.

President-elect Abraham Lincoln stops at Independence Hall in Philadelphia to raise the flag bearing the Kansas star.

March   Lincoln is inaugurated as the sixteenth president.

April   James Lane and Samuel Pomeroy are selected by the new state legislature to represent Kansas in the Senate.

The Civil War begins when the Confederacy attacks federal forces at Fort Sumter, in South Carolina. Lincoln calls for 75,000 volunteers to put down the rebellion.

Virginia secedes from the Union and is soon followed by Arkansas, Tennessee, and North Carolina.

To protect the president, James Lane forms the Frontier Guard, partly consisting of Kansans in the capital for Lincoln's inauguration, where they serve from April 18 to May 3.

Lincoln's initial militia call is answered by 650 Kansans, even though Kansas was not asked to supply troops.

May   The First Kansas Infantry is mustered at Leavenworth.

June   Martin Conway is elected to the House of Representatives.

Governor Robinson calls for more troops and the Second Kansas Infantry is mustered at Kansas City, Missouri, for three months.

James Lane announces his appointment as brigadier general.

July   The Fifth Kansas Cavalry is organized.

The Third Kansas Infantry is organized, with James Montgomery as its colonel. The Third and Fourth Kansas Infantries are merged to form the Tenth Kansas Infantry in April 1862.

The battle of Bull Run is fought in Virginia.

August   The battle of Wilson's Creek is fought south of Springfield, Missouri, with troops from the First and Second Kansas Infantry regiments.

John C. Frémont issues a proclamation freeing the slaves in Missouri.

September   Humboldt is raided by bushwhackers.

Lincoln revokes Frémont's proclamation.

Lane leads a sack of Osceola, Missouri.

October	Humboldt is raided again.
	The Eighth Kansas Infantry is organized.
November	The Department of Kansas is established under Major General David Hunter.
December	One hundred contrabands, freed by Colonel Daniel R. Anthony in Independence, Missouri, arrive at Leavenworth.

1862

January	Defeated in Indian Territory, Union Indians retreat into Kansas.
	Investigations regarding the Bond Swindle begin.
February	Ulysses S. Grant captures Forts Henry and Donelson, in Tennessee.
March	William Quantrill attacks Aubrey, in Johnson County, killing three Kansans.
April	The battle of Shiloh is fought in Tennessee.
May	General James Blunt takes command of the Department of Kansas.
	The First Regiment, Indian Home Guard, is formed at Le Roy by Robert Furnas.
	Congress appropriates $100,000 to pay the Lane brigade.
	The First, Seventh, and Eighth Kansas Infantry regiments as well as the Second Kansas Battery head to Corinth, Mississippi.
June	Kansas troops reoccupy part of Indian Territory, marching almost to Fort Gibson.
	The Second Regiment, Indian Home Guard, is raised.
July	President Lincoln signs the Pacific Railway Act.
August	James Lane begins recruiting African American troops.
September	Quantrill raids Olathe, killing several men and destroying the offices of two newspapers.
	Lincoln issues the preliminary emancipation proclamation.
October	The First Kansas Colored Infantry is organized near Fort Lincoln, Bourbon County.

1863

January   The First Kansas Colored Infantry is mustered at Fort Scott.

               Fort Scott is reestablished as a permanent military post.

March   The Union passes its first conscription act.

June   Confederate general Robert E. Lee invades the North.

July   Colonel James Williams, with 800 men of the First Kansas Colored
               Infantry and 500 Americans Indians, defeats a force of Texans
               under the Cherokee Stand Watie at Cabin Creek.

               The battle of Gettysburg is fought in Pennsylvania.

               Vicksburg surrenders with troops of the First Kansas Infantry
               taking part in the campaign.

               Blunt has a victory over Confederate Douglas Cooper at Honey
               Springs, south of the Arkansas River, in Indian territory.

August   The Lawrence massacre is perpetrated by Quantrill's raiders,
               killing more than 160 men and boys and burning 200 buildings.

September   The Fifteenth Kansas Cavalry is organized to protect the border
               with Missouri.

               Members of the Eighth Kansas Volunteer Infantry take an active
               part in the battle of Chickamauga, in Georgia. The Union is forced
               to fall back to Chattanooga, Tennessee.

October   General Blunt and a small escort are attacked near Baxter Springs by
               Quantrill and his raiders. Blunt escapes, but most of his men are killed.

               Colonel Powell Clayton and the Fifth Kansas Cavalry take part in
               the battle of Pine Bluff, Arkansas.

November   Lincoln delivers the Gettysburg Address.

               The battles of Chattanooga, Lookout Mountain, and Missionary
               Ridge help end the Confederate threat in Tennessee, with the
               Eighth Kansas participating.

December   Colonel William Phillips defeats a rebel force near Fort Gibson.

1864

January	General Samuel Curtis takes command of the Department of Kansas.
April	The Thirteenth Amendment passes the Senate.
	The battle of Poison Spring, Arkansas, is fought.
May	The battle of the Wilderness is fought in Virginia.
June	The battle of Cold Harbor is fought in Virginia.
	Lincoln is renominated for president on the Union ticket.
July	Confederate general Richard M. Gano captures Captain David F. Medford and eighty-two of his Sixth Kansas men at Fort Smith, Arkansas.
September	Atlanta falls.
October	Governor Thomas Carney calls out the state militia under Major General George Deitzler in response to reports that Confederate general Sterling Price is advancing toward Kansas.
	General Curtis proclaims martial law in Kansas.
	The battle of the Little Blue in Missouri ends with a Union victory.
	At the battle of Westport, Missouri, the Confederates are defeated and begin to retreat.
	At the battle of Mine Creek, Kansas troops defeat Confederate troops.
November	Abraham Lincoln is reelected president.
	The pursuit of Sterling Price is called off when Generals Curtis and Blunt reach the Arkansas River.
	Sherman begins his march to the sea.
December	Sherman captures Savannah.
	The draft is ordered in Kansas.

1865

January   The Kansas senate reelects James Lane to his U.S. Senate seat.

              The Thirteenth Amendment passes the House of Representatives.

February   The draft begins in Kansas for the first time.

              The Eleventh Kansas Cavalry leaves Fort Riley for Fort Kearny.

March   Lincoln is inaugurated for his second term.

              The draft in Kansas is suspended after the state is given proper
              credit for its volunteers.

              Five Kansas regiments leave for Fort Smith.

April   The Civil War ends.

              John Wilkes Booth assassinates President Lincoln.

December   The Thirteenth Amendment is ratified.

1866

July   James Lane commits suicide.

1867

April   Hancock's Army burns an abandoned Indian village near
              Fort Larned.

July   Congress creates a peace commission to negotiate with northern
              and southern Plains tribes.

              The United States and representatives of five tribes sign the
              Medicine Lodge Treaty.

1868

November   Governor Samuel Crawford resigns to take command of the
              Nineteenth Kansas Volunteer Cavalry, which will serve in Philip
              Sheridan's campaign against the Plains Indians.

1873

Singleton's colony is established in Cherokee County.

1874–75

Winter   The exodus of African Americans out of the South begins.

1875

April   A call is issued to the "colored people of Tennessee" to go to Kansas.

1877

July   The Nicodemus colony is settled in Graham County by thirty settlers.

September   From the South, 350 more settlers arrive in Nicodemus.

1878

"Ho for Kansas!" flyers appear in the South.

1879

March   The Kansas Fever exodus begins as 6,000 African Americans leave Louisiana, Mississippi, and Texas for Kansas.

May   The Kansas Freedman's Relief Association is formed.

1880

April   Benjamin Singleton testifies before the Senate on the Exodus.

Discussion Questions

CHAPTER 1: SETTLEMENT AND STRIFE

1. Why was the passage of the Kansas-Nebraska Act so controversial? How did popular sovereignty change the settlement experience? Compare the traveling accounts of Wells and Hoole. What do they tell us about why people left their homes to settle in Kansas?

2. Why did the Kansas legislative assembly pass such a restrictive law regarding slavery? How did this law contribute to the conflict between proslavery and antislavery factions in the territory? Did this law violate American expectations regarding those freedoms they had enjoyed in their home states?

3. Why did the conflict between advocates of slavery and advocates of freedom move beyond debate to violence? How did the territory's Bleeding Kansas reputation affect the national debate on slavery?

4. Why did it matter whether Kansas joined the Union as a slave state or a free state? Was it truly an outpost in a larger battle?

CHAPTER 2: JOINING THE UNION

1. Did Kansans, as Robert Walker argued, have the power to silence the country's antislavery agitation? Had it been peaceably brought into the Union in 1858, would civil war have been averted?

2. For Kansans, how did their experiences in the 1850s affect their understanding of events after Abraham Lincoln's election? What did admission to the Union represent for Kansans?

3. What was Kansas's initial experience of statehood? How did war breaking out just weeks after their joining the Union change their perspective?

CHAPTER 3: PATRONAGE AND POLICY

1. How did politics within Kansas affect the state's prosecution of the war? How did Kansas's recent admission to the Union affect its ability to protect itself? How did it affect the state's ability to work with the federal government during wartime?

2. How did James Lane gain so much power in Kansas? How was he viewed within the state? How was he viewed by federal authorities?

3. Given that both Kansas and Missouri were Union states, how should border troubles have been addressed? What was the government's responsibility in ameliorating border tension? Are there limits to what the government can do in such conflicts?

CHAPTER 4: KANSAS'S MEN IN BLUE

1. What were some of the unique challenges soldiers in Kansas faced? How did a soldier's war experience differ if he served in the army or in the militia? If he was dispatched to New Mexico or Indian Territory? To Missouri or Tennessee?

2. How was the experience of fighting for the Union different for an African American soldier? How was it different for a member of the Indian Home Guard?

3. How did Kansans' territorial experience affect soldiers' reasons for fighting? Did it inform their views of the home front? How did Kansans react as they moved into the South with their regiments?

4. How were soldiers affected by their service? What were their concerns during wartime? How did these concerns differ from those of civilians?

CHAPTER 5: WARFARE ALONG THE KANSAS-MISSOURI BORDER

1. How do you explain the distrust between Kansans and Missourians? How did having jayhawking soldiers like George Packard serving in the region contribute to the cycle of violence?

2. How did the uncertainty of border life affect Kansans? Why did border residents like the Earl sisters remain instead of seeking refuge in the interior of the state?

3. What was the response to the Lawrence massacre? Was the state or federal government culpable in the Lawrence massacre? Could the massacre have been avoided?

CHAPTER 6: KANSANS AND ANTISLAVERY

1. Should the outbreak of war have affected how laws like the Fugitive Slave Law were implemented in Kansas? How did having a slave state bordering Kansas affect its citizens? How did it shape their views on emancipation and civil rights for African Americans?

2. Did government policy keep pace with changes regarding slavery within Kansas? How do you weigh the rights of property holders in a time of war?

3. How did the struggle of the 1850s affect Kansans' views of the institution of slavery? Did the influx of contrabands into the state change their views?

4. Why was arming African Americans as soldiers so controversial? What is the difference between contributing to the war effort through labor or through battle?

CHAPTER 7: POLITICS AND PROSPERITY

1. What do the documents in this chapter tell you about the parameters of dissent? How did Kansans define loyalty?

2. How did the war transform daily life in Kansas? How does wartime Kansas compare with territorial Kansas? What do these documents tell us about the economic opportunities to be found in the state?

3. As a frontier state, what were some of the challenges faced by the state in how it contributed to the war?

CHAPTER 8: THE CONTINUING MISSION

1. What led to the conflict between Kansans and American Indians? What did Kansans want from Indian tribes in the state? What did Indian tribes want from Kansas and the federal government?

2. How did the location of Indian Territory directly to Kansas's south affect the state's experiences in the Civil War? How did national goals complement or conflict with state goals?

3. How do you think Kansas soldiers felt about continuing to wage war in the West once the American Civil War had ended? What was the connection between this war against American Indians and the Civil War itself?

CHAPTER 9: THE PROMISE OF KANSAS

1. How was Kansas transformed by the Civil War? What were some of the challenges facing Kansas as the war ended?

2. Why was Kansas so attractive to the freed people of the South? How do you think their expectations fit with the reality of the state? How did Kansans react to the influx of so many refugees?

3. What did the railroad represent to Kansans? How would decisions about its route affect towns and residents? Did the railroad represent progress? Were there any who were adversely affected by the extension of the railroad?

Notes

PREFACE

1. *Burlingame Osage Chronicle,* January 30, 1864.
2. Homer E. Socolofsky and Huber Self, *Historical Atlas of Kansas,* 2nd ed. (Norman: University of Oklahoma Press, 1972, 1988), maps 38, 39.

INTRODUCTION

1. *Leavenworth Conservative,* January 31, 1861, quoted in "When Kansas Became a State," *Kansas Historical Quarterly* 23, no. 1 (Spring 1961): 4.
2. Kansas, Adjutant General's Office, *Report of the Adjutant General of the State of Kansas, 1861–1865,* vol. 1 (Leavenworth: Bulletin Co-operative Printing Company, 1867), xxvii, xlviii.
3. Dudley Taylor Cornish, *The Sable Arm: Black Troops in the Union Army, 1861–1865* (Lawrence: University Press of Kansas, 1987), 78.
4. *Emporia News,* February 6, 1864.
5. Members of the Democratic Party who opposed the war, who found fault with many of the Republican administrations' domestic policies, and who wanted to pursue immediate peace with the South were commonly referred to as copperheads, thus connecting such antiwar attitudes with the dangerous nature of the venomous snake.
6. *Leavenworth Weekly Inquirer,* April 17, 1862.
7. *Marysville Big Blue Union,* July 17, 1862.
8. *Emporia News,* July 2, 1864.

CHAPTER 1: SETTLEMENT AND STRIFE

1. Paul Wallace Gates, *Fifty Million Acres: Conflicts over Kansas Land Policy, 1854–1890* (Ithaca, NY: Cornell University Press, 1954), 17.
2. Russell Hickman, "The Reeder Administration Inaugurated, Part II—The Census of Early 1855," *Kansas Historical Quarterly* 36, no. 4 (Winter 1970): 425.
3. Joseph B. Herring, *The Enduring Indians of Kansas: A Century and a Half of Acculturation* (Lawrence: University Press of Kansas, 1990), 1, 13–15, 27.
4. Ralph Volney Harlow, "The Rise and Fall of the Kansas Aid Movement," *American Historical Review* 41, no. 1 (October 1935): 1.
5. Kevin Abing, "Before Bleeding Kansas: Christian Missionaries, Slavery, and the Shawnee Indians in Pre-Territorial Kansas, 1844–1854," *Kansas History: A Journal of the Central Plains* 24, no. 1 (Spring 2001): 58.
6. James C. Malin, *John Brown and the Legend of Fifty-Six* (Philadelphia: American Philosophical Society, 1942), 49–50.
7. Dale E. Watts, "How Bloody Was Bleeding Kansas? Political Killings in Kansas Territory, 1854–1861," *Kansas History* 18, no. 2 (Summer 1995): 117.

CHAPTER 2: JOINING THE UNION

1. Daniel Webster Wilder, *The Annals of Kansas* (Topeka: T. Dwight Thacher, Kansas Publishing House, 1886; New York: Arno Press, 1975), 90–106.

2. Gunja SenGupta, *For God and Mammon: Evangelicals and Entrepreneurs, Masters and Slaves in Territorial Kansas, 1854–1860* (Athens: University of Georgia Press, 1996), 123. Although 450 is not a significant number of slaves, SenGupta argues that the plantation system in territorial Kansas was growing.

3. Frank Heywood Hodder, "Some Aspects of the English Bill for the Admission of Kansas," *Annual Report of the American Historical Association for the Year 1906* (Washington, DC: Goverment Printing Office, 1908), 1:203–4.

4. William Frank Zornow, *Kansas: A History of the Jayhawk State* (Norman: University of Oklahoma Press, 1957), 86.

CHAPTER 3: PATRONAGE AND POLICY

1. See John L. Madden, "The Financing of a New Territory: The Kansas Territorial Tax Structure, 1854–1861," *Kansas Historical Quarterly* 35, no. 2 (Summer 1969): 155–64.

2. Albert Castel, *Civil War Kansas: Reaping the Whirlwind* (Lawrence: University Press of Kansas, 1997), 19–20. For an assessment of Lane that illuminates what Lincoln may have seen in him, see Craig Miner, "Lane and Lincoln," *Kansas History: A Journal of the Central Plains* 24, no. 3 (Autumn 2001): 186–99.

3. Castel, *Civil War Kansas*, 35.

4. Mark A. Plummer, *Frontier Governor: Samuel J. Crawford of Kansas* (Lawrence: University Press of Kansas, 1971), 13.

5. Charles Robinson to James Montgomery, May 4, 1861, George W. Collamore Collection, Kansas Collection, RH MS 33, Kenneth Spencer Research Library, University of Kansas Libraries.

6. Plummer, *Frontier Governor*, 38–42.

7. Castel, *Civil War Kansas*, 202.

8. *St. Louis Democrat*, June 4, 1866, quoted in *New York Times*, July 8, 1866.

9. *Wyandotte Commercial Gazette*, July 14, 1866.

CHAPTER 4: KANSAS'S MEN IN BLUE

Unless otherwise noted, all the troop data in this chapter is derived from Kansas, Adjutant General's Office, *Report of the Adjutant General of the State of Kansas, 1861–1865*, vol. 1 (Topeka: Kansas State Printing Company, 1896).

1. George Packard Letters, Kansas State Historical Society. "Jayhawkers" were antislavery adherents while "bushwhackers" (or "border ruffians" in the territorial period) were their proslavery opposites.

2. H. D. Fisher Papers, Collection 343, Kansas State Historical Society.

3. Mark A. Plummer, *Frontier Governor: Samuel J. Crawford of Kansas* (Lawrence: University Press of Kansas, 1971), 47–50.

4. See Albert Castel, *Civil War Kansas: Reaping the Whirlwind* (Lawrence: University Press of Kansas, 1997), 116–17; Jay Monaghan, *Civil War on the Western Border, 1854–1865* (Lincoln: University of Nebraska Press, 1984), 323.

5. George Packard Letters, Kansas State Historical Society.

6. Hugh D. Fisher, *The Gun and the Gospel: Early Kansas and Chaplain Fisher* (Chicago: Kenwood, 1896).

CHAPTER 5: WARFARE ALONG THE KANSAS-MISSOURI BORDER

1. *Illinois State Journal,* December 12, 1859, in *The Collected Works of Abraham Lincoln,* ed. Roy P. Basler, 9 vols. (New Brunswick, NJ: Rutgers University Press, 1953–55), 3:497–502.

2. James Montgomery to Franklin B. Sanborn, January 14, 1861, and James Montgomery to George Stearns, June 21, 1861, George L. Stearns Letters, Collection 507, Kansas State Historical Society.

3. Albert Castel, *Civil War Kansas: Reaping the Whirlwind* (Lawrence: University Press of Kansas, 1997), 42–43.

4. Ibid., 44–46.

5. Jay Monaghan, *Civil War on the Western Border, 1854–1865* (Lincoln: University of Nebraska Press, 1984), 181.

6. Donald L. Gilmore, *Civil War on the Missouri-Kansas Border* (Gretna, LA: Pelican, 2006), 134–35.

7. Castel, *Civil War Kansas,* 57, 61, 62.

8. Ibid., 102–5.

9. Ibid., 129, 137, 152. A stand of arms is a complete set of equipment for one Civil War soldier: rifle, bayonet, cartridge belt, and box of ammunition.

10. Ibid., 122, 142, 153. For a more critical view of these orders, see Gilmore, *Civil War on the Missouri-Kansas Border,* chaps. 11–12.

CHAPTER 6: KANSANS AND ANTISLAVERY

1. E. B. Whitman to George Stearns, September 7, 1862, Stearns Letters, Collection 507, Kansas State Historical Society.

2. Hamilton Gamble to Abraham Lincoln, September 9, 1862, Abraham Lincoln Papers at the Library of Congress, Manuscript Division (Washington, DC: American Memory Project, 2000–2002), http://memory.loc.gov/ammem/alhtml/malhome.html.

3. Albert Castel, *Civil War Kansas: Reaping the Whirlwind* (Lawrence: University Press of Kansas, 1997), 55–56.

4. Ibid., 91–94.

5. The Independent Battery, U.S. Colored Light Artillery, better known as Douglas's Battery, is noteworthy because it was commanded by black officers. See Roger D. Cunningham, "Douglas's Battery at Fort Leavenworth: The Issue of Black Officers during the Civil War," *Kansas History: A Journal of the Central Plains* 23, no. 4 (Winter 2000–2001): 200–217.

6. *The War of the Rebellion: A Compilation of the Official Records of the Union and Confederate Armies,* ser. 1, vol. 34 (Washington: Government Printing Office, 1891), 746.

7. Dudley Taylor Cornish, *The Sable Arm: Black Troops in the Union Army, 1861–1865* (Lawrence: University Press of Kansas, 1987), 177.

8. Isaiah Morris Harris Collection, Kansas Collection, RH MS P60:B, Kenneth Spencer Research Library, University of Kansas Libraries.

9. Nicole Etcheson, *Bleeding Kansas: Contested Liberty in the Civil War Era* (Lawrence: University Press of Kansas, 2004), 231.

CHAPTER 7: POLITICS AND PROSPERITY

1. Samuel Ayers Papers, Kansas State Historical Society.

2. Albert Castel, *Civil War Kansas: Reaping the Whirlwind* (Lawrence: University Press of Kansas, 1997), 212–14.

3. *Neosho Valley Register,* reprinted in the *Leavenworth Daily Conservative,* November 12, 1862.

4. John L. Madden, "The Financing of a New Territory: The Kansas Territorial Tax Structure, 1854–1861," *Kansas Historical Quarterly* 35, no. 2 (Summer 1969): 157, 161–62.

5. Castel, *Civil War Kansas,* 204.

6. Ibid., 207–8.

7. Ibid., 213.

8. For more on prewar land policy and its effect on state politics, see Paul Wallace Gates, *Fifty Million Acres: Conflicts over Kansas Land Policy, 1854–1890* (Ithaca, NY: Cornell University Press, 1954).

9. Castel, *Civil War Kansas,* 94–96.

10. Mark A. Plummer, *Frontier Governor: Samuel J. Crawford of Kansas* (Lawrence: University Press of Kansas, 1971), 37–38.

11. Powell Clayton to John Halderman, October 21, 1864, John A. Halderman Collection, Kansas State Historical Society.

12. Plummer, *Frontier Governor,* 38.

13. Castel, *Civil War Kansas,* 180–81.

14. Ibid, 180.

CHAPTER 8: THE CONTINUING MISSION

1. William E. Unrau, *Indians of Kansas: The Euro-American Invasion and Conquest of Indian Kansas* (Topeka: Kansas State Historical Society, 1991), 72.

2. Albert Castel, *Civil War Kansas: Reaping the Whirlwind* (Lawrence: University Press of Kansas, 1997), 218–19.

3. Clarissa W. Confer, *The Cherokee Nation in the Civil War* (Norman: University of Oklahoma Press, 2007), 46.

4. Garrick Bailey and Roberta Glenn Bailey, "The Civil War in Indian Territory," in Frederick E. Hoxie, ed., *Encyclopedia of North American Indians* (Boston: Houghton Mifflin, 1996), 124. Among these tribes were three with lands in southern Kansas: the Quapaws, the Osages, and the Cherokees. See Gary Cheatham, "Within the Limits of the Southern Confederacy: The C.S.A.'s Interest in the Quapaw, Osage, and Cherokee Tribal Lands of Kansas," *Kansas History: A Journal of the Central Plains* 26, no. 3 (Autumn 2003): 172–85.

5. Bailey and Bailey, "Civil War in Indian Territory," 124; Confer, *The Cherokee Nation,* 59-65; and Thom Hatch, *The Blue, the Gray, and the Red: Indian Campaigns in the Civil War* (Mechanicsburg, PA: Stackpole Books, 2003), 8–21.

6. Castel, *Civil War Kansas,* 97–99.

7. Ibid., 160.

8. Bailey and Bailey, "Civil War in Indian Territory," 125.

9. *The War of the Rebellion: A Compilation of the Official Records of the Union and Confederate Armies*, ser. 1, vol. 41 (Washington: Government Printing Office, 1893), 462.

10. Mark A. Plummer, *Frontier Governor: Samuel J. Crawford of Kansas* (Lawrence: University Press of Kansas, 1971), 114–15.

11. H. Craig Miner and William E. Unrau, *The End of Indian Kansas: A Study of Cultural Revolution, 1854–1871* (Lawrence: Regents Press of Kansas, 1978), 139.

CHAPTER 9: THE PROMISE OF KANSAS

1. William Connelley, *A Standard History of Kansas and Kansans*, 5 vols. (Chicago: Lewis, 1918), vol. 2, chap. 39.

2. James R. Shortridge, *Peopling the Plains: Who Settled Where in Frontier Kansas* (Lawrence: University Press of Kansas, 1995), 8, 10.

3. Richard B. Sheridan, "From Slavery in Missouri to Freedom in Kansas: The Influx of Black Fugitives and Contrabands into Kansas, 1854–1865," *Kansas History: A Journal of the Central Plains* 12, no. 1 (Spring 1989): 36–37.

4. Shortridge, *Peopling the Plains*, 29, 39, 42.

5. Quoted in Robert G. Athearn, *In Search of Canaan: Black Migration to Kansas 1879–80*, (Lawrence: Regents Press of Kansas, 1978), 256, 276–77.

6. Nell Irvin Painter, *Exodusters: Black Migration to Kansas after Reconstruction* (New York: Alfred A. Knopf, 1977), 259.

7. Homer E. Socolofsky and Huber Self, *Historical Atlas of Kansas*, 2nd ed. (Norman: University of Oklahoma Press, 1972, 1988), numbers 30, 31.

8. Mark A. Plummer, *Frontier Governor: Samuel J. Crawford of Kansas* (Lawrence: University Press of Kansas, 1971), 55.

9. H. Craig Miner, *West of Wichita: Settling the High Plains of Kansas, 1865–1890* (Lawrence: University Press of Kansas, 1986), 15.

10. Ibid.

11. Quoted in Douglas C. Jones, *The Treaty of Medicine Lodge: The Story of the Great Treaty Council as Told by Eyewitnesses* (Norman: University of Oklahoma Press, 1966), 156.

12. Roger C. Smith, "An Analysis of 100 Years of Grasshopper Populations in Kansas (1854–1954)," *Transactions of the Kansas Academy of Science* 57, no. 4 (December 1954): 397–433.

Selected Bibliography

CHAPTER 1: SETTLEMENT AND STRIFE

Etcheson, Nicole. *Bleeding Kansas: Contested Liberty in the Civil War Era.* Lawrence: University Press of Kansas, 2004.

Malin, James C. *John Brown and the Legend of Fifty-Six.* Philadelphia: American Philosophical Society, 1942.

Mullis, Tony. *Peacekeeping on the Plains: Army Operations in Bleeding Kansas.* Columbia: University of Missouri Press, 2004.

Oertel, Kristen Tegtmeier. *Bleeding Borders: Race, Gender, and Violence in Pre–Civil War Kansas.* Baton Rouge: Louisiana State University Press, 2009.

Shortridge, James R. *Peopling the Plains: Who Settled Where in Frontier Kansas.* Lawrence: University Press of Kansas, 1995.

CHAPTER 2: JOINING THE UNION

Berwanger, Eugene H. *The Frontier against Slavery: Western Anti-Negro Prejudice and the Slavery Extension Controversy.* Urbana: University of Illinois Press, 1967.

Gates, Paul Wallace. *Fifty Million Acres: Conflicts over Kansas Land Policy, 1854–1890.* Ithaca, NY: Cornell University Press, 1954.

Monaghan, Jay. *Civil War on the Western Border, 1854–1865.* Lincoln: University of Nebraska Press, 1984.

Rawley, James A. *Race and Politics: "Bleeding Kansas" and the Coming of the Civil War.* Philadelphia: Lippincott, 1969.

SenGupta, Gunja. *For God and Mammon: Evangelicals and Entrepreneurs, Masters and Slaves in Territorial Kansas, 1854–1860.* Athens: University of Georgia Press, 1996.

CHAPTER 3: PATRONAGE AND POLICY

Bailes, Kendall E. *Rider on the Wind: Jim Lane and Kansas.* Shawnee Mission, KS: Wagon Wheel Press, 1962.

Collins, Robert. *Jim Lane: Scoundrel, Statesman, Kansan.* Gretna, LA: Pelican Publishing, 2007.

Robinson, Charles. *The Kansas Conflict.* Lawrence: Journal Publishing, 1898.

Spurgeon, Ian Michael. *Man of Douglas, Man of Lincoln: The Political Odyssey of James Henry Lane.* Columbia: University of Missouri Press, 2008.

Zornow, William Frank. *Kansas: A History of the Jayhawk State.* Norman: University of Oklahoma Press, 1957.

CHAPTER 4: KANSAS'S MEN IN BLUE

Brownlee, Richard S. *Gray Ghosts of the Confederacy: Guerrilla Warfare in the West, 1861–1865.* Baton Rouge: Louisiana State University Press, 1958.

Cornish, Dudley Taylor. *The Sable Arm: Black Troops in the Union Army, 1861–1865.* Lawrence: University Press of Kansas, 1987.

McPherson, James M. *Battle Cry of Freedom: The Civil War Era.* New York: Oxford University Press, 1988.

Mitchell, Reid. *The Vacant Chair: The Northern Soldier Leaves Home.* New York: Oxford University Press, 1993.

Starr, Stephen Z. *Jennison's Jayhawkers: A Civil War Cavalry Regiment and Its Commander.* Baton Rouge: Louisiana State University Press, 1974.

CHAPTER 5: WARFARE ALONG THE KANSAS-MISSOURI BORDER

Castel, Albert. *Civil War Kansas: Reaping the Whirlwind.* Lawrence: University Press of Kansas, 1997.

Fellman, Michael. *Inside War: The Guerilla Conflict in Missouri during the American Civil War.* New York: Oxford University Press, 1990.

Gilmore, Donald L. *Civil War on the Missouri-Kansas Border.* Gretna, LA: Pelican, 2006.

Goodrich, Thomas. *Black Flag: Guerrilla Warfare on the Western Border, 1861–1865.* Indiana University Press, 1999.

Neely, Jeremy. *The Border between Them: Violence and Reconciliation on the Kansas-Missouri Line.* Columbia: University of Missouri Press, 2007.

Schultz, Duane. *Quantrill's War: The Life and Times of William Clarke Quantrill, 1837–1865.* New York: St. Martin's, 1996.

CHAPTER 6: KANSANS AND ANTISLAVERY

Cornish, Dudley Taylor. "Kansas Negro Regiments in the Civil War." *Kansas Historical Quarterly* 20, no. 6 (May 1953): 417–29.

Cunningham, Roger D. *The Black Citizen-Soldiers of Kansas, 1864–1901.* Columbia: University of Missouri Press, 2008.

Morrison, Michael A. *Slavery and the American West: The Eclipse of Manifest Destiny and the Coming of the Civil War.* Chapel Hill: University of North Carolina Press, 1997.

Oates, Stephen B. *To Purge This Land with Blood: A Biography of John Brown.* Amherst: University of Massachusetts Press, 1984.

Trudeau, Noah Andre. *Like Men of War: Black Troops in the Civil War, 1862–1865.* Boston: Little, Brown, 1998.

CHAPTER 7: POLITICS AND PROSPERITY

McNall, Scott G. *The Road to Rebellion: Class Formation and Kansas Populism, 1865–1900.* Chicago: University of Chicago Press, 1988.

Plummer, Mark A. *Frontier Governor: Samuel J. Crawford of Kansas.* Lawrence: University Press of Kansas, 1971.

Socolofsky, Homer E. *Kansas Governors.* Lawrence: University Press of Kansas, 1990.

Stuewe, Paul K., ed. *Kansas Revisited: Historical Images and Perspectives.* Lawrence: University of Kansas: Division of Continuing Education, 1990.

CHAPTER 8: THE CONTINUING MISSION

Confer, Clarissa W. *The Cherokee Nation in the Civil War.* Norman: University of Oklahoma Press, 2007.

Herring, Joseph B. *The Enduring Indians of Kansas: A Century and a Half of Acculturation.* Lawrence: University Press of Kansas, 1990.

McQuillan, Aidan. *Prevailing over Time: Ethnic Adjustment on the Kansas Prairies, 1875–1925.* Lincoln: University of Nebraska Press, 1990.

Miner, H. Craig, and William E. Unrau. *The End of Indian Kansas: A Study of Cultural Revolution, 1854–1871.* Lawrence: Regents Press of Kansas, 1978.

Unrau, William E. *Indians of Kansas: The Euro-American Invasion and Conquest of Indian Kansas.* Topeka: Kansas State Historical Society, 1991.

CHAPTER 9: THE PROMISE OF KANSAS

Athearn, Robert G. *In Search of Canaan: Black Migration to Kansas 1879–80.* Lawrence: Regents Press of Kansas, 1978.

Miner, H. Craig. *West of Wichita: Settling the High Plains of Kansas, 1865–1890.* Lawrence: University Press of Kansas, 1986.

Napier, Rita, ed. *Kansas and the West: New Perspectives.* Lawrence: University Press of Kansas, 2003.

Painter, Nell Irvin. *Exodusters: Black Migration to Kansas after Reconstruction.* New York: Alfred A. Knopf, 1977.

Shortridge, James R. *Peopling the Plains: Who Settled Where in Frontier Kansas.* Lawrence: University Press of Kansas, 1995.

Index